Failing Grade

Oregon's Higher-
Education System
Goes Begging

Failing

Grade

Oregon's Higher-Education System Goes Begging

DAVID SARASOHN

NEW OREGON PUBLISHERS · PORTLAND, OREGON

Published by New Oregon Publishers, Portland, Oregon
Distributed to the trade by Publishers Group West, 1700 Fourth St., Berkeley,
CA 94710, www.pgw.com

First U.S. edition 2010
Printed in Canada
Interior design by Janet Parker
www.tinhouse.com

Contents

Foreword by Win McCormack 1

Introduction by Dave Frohnmayer 7

Preface by David Sarasohn 15

State System Sinking in '90s 25

Higher Education Heading Even Lower 33

In Higher-Ed Playoff, Oregon's Trailing 36

Oregon Studying to Be a Sidekick State 39

Rising Students for Sinking Colleges 43

An Address to the 1992 Escapees 48

Higher Education Quietly Getting Lower 51

"It'll Be Like a T-Shirt That Says USSR" 54

Washington Invests 57

On Higher Ed, Not Quite High Enough 60

U of O President Won't Duck the Future 63

Portland State Ventures into Portland 66

Oregon's Rising Role: Collegiate Colony 69

State Colleges: Onward and Downward 72

The Future Is Exciting—Next Door 75

Llamas Carry the Load for Higher Ed 78

HIGHER ED: A Motto to Match Its Money 81

Oregon Offers Breaks Instead of Brains 84

The Eyes of Texas Are on Research 87

Starved Colleges Turn on Each Other 90

A Prayer, and a Wing, for Higher Ed 93

OREGON HIGHER ED: Last Known Address 96

Higher Ed: Washington's Got a Secret 99

Billing Our Children 102

Viking Queen Sets Sail 107

Degrees of Deeper Debt 110

Irate PSU Alumni Report 113

Making a University 116

THE FUTURE IS SIGHTED ELSEWHERE: *Newsweek*'s Hottest
    Tech Cities All Boast Higher-Ed Engines—
    and Guess Who Didn't Qualify 119

Market Rises for Faculty, Not Oregon 122

Trying to Catch Up with Old Wash Tech 127

Again Oregon Tries the Old College Trash 130

Salem Needs Some Higher Education 133

World-Class Universities, Discounted 136

Oregon's Newest Varsity Letter Is an F 139

Oregon's Idea of a Research University 142

EDUCATION FUNDING: At Least We Should Savor Oregon's
    Comic Aspects 145

THE LEGISLATURE: On Higher Ed, No Reasonable Offer Received 150

School Systems Worlds Apart: Standing on the Wrong Side
    of the Entrance to the Future 153

Oregon's Universities: In Politics, Higher Ed Rarely Comes Up,
    As It Goes Down 156

An Assignment for Higher Ed 159

KNOWLEDGE IS POWER: Oregon Sees the Light 164

FUNDING HIGHER ED: Universities Find a Cheerleader,
    Still Need a Victory 168

Losing by Degrees—On Higher-Ed Board, Francesconi Faces
    Another F 171

HIGHER EDUCATION: How Dumb Can We Get When It Comes to
    Cutting Budget? 174

OREGON'S COLLEGES: Lincoln Hall's Leaky Roof Is Metaphor for
    Higher Ed 177

HIGHER EDUCATION: Budget As If the Future Were Coming 180

Oregon Universities: Bernstine's Exit Underscores the Erosion
    in Higher Education 184

Subtracting Higher Ed 187

HIGHER EDUCATION: Legislature to Students: Let Them Eat
    Cake (or Cookies) 190

HIGHER ED: If You Build It, They'll Help Pay the Bill.......................... 194

Community College Funding: Lower-Income Kids' Access to
    Higher Ed Sinking 198

HIGHER EDUCATION: We're Losing the Tony Trans As Oregon's
    Universities Spiral Down... 202

Higher Ed's Tsunami.. 206

HIGHER EDUCATION: Recruiting Difficulties Reflect the Sorry
    State of Oregon's Colleges 210

It's a Wrap 213

On a Shuttered Library, Words of Caution for Higher Ed.................. 217

U.S. NEWS NUMBERS: Rankings of the Oregon Universities
    Not Classy 221

The Key College Ranking: How Many Make It to College Oregon
    Education 224

INVESTMENT FOR A FUTURE: Commitment to Higher Ed
    Takes Sharp Bounces 227

INVESTING IN EDUCATION AND COMMUNITY: Public-Private
    Partnerships Could Help Portland Students................................. 230

EDUCATION: Oregon Could Learn from the Celtic Tiger................... 235

PRESIDENTIAL POLITICS: Clinton Gets It: Kids Need Access
    to College 239

E-BOARD EDUCATION: Facing Another Lowering of Higher Ed........ 244

THINKING BIG FOR OREGON: Save the Future 247

Emerald Opportunity: Oregon Higher Ed Has Reason to Get Its
    Irish Up 251

COLLEGE TRACK: Marathon Run for Education.................................. 254

HIGHER EDUCATION: A Quick Way to Connect Jobs to Relief
and a Route to the Future 257

HIGHER-ED FUNDING: Federal Investment at College Level
Needed 260

FINANCIAL AID: College Students' Next Lesson: Bad Economics...... 263

HIGHER EDUCATION: When Two Trends Collide on Campus
Heading Toward a Collision Course... 266

THE UNIVERSITIES' BUDGET: In Beaver State, Higher Ed Plucked
Like a Turkey... 269

EXPERIENCE CORPS: With Kids, It Turns Out Experience
Does Count 272

Farewell to Frohnmayer: UO's Departing Chief Fought
Funding Crises.. 275

HIGHER ED'S WEEK: For Students: More Help, Higher Hurdles........ 278

PUBLIC CORPORATIONS: In Colleges, Rearranging Can't Avoid
Refinancing 281

BUILDING A BRIDGE TO COLLEGE: Offering Portland Kids a
Life after High School.. 284

GLOBE IS GAINING: Higher Ed Cuts True Madness of This March 287

OREGON GOVERNOR'S RACE: Higher-Ed (Gasp!) Gets Campaign
TV Time 290

RESETTING EXPECTATIONS: Recognize the Realities of Reset—
and Its Cost.. 293

ESCAPING THE LEGISLATURE: Flexibility for Higher Ed, and
Maybe Some Help... 296

Foreword

Higher Education for the Oregon Legislature

I have been reading David Sarasohn's *Oregonian* columns on higher education over the past twenty years with growing dismay, ever since his very first one, "State System Sinking in the '90's," appeared in the July 15, 1990, edition of the newspaper. In that column, David cited the stunning fact that the University of Oregon was ranked 110th out of the 120 doctorate-granting public universities in the salary levels of its professors. He then drew a comparison between efforts underway in our neighboring state of Washington to expand and upgrade its higher-education system—Washington was launching a program to increase the capacity of its system by 30 percent before 2010—and Oregon's apparent intention simply to go on treading water with what it already had in place.

David did not stop with a comparison to Washington in that column, however. Conceding that Washington is a larger, wealthier state that might have something of an advantage and a head start, he went on to compare the level of support for higher education in Oregon with the level of support in Iowa, a state that, at the time, almost exactly matched Oregon in both population and per-capita income. He found that Iowa ranked 12th out of the fifty states in per-capita spending on higher education, while Oregon ranked 34th. He also found that the University of Iowa and Iowa State University, each about 60 percent larger than the University of Oregon or Oregon State, respectively ranked 18th and 36th on the salary scale for professors at research universities. He quoted a professional administrator in the field of higher education who called Iowa a "high-effort state." Oregon was, by obvious implication, a low-effort state, though the administrator would not characterize it exactly that way.

According to figures David cites in a May 5, 2006, column, between 2001 and 2006 the average state appropriation for higher education in the United States increased 9.9 percent, and during that time Washington's rose 14.9 percent, while in the same period the Oregon legislature cut Oregon's funding for higher education by 8 percent. By my reckoning, that translates into Oregon's higher-education system falling behind in funding on a national scale by 17.9 percent in just those five years, and, relative to Washington, by 22.9 percent.

The results of twenty years of disinvestment in higher education in Oregon are as you would expect, or even worse. In David's final column that appears in this book, of July 18, 2010, he cites findings from a report called *Trends in College Spending 1998–2008* produced by the Delta Project on Postsecondary Education Costs, Productivity and Accountability. According to this report, the amount of Oregon's per-capita spending from its general fund on university students in that period was 44th in the country, and its per-student spending at its two research universities—meaning combined spending from general fund money and money from tuition—totaled $11,800, 8th from last. Washington, on the other hand, was next to the top in that second category.

The report also states that in Washington, 42 percent of the cost of educating a student came from tuition, whereas in Oregon, tuition provided 67 percent of the cost. Thus it is no accident that in 2007, according to the table ("Average debt at graduation per borrower, public 4-year,

2007") on pages 105–106 of this book, Oregon ranked 19th out of the 50 states in the debt burden carried by its four-year-college students at graduation.

I know that members of the Oregon legislature believe that the cuts they have made to Oregon's higher-education system, or the monies they have not provided for it, are a matter of fiscal necessity or fiscal prudence: they have made do, they think, the best they could with the funds Oregon's tax system provides, carefully balancing the needs of that system against other important needs, including K–12 education and human services. Here David begs to differ, or, at least, to offer a different perspective, one that views higher education not as an obligatory drain on the state's resources or only a means to enrich its students' personal and professional lives, but as a potential powerful engine of economic growth for the state, as it has been for other states.

"In Washington, there doesn't seem to be any big controversy to say that higher education fuels our economy," the government affairs manager for the American Electronics Association of Oregon, Jim Craven, declares in a Feb. 26, 1995, column. "Here, when higher-ed folks are cutting 8% instead of 15%, that's a great victory." In a Nov. 22, 1998, column, "The Future is Sighted Elsewhere: *Newsweek*'s Hottest Tech Cities All Boast Higher-Ed Engines—and Guess Who Didn't Qualify," David reports, "To Oregon, of course, Seattle and the UW are a different world. But just a bit further down the road in the magazine's listing of the future is Boise—poised to draw support from a brand-new engineering school at Boise State." And in a June 15, 2008, column, Ron Fox, executive director of the Southern Oregon Economic Development Inc., comments, "Oregon invests in fixing potholes, not in changing paradigms. If you think about it, Oregon is West Virginia with a beach. It's a pretty scary future we have in terms of the global market."

What accounts for this disastrous downward drift of Oregon college and university education toward mediocrity and, inevitably, if the trend continues, outright inferiority compared even to a state such as Idaho?

As former state legislator and former University of Oregon president Dave Frohnmayer suggests in his introduction, one of the principal reasons is Oregon's inadequate and unbalanced tax system, whose problems begin, but do not end, with the state's lack of a sales tax. The sales tax is an instrument desperately needed in Oregon to counterbalance the wild fluctuations of revenue from the income tax, which make accurate state budgeting a virtual impossibility. There is an equal need to abolish, completely, the so-called "kicker," which in good economic times refunds "surplus revenues" from the income tax to individual and corporate taxpayers based on two-year advance estimates by state economists. This irrational mechanism, used nowhere else in the world, prevents the state from accumulating a meaningful "rainy day fund" to offset real-time deficits during an economic crisis.

However, it would not be enough simply to have a more rational and balanced tax system in order to reverse the steady decline of Oregon's higher-education system, though that is certainly a necessary precondition. Oregon also needs a dynamic economy with cutting-edge businesses and a prosperous middle class, so that there is a base to tax. Here, vis-à-vis the role of higher education in such a process, there is clearly a vicious circle operating, in which the legislature finds itself short of funds to finance a first-class system, and the lack of leading intellectual centers in the state impedes the development of a tax base strong enough to provide such funds, etc. Ad infinitum? Let us pray not. This vicious circle is also a downward spiral, and must be broken if Oregon is to have a real future.

As with any vicious circle, breaking this one cannot but be arduous and painful, and will require a number of things not seen around these parts for a while—for instance, strong leadership from the business community, which depends on an educated labor force for its success. In closing, though, I would like to address our esteemed friends in the Oregon legislature by drawing attention to David's July 19, 1996, column, entitled "Higher Ed: Washington's Got a Secret," which begins with the lead "To an Oregonian, seeing Washington state's ideas about higher education can be like looking at a Victoria's Secret catalogue. There's the same powerful sense of allure and unattainability—and it's always impressive to look at the figures ... At least until it's time to return to the shapeless higher-ed debate in Oregon." David continues on to explain Washington's big secret: "Up there you find Democrats and Republicans arguing over who's the stronger and most effective supporter of the state's higher-ed system." Then he offers this line, wry or mournful depending on your interpretation of it: "You won't find a pose like that in the Victoria's Secret catalogue—or anywhere in Oregon."

—WIN McCORMACK
Publisher

Introduction

Higher Education in Oregon: An Endangered Species?

The protagonist in Franz Kafka's memorable short story "Ein Hungerkünstler" ("A Hunger Artist") is a devoted circus performer whose art is to display his heroic capacity to survive in the face of deliberate self-starvation. At first, crowds of onlookers applaud in amazement and celebrate the artist's stoic endurance. But as the duration of the artist's fasting increases, the support of passing audiences wanes. The performer ultimately dies in his straw-filled cage, alone and unwatched.

In student days long ago, I painstakingly translated this Kafka master-piece word by word from the original German. Its impact has never quite left me. David Sarasohn's *Failing Grade*, which chronicles the past two decades of public higher education in Oregon, unexpectedly reminded me of the story.

The Oregon Admission Act of February 14, 1859, gave us statehood, the nickname "Valentine State," and surprisingly few obligations. The two most notable commitments were promises in exchange for sub-stantial land grants. The first was that endowed lands would be used for

7

the support of a system of "common and uniform schools"; the second was the establishment of "a public university." But the timber barons of the late nineteenth century squandered or stole much of the land-grant endowments, and the remarkable legacy of a mid-nineteenth-century population—of which less than one percent had attained a college degree—was tragically wasted.

David Sarasohn writes not of the past, however, but of late-twentieth and early-twenty-first-century errors, born less out of personal greed than shortsighted public decisions that have stood in the way of higher education's promise for our own times. He scans the contemporary economic and political landscape repeatedly, but its broad contours are worth recapping here.

Oregon's timber- and resource-based economy supported a wide variety of family-wage jobs well into the 1970s. But in recent years, the vulnerability of the timber industry, first to the sharp cycles of the national housing market, then to growing environmental concerns about diminishing old-growth stands, has made this mainstay precarious. A strong reliance of state finances on the personal income tax has exaggerated the volatile impacts of the national business cycle on state budgeting, and the absence of a state sales tax has made escalating property taxes a target for an all too accessible initiative process.

The shortcomings of legislation by plebiscite in Oregon are notable and beyond the scope of this introduction. But initiatives are not, as is the legislature, bound by a constitutional requirement to balance budgets. And two of the worst initiatives in Oregon's history set the tone of the fiscal landscape for the decades in which Sarasohn's essays were written.

In 1990, Measure 5 sharply cut property-tax revenues for schools and required the state general fund to backstop local government and school revenues for six years. While it provided no new offsetting revenue for state government operations, it mandated that the general fund replace property-tax losses to local schools. This reduced the level of outcry from school districts but set up a hugely destructive competition between K–12 advocates and higher-education interests. As Sarasohn notes, university professors cannot descend on Salem in the same numbers or with the same innate appeal as children disembarking from hundreds of yellow school buses at the capitol. Measure 11, 1994's mandatory-sentencing initiative, allocated billions of dollars for prison construction and operational requirements, diverted state revenues from traditional objects such as higher education, and, again, provided no revenue source to fund its mandated costs. Although it still is impolitic to say so in some quarters, these two reckless political actions resulted in a long-term, double-dip, voter-induced recession from which Oregon has not yet recovered.

Ironically, "kicker" legislation enacted in 1979 to quell a growing tax revolt magnified the problems created by Measures 5 and 11. The "kicker" mandates a rebate to tax payers whenever the amount of personal income-tax revenue received by the state exceeds 2 percent of the figure the state economist estimated at the beginning of the state budget process. This artifice, for which this author (to his great regret) voted, requires an unattainable degree of forecasting clairvoyance, stunts the capacity to build back state-funded assets in times of plenty, and does nothing to cushion inevitable budget shortfalls in times of economic distress.

Devastating as Measures 5 and 11 were, their effects were alleviated in the short term by a 1991 decision to legalize and regulate a booming illegal video-poker problem, which meant that a suddenly engorged state lottery could backfill and partially disguise otherwise catastrophic budget problems.

And, finally, even while the spotted owl decision, under the federal Endangered Species Act, fractured the state politically and diminished income-tax receipts from the timber industry and its highly paid workforce, the sudden boom in high-tech and construction jobs and the high-wage in-migration (largely to the Portland tricounty area) of the 1990s provided welcome—if temporary, regionally limited, and cyclical—wage and state-revenue relief.

Sarasohn watched all of these trends unfold and reported insightfully how their disparate impacts hindered the support of higher education by paralyzing or diverting the legislature's attention: "About once a decade, a legislative session remembers that Oregon has a higher-education system" (June 10, 2007).

In the years of my own legislative service (1975–80), one could comfortably cross a party line for a good idea. Party loyalty was expected on organizational issues; representation of one's constituency gave one political independence and usually routine acceptance. Ideological issues involving personal choice and private behavior, taxation policy and regional allegiance made a difference among fellow party members, but did not lead to ostracism from the party caucus. Political-action committees and their funding dominance, staggering campaign costs and the vulnerability of candidates to twenty-four-hour multimedia attack smears were absent from the political scene. It is not hard to view the past as a better time for principled advocacy of long-term objectives.

Sarasohn knows that higher-education advocates fare poorly in this new era of binding caucus politics and hot-button appeals, which make the long term seem irrelevant, and the next election cycle utterly commanding. He watches and reports the sad, obsessive political death dance in which legislators and governors neither help nor let go of their public higher-education partners. If lip service were currency, our public universities would be billionaires. Instead, they are supplicants waiting for the next revenue forecast and instructions that tell them to tighten belts while keeping down tuition costs; to meet increasing enrollments with existing quality standards; and to resist, at all costs, saying in public that present budget strategies are unsustainable and that double-digit reductions in state support levels are a deplorable betrayal of the next generation.

The unscripted dance, as Sarasohn's columns disclose, has multiple partners. Budget decisions by governors are singularly important to define priorities, but the incremental add-ons seem glacially slow and

10

acutely vulnerable. The governor's administrative departments may have competing budget priorities that cause them, for example, to sequester for other purposes massive interest earnings on student tuition payments even when hailing the need for reductions in tuition rates generally. Legislative Democrats praise higher education's unique contributions while reserving their votes and attention to the K–12 share of budget negotiations and the teacher union stranglehold on their campaign-funding access.

Republican legislators, like their Democratic counterparts, appreciate the genuinely liberating power of college-degree attainment and show genuine support to free the system from onerous regulatory restrictions as long as higher education discounts its appropriation dollars even further against the unfunded and unrealized savings that might result from loosening these restrictions. They race away at the mere mention of a revenue-raising source of new support. Unusually powerful student lobbies work to take "high tuition/high aid" strategies utterly off the table and force debate into minuscule tactics to "buy down" tuitions and ignore the resource capabilities and differing missions of each institution.

Legislators of both parties cannot seem to let go of tuition control, even though formal delegation to set these rates has rested with the Oregon State Board of Higher Education for almost one hundred years. Here, politics trumps legal formalism, as Sarasohn so well knows. He recounts repeatedly how, in the absence of resources, "solutions" for higher education were diverted to questions of process and endless structural tinkering, some of it meaningful only as valiant symbolism, not substance. Of one of my own efforts, he wrote that it was a "classic Oregon solution. It's creative, elegant—and doesn't come near to solving the problem" (November 29, 2009).

For all of the facts he sifts, for all of his thoughtfully chosen sources of expertise, for all of his careful historian's abilities to extrapolate trends, Sarasohn never loses sight of the human faces. He reminds us that, since the implementation of Measure 5 and the program- and opportunity-cutting bloodbath that followed, 5,000 of those faces annually didn't have a chance at higher education. He finds and names students for whom even a modest tuition increase will mean dropping out. He worries, as should we all, about how mountains of student debt will affect job decisions, marriage plans, and personal opportunity. He points to the growing demographic of ethnic-minority youngsters who have no family experience of educational support. He goads us to consider the striking contrast of Oregon's situation with the robust support higher education garners elsewhere nationally (for example, in our neighboring state of Washington) and, increasingly, internationally. And he salutes higher-education investments in other states and countries that "paid off like an overenthusiastic slot machine."

Sarasohn's essays document the social consequences of decades of neglect of higher education: "In valuing universities the market doesn't grade on effort. It grades on investment and performance—and it grades over decades" (June 10, 2007). He urges us to worry deeply because the present generation of Oregonians aged 25 to 34 is less well educated than its parents—a development unique in American history! He notes the consensus that higher education is a central asset that ensures economic competitiveness and personal well-being. He wonders if Oregon's aspiration is "to be mediocre more cheaply" (Feb. 26, 1995).

Higher education makes an easily demonstrable contribution to individual economic well-being. Ironically, this measurable personal benefit is sometimes cited by critics who claim that this "private good" should be paid for, regardless of the amount of debt accrued, by its recipients. Sarasohn knows this dodge and looks to the larger "public goods" from educational achievement that economists find real, but less quantifiable: national economic competitiveness; literacy; civic participation; reduced levels of crime, delinquency, and abuse; and engaged personal and family opportunity. As befits his deserved but unofficial title as Oregon journalism's most powerful higher-education advocate, Sarasohn's support for higher education serves values far deeper and richer than the cause of personal economic advancement alone.

There are bright spots, though. To the surprise of pessimists, Sarasohn accurately reports that Oregon's universities are far, far better than their balance sheets indicate. Respected "performance measures" gauge and show welcome and even surprising progress in quality and performance by nearly every institution. Sarasohn gratifyingly often salutes the dedication of my colleagues.

It is painful to contemplate recent scientific evidence that earthworms and laboratory animals live substantially longer on seriously restricted diets. Perhaps (and Kafka might agree) a modest degree of starvation is better for life and creativity than is corpulence. Oregon universities have no experience of the latter, so the test site—at a time when formerly wealthy institutions stagger from economic setbacks—must reside elsewhere. Operating on margins that are this thin, we do know one theme that Sarasohn's work reiterates: there is a very fine line between scarcity and mediocrity. No one benefits from, nor ultimately will pay for, mediocre higher education.

In Sarasohn's work, there is no political naiveté. He avoids glib "pox on both their houses" rhetoric and invokes the absurd and sardonic rather than taking cheap cynical shots. He is equally adept at dissecting wine varieties and national political issues. He includes research that is authoritative beyond mere anecdote, a tribute to the rigor of his own academic training. His writing flashes throughout with humor, biting or rich, usually unexpected but always welcome, as in his passing observation of May 30, 1997, that in terms of the state's attention "it's been a lot better to be a felon than a freshman," or his tale of how the use of llamas in a lobbying effort helped save the highest-cost program in the system, veterinary medicine, in the face of much more highly ranked priorities. (The latter example is my personal favorite, and well worth the price of the book alone.) Higher-education champions are supremely fortunate to have his enduring commitment.

An introduction should provide context for the reader's journey into great ideas. It is my honor to invite you to share David Sarasohn's reflections on Oregon's unhappy efforts to keep a promise made long ago to public higher education. In this journey we meet ourselves: flawed leaders, flawed followers, imperfect visions, and disagreements over means, ends, or egos, or all three. But those components are universal to the human condition, and Sarasohn urges us to move above and beyond them, if we can. He is deeply witty, deeply wise, and he hasn't given up. Neither should we. Hopefully this book will spur policymakers to give renewed attention to our state's original higher-education commitment.

Kafka's "A Hunger Artist" concludes with the circus masters clearing the artist's cage of his remains and introducing a young panther in hopes of reclaiming the crowds. David Sarasohn would remind us that even Kafka could not have predicted that panthers would become an endangered species.

—DAVE FROHNMAYER
former president, University of Oregon;
former dean, University of Oregon Law School;
professor of law, University of Oregon Law School, 1971–81;
former state representative, 1975–80;
former attorney general of Oregon, 1981–91

Preface
Thinning the Soup

*"We have to ask ourselves, what do the other
states know that we don't know?"*
—JOSEPH W. COX,
former chancellor of the Oregon State
System of Higher Education

In the spring of 2007, during one of various attempts by Oregon's higher-education system to get noticed at the state capitol, Mark Perlman, a philosophy professor at Western Oregon University, raised a point about the difficulty of hiring new professors in a system with a faculty pay scale somewhere between the national averages and lunch money. Seeking an Eastern philosopher, his department had focused on a candidate who was, understandably, a Buddhist.

"Buddhists are not known for monetary interests," said Perlman. "We offered him the job, and he turned us down over money.

"That's how bad it is now. Oregon can't even hire a Buddhist."

Although the faculty pay levels are ideal for people who don't eat meat.

If the hiring had worked out, it might have brought a useful perspective to a higher-education system that's often sounded like one hand clapping—and that has given neither hand much to clap about.

The Buddha sat under a bo tree for seven weeks, and arose enlightened. Oregon has sat for decades under a declining timber economy without ever accepting that the world around it is changing. Despite what even Oregon politicians would piously call an emerging knowledge economy, the state has steadily disinvested in its higher-education system, even while bracketed by world-class research universities to the north and south.

In 1989–90, the Oregon higher-education system drew 55 percent of its teaching and educational funds from the state general fund and 37 percent from tuition. In 2009–11, the numbers were 26 percent from the state, 64 percent from tuition. When funding for research and other activities are included, the state's percentage becomes considerably smaller. Over that time, the percentage of the general fund going to higher education plunged from 8.22 percent to 4.78 percent. In that 20-year period, state funding for prisons caught up with and shot past higher-education funding, creating a state where, quite possibly, it's better to be a felon than a freshman.

Nationally, in the past 20 years, the percentage of state budgets going toward higher education has slipped. But there are a couple of particular circumstances why Oregon's varsity letter has been especially lower-case.

First, its universities were never in great shape to begin with.

Second, while other states' university budgets have been on the down escalator, Oregon's has been descending by elevator. Three times in the past three decades—during the timber recession of the early 1980s, after the passage of Measure 5 in 1990 and in the post-9/11 downturn—Oregon cut its per-student spending more sharply than any other state, sometimes when most other states weren't cutting at all, or were actually investing.

In 1994, Oregon cut its general-fund support for higher education by 10.5 percent. Only one other state—Montana—cut its spending at all.

"We have to ask ourselves," mused Joseph W. Cox, chancellor of what was then the Oregon State System of Higher Education (now the Oregon University System), "what do the other states know that we don't know?"

An even more interesting question is, Why don't we want to know it?

During years when states such as Washington, Illinois and Connecticut were declaring their determination to join the higher public-university elite, to contend with Berkeley or Michigan, it seemed that Oregon's dearest goal was to be mediocre more cheaply.

Just about the same time Perlman was explaining the problems of Oregon hiring, Washington Governor Christine Gregoire was explaining her state's strategy.

"We invested in our research institutions," she declared. "We absolutely believe that the U of W and WSU are two of the greatest economic-growth engines in the state."

In the lecture halls and laboratories of the Northwest, Gregoire's declaration of intellectual dependence could be engraved next to a comment by Jim Craven, a longtime lobbyist for the American Electronics Association of Oregon: "Here, when the higher-ed folks are cutting 8 percent instead of 15 percent, that's a great victory."

Combined with Oregon's constant—and deepening—underfunding has been an intense overmanagement. As loath as legislators have been to let loose money, they've been even more reluctant to lose control. Oregon's legislature sends $6 billion to K–12, with virtually no strings attached. About one-tenth of that amount goes to universities, with thousands of separate line-item appropriations.

Months after his testimony before a legislative committee in February 2009, Oregon State president Ed Ray recalled, with only a small shudder, "I urged the legislators that whatever they were going to give us, not to micromanage us. I later heard from the chancellor's office that the legislators thought it was charming that I'd said those things, but that's not the way things work."

The state capitol's disdain for higher education has been bipartisan. Support has slid under Republican legislatures and Democratic governors, and it's been rare to hear calls from either side to make higher education a priority,

When asked about faculty salaries at a faculty-student meeting at OSU in 1990, Governor Neil Goldschmidt replied dismissively, "Faculties are paranoid. Faculties care about faculty business and very little else. . . . I don't think the world should be buffaloed when a university faculty tells us they want money for something, that somehow they just came down from Mount Sinai."

Certainly, Oregon never has been buffaloed.

The occasional lonely voice suggesting that higher education would shape the future of the state could also come from either side. In 1995, Rep. Del Parks, a Republican from Klamath Falls, argued, "When someone makes a higher income because of college, the state takes 10 percent off the top. For every extra $1,000 they make, the state gets another $100. It doesn't come back for 15 years, but then it comes back big-time."

Typically, this has been a calculation much too long-range for most elected officials in Salem to make. Only about once a decade—in 1985, 1999 and 2007—has the legislature actually taken notice of its universities, with each such session providing the brief relief of a canteen in the desert, temporary support that swiftly runs out.

For the past two decades, Oregon's thinking about its higher-education system has focused largely on strategies for dealing with underfunding. It's been a kind of academic shell game, trying to keep things moving things fast enough to hide the missing money. The strategies have extended from a frenzied hunt for duplication—the argument that it is wasteful for two universities to teach the same thing even if classrooms at both places are packed—in the 1980s, to Southern Oregon University's decision in 2010 to essentially cut its ten-week quarters to nine weeks.

In the 1990s, the system turned to an approach that Chancellor Bartlett referred to as "thinning the soup," reducing offerings and enlarging classes and student-faculty ratios. Since this strategy was paired with a dramatic increase in tuition, shifting the funding responsibility from the state to the student, it resulted in students explicitly being charged more for less.

One briefly successful financial ploy, helped by short-term university problems in California, was "spreading the net," which entailed sharply increasing the number of out-of-state students paying out-of-state tuition—particularly at the University of Oregon and Southern Oregon. At one point, approximately half the U of O freshman class came from out of state, and U of O President Myles Brand urged faculty members making out-of-state appearances to ask if they could speak to some high school students. A hundred more students paying out-of-state tuition, he pointed out, came to a million dollars, and while 100 students weren't a lot of students, a million dollars was a lot of money. By the mid-'90s, the Oregon state system had 5,000 fewer students—and perhaps 10,000 fewer Oregon students.

The impact might have been called a neutron bomb effect—the university buildings were still there, but many of the Oregon students were gone.

By the time of the Great Recession, the approach had turned more to increasing considerably both the tuition and the numbers of Oregon students, while still not examining too closely what the customers were getting for their money.

In some cases, state universities seeking cost savings that wouldn't be noticed in their academic output cut back on counselors and student services—a strategy that does indeed save money, until a large hunk of your freshman class doesn't return for sophomore year.

The state also turned to the popular bureaucratic stratagem of deferred maintenance, until by 2007 the system had a maintenance shortfall of $650 million. The situation's poster boy was Portland State's Lincoln Hall, a building already old when the Portland school system gave it to Portland State College in the middle of the last century, a building still open mostly because the city had never sent an inspector to close it down. When Governor Ted Kulongoski visited the building's roof that spring to garner backing for capital reinvestment, PSU President Dan Bernstine said he appreciated the governor's support but he wasn't going up there.

In Oregon, there has always been the confidence that reorganization can create what other states have to spend money to achieve. As former Portland State president Judith Ramaley once remarked, "I've never seen any place that had such faith in moving around boxes." The problem with reorganization, she went on to note, was, "All you're doing is taking a bunch of underfunded institutions and putting them together to share our poverty."

After decades, the debate has changed remarkably little. In the mid-1980s, Oregonians argued that the system had too many campuses, and could save money by selling the Oregon College of Education to the state to use as a prison. Two decades later, the institution was renamed Western Oregon University, but Oregon higher-education board vice chairman Kirby Dyess was warning that at the current level of funding, Oregon could not afford all its campuses and might have to sell one.

So to deal with Portland's status as the largest major metropolitan area without a major research university, the idea of merging Portland State University with Oregon Health and Science University was proposed. The resulting institution might not have research university doctoral programs, but it would have a research university letterhead.

Over those same decades, both the University of Washington and Washington State University opened three new campuses.

With livability such a major priority in Oregon, it's sometimes hard to see why higher education isn't. "Leadership is a puzzle. This is a state based on lots of small enterprises, and very mixed cultures," Bartlett noted, after completing five frustrating years as chancellor of the state system in the nineties.

"I don't understand why the business leaders of this state don't understand how important higher education is to them. It just didn't happen here the way it happened all around us.

"There's been an attitude on the part of some of our political leaders that the real folks are the ones who go no further than community college," he continued. Yet, "it's clear that if we want to go to the kind of high-value-added society we want, people can't stop at community college—unless we want to import our talent. We can do that, and imperceptibly colonize ourselves."

Possibly, this attitude comes from the time when Oregon was rich with family-wage jobs, in forests and fish, that didn't require higher education. The attitude endured even after the forest issue had changed entirely—to Oregon's banking its economic future on being the "Silicon Forest," even though it's not really your nickname when you're the only one who uses it. Despite repeated warnings by the high-tech industry that Oregon lacked the academic-research firepower to be a real technology center, Oregon assumed its status had to be permanent—until the Great Recession reminded the state where the real high-tech centers are.

Now, Oregon has a system not only hard-pressed to produce economic energy but also hard-pressed to produce enough graduates. We're at a point where the people moving to Oregon are better educated than the people who grew up here, and Oregonians in their 40s and 50s are better educated than Oregonians in their 30s. Oregon's state benchmarks call for 40 percent of Oregonians to have four-year degrees. Just to match our current level of 28 percent, in the next two decades we'd need a capacity increase the size of the University of Oregon. To reach 40 percent, we'd need three more Oregon States.

That would take a real Beaver believer.

There may be another reason why Oregon's leadership has never felt a tight connection with the state's higher-education system. Oregon has always been a place of changing population; its only Pulitzer Prize–winning novelist, H. L. Davis, once said it is a place where stories that begin somewhere else end, or where stories begin that will end somewhere else. Accordingly, these days not quite half the membership of the Oregon legislature was born here, let alone went to a state university.

By contrast, the University of Georgia has produced 12 of the state's U.S. senators, and 25 of its governors. One alumnus who filled both jobs, Zell Miller, created the Georgia Hope Scholarship program, where a B average in a state high school provides free tuition to a state university. It's surprising how effective this is as a recruiting device, how the University of Georgia has recently advanced from 26th to 20th nationally among public universities, and how Georgia legislators' question about the university system isn't "What can we cut next?" but "How 'bout them Dawgs?"

If Oregonians—and Oregon legislators—actually identified with the state's universities, the universities in turn would redefine Oregon. We would have a higher-education system that provided a desperately needed economic engine, a system that provided the university access Oregon children deserve, a system that gave Oregon a national and international presence beyond rose gardens and recycling.

Or at the very least, we would have a system that could afford to hire a Buddhist.

—DAVID SARASOHN

The *Oregonian* columns

July 15, 1990 - July 18, 2010

State System Sinking in '90s

Over the next 10 years, as present trends develop, the quality of Oregon's public university faculty will get worse and worse.

At the same time, due to competition caused by enrollment pressures that the system is in no condition to meet, the quality of students should be getting better and better.

Maybe around 1998, the two will meet, and Oregon will have drowned in two different demographic waves at once.

Nationally, the 1990s will begin a time of faculty scarcity and student increase. The next governor of Oregon will inherit a higher-education system that is in no shape to deal with either one.

To see the full extent of the problem, we have to make a short tour of the Incredible Shrinking Law School, the Compression Chamber, the Advice that Got Taken, the Echo Boom and, finally, head off on the Iowa Trail.

But first, we have to meet the Wolf Who Showed Up.

For years, faculty in the Oregon state system have been complaining about their salaries, consistently in the lowest third of the national rankings. But for years, despite the professors' insistence that the wolf was at the door and was already eating away at their morale, it hardly mattered: During the 1970s and early 1980s, there was a national professor surplus, and even a state paying the way Oregon was could pick up some bargains.

Oregon has taken full advantage of the situation.

From 1978 to 1988, Oregon's per capita state support of higher education dropped from 17th to 34th in the country, tying it with Nevada for fastest ride downhill. A substantial faculty pay increase in Gov. Vic Atiyeh's last legislative session improved the situation temporarily, lifting Oregon State University to 79th and the University of Oregon to 90th in pay ratings out of 111 doctorate-granting public institutions.

Since then, however, during the Goldschmidt administration, the system has slid like a base-stealer. In the next year, OSU and the UO fell to 95th and 104th out of 117, and in the newest rankings, they are 103rd and 110th out of 120. The University of Oregon is now three spots below Northern Arizona and three spots above Texas Southern.

"Faculties are paranoid," Gov. Neil Goldschmidt told an Oregon State faculty-student meeting in March, responding to a question on faculty pay. "Faculties care about faculty business and very little else . . . I don't think the world should be buffaloed, when a university faculty tells us they want money for something, that somehow they just came down from Mount Sinai."

On higher-education issues, Goldschmidt has been a rebel without a clue.

Because the wolf is finally showing up.

Nationally, the professors tenured in the academic boom years of the '50s and '60s are about to turn in their lecture notes. The University of Oregon, like many across the country, is going to have to replace one-third to one-half of its faculty during the 1990s.

At these prices, that's going to be tricky—especially since, in fields such as business, science, engineering and even foreign languages, universities now compete increasingly not only with each other, but also with corporate hiring.

26

In fact, it already is tricky, which gets us to the Incredibly Shrinking Law School.

During each of the last few years, the University of Oregon Law School has set out to hire three or four professors. In that time, it has offered permanent jobs to ten applicants.

It has hired only one person.

This year, the American Bar Association has placed the law school on probation.

Something about understaffing—and insufficient resources.

"Here we have a national organization saying the law school is underfunded," said UO President Myles Brand, "but on the campus, the law school is funded above the average."

The wolf is showing up at a lot of other schools and departments in the system. At Oregon State, the School of Veterinary Medicine has also been put on probation.

And, as Executive Vice Chancellor W.G. Lemman points out, those are just the schools that have been assessed lately.

"If we were undergoing review in other areas," said Lemman, "we might be in as much trouble in those."

A lot of faculty members aren't waiting for the wolf. According to a five-year study at Oregon State, professors leaving for other places are getting an average pay increase of 47 percent.

The proudest recent boast of higher education around here has been the creation of centers of excellence at each university campus, such as in engineering at Oregon State. But it's already clear that the centers cannot hold; an OSU associate professor of nuclear engineering, earning $25,582, was hired away by Texas A&M for $47,872. Oregon State has been unable to hire a chairman for its department of chemical engineering.

Oregon Health Sciences University, which thanks to Sen. Mark Hatfield has had a building boom, is having trouble finding men (or women) to match its mountaintop. It has been unable to hire chairmen for its departments of microbiology, medical genetics, radiation oncology and pathology.

Portland State University calculates that it has recently been outbid on 26 job offers, as well as losing current faculty members. Its losses are not only in business and the hard sciences, but even in areas such as history, foreign languages and music, where just a few years ago colleges could buy professors at $1.98 a pound.

These days, even the wolf knows better.

"We don't have to be at the top of the salary scales," said Brand, noting that some faculty will take a bit less to be in Oregon. "If you give me average salaries, I can build a hell of a university."

At the moment, of course, Brand is not being given average salaries, but he and his associates still have to find bodies to teach their classes. That gets us to the Compression Chamber.

That's where senior and junior salaries get pushed together.

"When institutions recruit young professors," said Lemman, "often they have to be paid more than colleagues who have three, four, six or ten years' experience."

The popularity of this approach among senior faculty can be imagined.

"Current personnel practices have caused me to realize that this institution has little loyalty to its faculty and is owed little in return," said Robert Jones, a psychology professor at PSU.

Portland State still tries to recruit the best, says Jones, "but the best new people don't stay long. The day after they're hired, they start losing against the national average."

In any compression, something escapes. What's escaping here is faculty.

And the state system's position continues to crumble, as other states make substantial investments in their higher-education programs. In the last two legislatures, university faculty were given raises considerably below the national average.

"We're shooting at a moving target," says higher-education Chancellor Thomas Bartlett. "Once you get behind in the game, you have to run twice as fast just to keep up."

Up to now, the state has shown little interest in breaking into a trot. Goldschmidt said he would ask the next Legislature for a $45 million increase for faculty salaries, but by the time the money gets into the system, other states' increases will have sent Oregon's universities even further down the river.

One answer, as Bartlett points out, is to shrink the system, to give the state the universities it's paying for. This is happening already, and the squeeze is going to get a lot tighter.

Putting it another way, there are a lot of eighth-graders now thinking about being a Duck or a Beaver who'd better learn the mascot of their local community college.

"If we were to take all the students who qualify, there would be at least a couple thousand more here," says Graham Spanier, provost of Oregon State. "We consider ourselves the people's university. We're very uncomfortable turning away people who are qualified to be here."

At PSU, according to Provost Frank Martino, the situation is worse: "We could increase enrollment by 5,000 overnight. We have to turn them away with baseball bats."

One reason Oregon's registrars have been getting out the Louisville Sluggers—and will be taking a lot more batting practice in the next few years—is the Advice That Got Taken.

Throughout the 1980s, the number of 18-year-olds was declining, and people were contemplating turning colleges into planters. But at the same time, students were being told that their only hope for the future was college.

Rotten kids. They always do what you tell them.

As a result, although the number of potential college students dropped, the percentage of high school students going on to college increased, and they were joined by a lot of people too old for fraternity hazing.

That's why state university admissions standards keep going up. The alternative is to have classrooms that get declared overcrowded by the fire marshal.

And these are the good times.

That roaring you hear in the distance is called the Echo Boom, meaning that all the baby boomers who failed to have children on time finally got around to being fruitful and multiplying.

In 1991, the number of Oregon high school graduates bottoms out, at 25,635. Then it starts to shoot upward, until in 2000 it reaches 33,785.

All this happens at the same time the percentage of graduates going to college keeps rising, at the same time newcomers keep moving into the state.

By the year 2000, it could be tougher to get into the University of Oregon than into the NBA finals.

Oregon is not, of course, the only state to face this kind of challenge. The difference is that other states are doing something about it.

California—admittedly not an exact parallel, although its projected growth rate is just slightly higher than Oregon's—is planning three new University of California campuses by 2000, increasing UC enrollment from 165,000 to at least 232,000. The California State University system will grow from about 350,000 students now to 547,000 by 2005.

Soon, our football teams will be able to lose to UC Modesto.

Washington has launched a growth program to increase the capacity of its system by 30 percent by 2010, including two new University of Washington campuses and three new Washington State University campuses—the largest in Vancouver.

The system is working on a program to make itself one of the top five in the country by 1995.

California and Washington, it is immediately pointed out, are larger, wealthier states, which have cities and everything. But there are other models.

There is, for example, Iowa, which with just a little more sagebrush would resemble Oregon completely. In 1988, Iowa was the 29th-largest state, with a population of 2.8 million and per capita income of $14,764.

Oregon is the 30th state, with 2.7 million people and per capita income of $14,982.

Oregon is the smallest state in the Pac-10 while Iowa is the smallest state in the Big 10, although they've been to the Rose Bowl more recently.

But in direct state support of higher education—community colleges to graduate schools—Iowa is 12th in per capita spending, paying $180 per citizen, while Oregon is 34th, paying $140. The difference means that Iowa supports two major universities, each about 60 percent bigger than Oregon and Oregon State, with the University of Iowa 18th on the salary charts and Iowa State 36th. It also supports a sizable regional institution, the University of Northern Iowa, and provides $2,600 a year for each Iowa student attending an Iowa private college.

"I've been here 8½ years, and I've seen tremendous growth in our effort to keep our students in Iowa," said John Heisner, director of program administration for the Iowa College Aid Commission. "There's never enough money, but there's been a commitment in the Legislature to maintaining our level."

The Iowa system is in the early stages of designing a long-term growth plan.

"Iowa is what we call a high-effort state," said Edward R. Hines, director of the Center for Higher Education at Illinois State University. "Oregon has been having some problems recently."

Maybe what Oregon needs is more corn.

At the moment, Oregon is in no position to consider a program to increase its enrollment and maintain its present level of higher-education opportunity. The best it could do is ask some departing faculty to take some students with them.

But the accessibility question is one the system can't avoid. There have already been complaints about the University of Oregon's elevated new admissions hurdles; as the steps to all the institutions get steeper and narrower, legislators will have lots of interesting conversations with parents and students.

"One thing the system is very responsive to is political pressure," said state Sen. Cliff Trow, D-Corvallis. "At that point, something will probably happen."

Unfortunately, that point just gets you back to the first point, where the Wolf Who Showed Up hasn't gone away.

"My own opinion," UO President Brand added, "is that we can't even begin to think about expanding until we repair the cracks in the foundation. And if we don't make substantial progress by the midpoint of the decade, we'll have too hard a job."

That job is waiting for the next governor.

He'll find the higher-education system waiting over by the wolf.

THE OREGONIAN, JULY 15, 1990

1. State General Fund contribution to university budgets

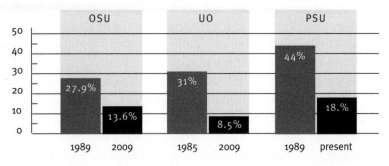

SOURCE: OUS Controller's Division and published financial statements

Demonstrates drop in amount of funds Oregon state contributed to its public universities from 1989 to 2009.

Higher Education
Heading Even Lower

In California, they say that the difference between Gov. Ronald Reagan and Gov. George Deukmejian was that Deukmejian meant it. Over the last eight years, Deukmejian greatly expanded prison capacity, opposed new taxes, and took a Grinchlike view of health, education and social spending.

With one exception.

When Deukmejian became governor in 1983, according to University of California president David Gardner, he asked Gardner three questions: What was the condition of the university system? What was the significance of that? What could he do to help?

Because of the answers Gardner gave, state funding of the UC system doubled during Deukmejian's two terms. Enrollment went up, quality improved and the system is now writing fight songs for three new campuses.

If you didn't know that Deukmejian was a conservative, you might almost call his higher-education spending liberal.

Right now, people are also asking three questions about the Oregon higher-education system:

Do we really need one?

How small can we make it?

Can't we get cheaper faculty?

The last higher-education system getting this kind of support was the American University of Beirut.

From this legislative session, Oregon's colleges and universities were hoping for a rebuilding bonus after two decades of neglect. What they're getting is a $90 million bill for their share of Measure 5.

It's hard to know exactly what kind of condition the state's higher-education system will be in two years from now. That's because nobody's sure about one question:

What's the level below mediocre?

Deukmejian was moved to make higher education a priority after Gardner told him that only 71 percent of UC's first-choice job offers were accepted. The governor piloted through a substantial pay increase, and UC's acceptance rate returned to 90 percent.

There is no comparable figure at the University of Oregon, because most of your first-choice faculty candidates would never apply to a school in the bottom 15 percent of pay range in the first place. Just because you have a doctorate doesn't mean you're stupid.

The meaningful calculations in the Oregon system aren't about professors who are arriving, they're about professors who are leaving. That was the situation before Measure 5; now, of course, the gravy train is over.

"Oregon could easily stumble into a Third World system from which it would take decades to recover," says Chancellor Thomas Bartlett. "We need programs that are competitive outside Oregon."

To try to maintain some programs that won't make people in other states giggle, Bartlett has to reduce the total enrollment of the system. "Either we get rid of some students," he points out, "or we expand the class sizes and inflate the currency. That's not going to happen."

Just at the time when high schools are producing more graduates, and other states are increasing their college enrollment, Oregon will be shrinking its campuses. Oregon: Things learn differently here.

There is also the small matter of a recession, which traditionally causes students who are attending or considering private colleges to return to the state system.

Or at least to try to.

All of this amounts to a higher-education system, especially at the University of Oregon, that will be harder to get into than a bank vault. Then again, you might want to get into the vault first, because tuition now has to go up big-time.

All of this, of course, only happens in the first round of Measure 5 cuts. If we somehow go through all three rounds without finding some more money, Bartlett projects, in 1996 we'll have a state undergraduate system consisting entirely of Oregon State University and a branch campus in Portland.

This will at least solve one of Oregon's problems: whether the state can support two programs in the Pac-10.

Unless Oregon does something about its direction, we're building a unique kind of state here, with its own special attraction.

We will, from now on, have lower property taxes, or at least lower property tax rates. Most of public health care should survive, because the feds won't let the state cut it much. Higher education will be embarrassing, and K-12 perhaps not much better, but that only matters if you think you've got a future.

We may not ever get a governor like Deukmejian, who can put through a higher-education reconstruction plan, but we'll get lots of other California retirees.

Because what we're building is a terrific state to die in.

THE OREGONIAN, JANUARY 6, 1991

In Higher-Ed Playoff, Oregon's Trailing

Once again, it's time to play, "What Does Washington Know That Oregon Doesn't?"

This time, the category is Higher Education.

First question: Which state slid from 17th to 34th nationally in support of higher education during the 1980s, has faculty salaries in the bottom fifth of the country and is currently preparing for the future by cutting its higher-education enrollment by 10 percent?

Hint: Don't think of the Rose Bowl.

I'm sorry, hiding behind the *Chronicle of Higher Education* won't help.

Let's go to the next question: Which state currently has a plan to build five new university campuses, increase enrollment by 30 percent and become one of the top five state systems in the country by 1995?

Hint: Look at a dollar bill.

And if you live in a state that's moving into the next century with a third-rate higher-education system, you'd better look at one quickly.

Admittedly, Washington's momentum in higher education seemed to slow recently, when Gov. Booth Gardner produced a budget with $82 million in higher-education cuts—although still including an 8.2 percent faculty salary increase. But last month, when revenue forecasts came in, Gardner proposed putting $85 million back.

"We've made significant advances in our colleges and universities over the past six years," said Gardner, "and it's important to me to maintain the commitment to excellence."

But Gardner's plans may run into trouble with the Republican chairman of the Senate Higher Education Committee.

The senator wants to spend more.

In some ways, the Columbia is a very wide river.

Next question: Which state has an urban branch university that raised nearly $1 million in cash from local businessmen this year?

Sorry, it's not Oregon, home of Portland State.

It's the University of Washington at Tacoma—the Fighting Sea-Tacs?—which first opened its doors last September, won't have a real campus until 1996 and has just received $850,000 from the Executive Council for a Greater Tacoma.

"It's a nice welcome, a very nice welcome for our branch campus," said Marilyn Dunn, vice president for development.

After 40 years, Portland State University is still waiting for that kind of welcome. In fiscal 1990, Portland State raised $373,843 from local companies, plus another $80,813 in non-cash contributions. This year, things are running a bit better, thanks partly to $1 million in software from Mentor Graphics, but nobody's expecting $850,000 in cash to come walking in the door.

Historically, there have been lots of explanations for the limited support by Portland business for PSU: Portland's not a very big city; the college ties run to other places; power patrons around here usually aren't Portland State alumni. Yet in a smaller city, just down the road from mighty UW Seattle, $850,000 is collected for an institution with no alumni at all.

It looks like Washington does know something Oregon doesn't. Before anybody plans on the success of PSU's new action plan, requiring

$4 million in private funding, somebody had better figure out what it is.

But the next question gets us to the brighter side: One state is investing heavily in higher-education expansion in the Portland area. Which one?

Does the phrase, "First in war, first in peace, first in Seattle Mariners" suggest anything?

Last month, Washington selected a 350-acre site north of Vancouver for the construction of a $50 million local campus of Washington State University. By 1996, when the campus opens, WSU-Vancouver should enroll 2,500; by 2010, the total will be 5,000.

Of course, the figures can grow with Washington's demand—or Oregon's decay.

"In 20 years, there'll be a major higher-education institution in the Portland area," predicted a ranking PSU official last spring. "It will be in Vancouver."

With a visa, you'll be able to visit.

This gets us to the last question: Which state is now planning for the increasing need for higher education for Oregon students?

Hint: It has the same name as a large eastern city where George Bush lives.

With the coming enrollment cutbacks in Oregon, WSU is looking across the river at a whole new market.

"It's a major shock for students, and we're trying to let them know we encourage their applications," says Terry Flynn, Washington State admissions director. "We're not going to be like sharks after blood, but we're going to help them however we can."

It's nice of Flynn not to be specific about who's bleeding.

Time for one more round of "What Does Washington Know That Oregon Doesn't?"

This time, higher education isn't the category.

It's the answer.

THE OREGONIAN, APRIL 3, 1991

Oregon Studying to Be a Sidekick State

One of the great job descriptions in American culture is "sidekick." Large, friendly and not too bright, the sidekick's main role is to watch the hero admiringly.

There was Gabby Hayes for Roy Rogers, Goober on *The Andy Griffith Show* and the Wookie in *Star Wars*.

And in the Northwest, there's Oregon as a sidekick for Washington.

From what happened to the two states' higher-education system in the legislative sessions just past, it seems that "sidekick" may be Oregon's career objective.

Both states ended up with budgets that they hope will keep their quality levels about where they are. But Washington is postponing its plans to boost quality in order to expand enrollment by about 4 percent. Oregon, in order to keep from losing quality, is cutting its enrollment by about 4 percent.

Even in a national fiscal crisis in higher education, nobody else has felt the need to do that. According to Edward R. Hines, director of the

Center for Higher Education at Illinois State, "I'm not aware of any sys-tem-wide enrollment in any state that is going down," although for states in Oregon's condition, it's "an unfortunate but a rational approach."

The different decisions have nothing to do with different levels of demand, which will be rising in both states as numbers of high school graduates rise through the 1990s.

"The baby boomers' children are coming in, so let's get prepared for them," explains state Sen. Dan McDonald, a conservative Republican from Bellevue, Wash., who chairs the Senate Ways and Means Committee and pushed hard for higher-education budget increases.

Just as in Oregon, arguments about supporting higher education tend to say a lot about economic development.

"Clearly, that's the driver, that's what makes quality firms stay in a place," says McDonald. "But I think there are quality of life and mobility in society arguments as well."

Sidekicks, if you remember, hardly ever talk about qual-ity of life. Mostly they say things like, "By golly!" or in the case of the Wookie, "Arrrrgggggh!"

That is, curiously enough, just what Oregonians might say about the existing quality difference between Washington's and Oregon's systems— the situation that Oregon's cutbacks hope to preserve.

According to Washington's figures, the budget at Washington State University per full-time student is $12,002. By Oregon's figures, the spending per full-time student at Oregon State University is $8,645.

The gap between the University of Washington and the University of Oregon is even wider—$12,351 to $7,298—but that's partly because the UW has a medical school.

Lots of this, but not all of it, has to do with faculty salaries. In the cur-rent American Association of University Professors salary rankings for 123 doctorate-granting universities, the University of Washington is 38th, Washington State is 85th, Oregon State is 106th, University of Oregon 110th and Portland State is 112th.

Portland State is kind of the sidekick's sidekick.

Washington's long-term objective is to move into the top fifth. Oregon's long-term objective is to keep from falling off the chart.

Actually, Washington doesn't pay much attention to the AAUP lists. It compares its university salaries with a group of state universities that it considers comparable. The University of Oregon is not on the list.

"Oregon is just not a peer state to Washington," explained Dan Keller, associate director of the Washington Higher Education Coordination Board. "They've just not had the commitment in the past."

By golly.

Or possibly, "Arrrggggh."

By the past, Keller doesn't necessarily mean the deep, dark past. In 1973-75, higher education drew 17.4 percent of the state's budget. By 1989-1991, it was down to 15.2 percent, and for 1991-1993, it will be at 12.5 percent. Like Oregon, Washington's system took a pounding in the recession of the early 1980s; according to McDonald, the Washington Legislature set out actively in the following sessions to repair the damage.

For some, there's recently been a bright side to the Oregon funding levels: Faculty laid off as a result of the new budget haven't lost much.

"Often, the faculty we've had to ask to leave are ending up with very attractive appointments and better salaries," says Thomas Bartlett, Oregon's chancellor of higher education. "That's hard on the folks back home.

The general take on higher education's new budget was that, with Measure 5, things actually could have been much worse.

That's also the kind of thing the sidekick usually says.

"We've gotten into a trap of saying that this isn't really as bad as we thought it was going to be, rather than saying this is a major setback," says Bartlett. "In terms of what we've got to achieve, we are adding to our problems at every level—but not as much as we thought we would add."

And we've gotten further into a regional situation in which one state has a strong, expanding system and the other—which tries in some ways to be competitive—has a weak, shriveling one. While Washington is creating new campuses, Oregon is shutting down programs.

On the other hand, Oregon is offering its students one new major. You might call it Sidekick Studies.

THE OREGONIAN, JULY 28, 1991

Rising Students
for Sinking Colleges

Portland School Superintendent Matthew Prophet's plan to send every willing Portland high school graduate to college has everything going for it. The idea has leadership from Prophet, enthusiasm from the community and even the beginnings of some seed money.

In fact, there might be only one thing missing:

Colleges to send them to.

Tell Oregon's public colleges that you have a great plan to send them another thousand students a year, and they'll wonder how you missed the "No Vacancy" sign on the door.

After the first round of Measure 5 cuts, the ones that we're assured didn't actually hurt anything and were probably good for us, there are 2,500 fewer students in Oregon's higher-education system. The reductions were created largely by sharp increases in tuition to replace vanishing state support.

And that phase was the good part.

Prophet says he hopes to have his plan in place for Portland's graduating class of 1995. By that time, Measure 5 is scheduled to take another $2 billion out of the state budget. The only way higher education can deal with that is to turn state colleges into discount shopping malls.

At least the University of Oregon has a good location for it.

If the system tries to keep itself intact by raising tuition again, the 1993-94 school year could see another 50 percent increase. It won't go that high, but in a Measure 5 world, people raising money to send Portland graduates to college may find that the system has to increase tuition faster than they can come up with it.

Gov. Barbara Roberts insisted Thursday that there would not be another major tuition increase, even if campuses had to close. According to the higher-education system's newest projections, out Thursday, absorbing a 20 percent cut in state aid without any tuition increase would cut enrollment by 8,000 to 10,000. Then, of course, there'd be another equally large round of cuts in 1995 through 1997.

Considering that at the same time the places in the state system will be dropping, the number of Oregon high school graduates will be increasing, Portland's Class of 1995 might need more than financial aid to get into Oregon State.

It might need a crowbar.

The point isn't that there's anything wrong with Prophet's idea, which would be a terrific program for Portland to mount.

The point is just that on the present schedule Oregon's colleges may spend 1995 greeting more moving vans than students.

Of course, this level of denial is not limited to higher-education issues. Legislators keep urging new ways to put people in prison and keep them there longer, while in a matter of months we won't have room for the ones we've got locked up now. Political leaders point proudly to our new educational-reform program, without mentioning that it's a huge check written on an empty bank account.

Mentioning this situation now is considered a form of political bad taste. We are supposed to wait until the climate is right, something like the Bush administration's position on global warming.

In higher education, sometimes laughingly referred to as the engine of our economic future, people are starting to notice that it's getting pretty warm here already. In late February, a group of leaders of students, faculty and administrators urged the governor to move quickly on the issue.

"Higher education in the state of Oregon is heading for a disaster," said Jean Stockard, president of the Oregon Conference of the American Association of University Professors. "Unless substantial new sources of revenue are found within the next few months, the second phase of Measure 5 will require budget cuts that will amount to more than the closing of all of the regional state schools plus the Oregon Institute of Technology."

Last Thursday, a tutorial of Oregon's college presidents argued that the situation was not being helped by waiting. Universities and colleges are beginning their 1993-1995 budget planning now, and even faculty and students who won't end up getting cut are not eager to wait around Oregon to find out.

Even high school graduates, universally denounced these days as badly educated and unable to solve simple analytical problems, are able to figure out this one.

"There's a lot of confusion and anxiety out there, and more students want to go out of state," reports University of Oregon President Myles Brand about his institution's freshman recruiting. "We are developing a new export in this state—our best and brightest minds. We're sending them out of state."

This may, at least, solve the problem of where to send the 1995 Portland graduates whom Prophet plans to help to college. They can always go to college someplace else.

After all, the point is for them to get a good education.

THE OREGONIAN, MARCH 1, 1992

2. Higher education appropriations by state, per FTE

Rank	State	Higher education appropriations per FTE, public 2-yr and 4-yr, 2007
1	Wyoming	$14,709
2	Alaska	$11,525
3	New Mexico	$9,518
4	Georgia	$8,888
5	North Carolina	$8,854
6	Nevada	$8,336
7	Hawaii	$8,245
8	Connecticut	$8,210
9	New York	$8,127
10	Texas	$8,074
11	Idaho	$7,736
12	Kentucky	$7,662
13	Tennessee	$7,651
14	Maryland	$7,586
15	Oklahoma	$7,369
16	Massachusetts	$7,348
17	Arkansas	$7,292
18	New Jersey	$7,275
19	California	$7,083
20	Louisiana	$7,066
21	Illinois	$7,032
22	Nebraska	$7,025
23	Alabama	$7,001
24	Arizona	$6,871
	United States	$6,773
25	Washington	$6,736
26	Mississippi	$6,498

Rank	State	Higher education appropriations per FTE, public 2-yr and 4-yr, 2007
27	South Carolina	$6,317
28	Missouri	$6,253
29	Florida	$6,203
30	Wisconsin	$6,176
31	Delaware	$5,914
32	Minnesota	$5,875
33	Virginia	$5,842
34	Maine	$5,786
35	Utah	$5,774
36	Iowa	$5,723
37	Kansas	$5,627
38	Michigan	$5,353
39	Indiana	$5,351
40	Rhode Island	$5,229
41	Pennsylvania	$5,227
42	West Virginia	$5,045
43	North Dakota	$4,726
44	Oregon	$4,653
45	South Dakota	$4,575
46	Ohio	$4,486
47	Montana	$4,386
48	Colorado	$3,434
49	New Hampshire	$2,685
50	Vermont	$2,281

SOURCE: SHEEO, *State Higher Education Finance, FY 2007*. Excludes appropriations for medical schools and statewide public services.

The amount of financial support each state grants its universities, per full-time enrolled student.

An Address to the 1992 Escapees

(Music: "Pomp and Circumstance," or possibly "Louie, Louie.")

Members of the 1992 graduating class of the Oregon State System of Higher Education:

Gazing out over your eager, upturned faces, I want to congratulate you on your diligence, your perseverance and, except for the members of certain athletic teams, your success.

But mostly, I'd like to congratulate you on your timing.

You have all managed a last-minute escape from a higher-education system that is sinking like sixth-grade literacy. This is the first graduation I've attended where the parking lot is full of lifeboats.

According to recommendations made by the state Board of Higher Education last week, to meet the new budget projections under Measure 5, Oregon is about to have a system that many of you could not afford to attend. Those who enter the system anyway will not only pay more than you, but also will get less, and some of the degrees you're receiving will no longer be available.

On the other hand, at future graduations, seating will be much less crowded.

By 1994-95, according to the projections, tuition will be up 77 percent from what you all paid in 1990-91. Don't leap in your chairs like that; it scratches the gym floor.

The good news is that the increases make cutting the system's enrollment by 7,000 students pretty easy. "We do not have to keep students out with enrollment caps," said Chancellor Thomas Bartlett Monday. "We do it with tuition and instability."

At Portland State, for example, full-time-equivalency enrollment would drop from 10,130 in 1989 to 7,100 in 1995, the level of PSU in the early '70s. Departing with the students will be about 169 faculty and administrative positions.

They will be cutting down resources where PSU is already low. There are relatively few four-year Vikings receiving undergraduate degrees here today because PSU has one of the worst records in the country of graduating its freshmen. Partly this is because it has fewer degree programs, partly it is because of minimal student counseling and support. As those of you here today from Portland State know, the best way for a PSU student to get advice on how to graduate is to write Dear Abby.

If PSU students, like the others in the system, will be getting fewer services, at least they'll be paying more. But their contributions won't reach the level of students at some other state system institutions, such as the University of Oregon Law School.

In 1989, when you new lawyers sitting out there entered, law students paid 37 percent of the costs of their education. In your senior year, you paid 50 percent, and with tuition increases for next year, it will be 57 percent.

Rapidly—and I can tell this from the IOUs spilling out of your robes—U of O law graduates are winning the right to graduate in as much debt as alumni from private institutions. The only problem with this is if you thought a public law school might provide a little more access to poorer

49

students, or if you hoped some new lawyers might get interested in something like indigent defense instead of personal debt service.

Still, access is running low anyway. Ten years ago, the U of O law school accepted 60 percent of its applicants; now it's 19 percent. In 1987, when you all started cramming for the law boards, the school received 900 applications for 175 places; this year it's 2,100 applications for 145 places.

We could, possibly, squeeze along with fewer lawyers, although the test probably shouldn't be who can pay the higher tuition. But the case of the law school just demonstrates what's coming along for a system that's cutting itself away while facing increasing demand.

The number of high school graduates will rise by 33 percent in Oregon over the next decade; college and university spaces will be dropping.

"The state is absolutely wiping out capital assets right and left that will take a generation to rebuild," says Dave Frohnmayer, dean of the law school and former attorney general. "We know the kids are in the pipeline. We won't have the chairs."

Some of the kids will still manage to get into higher education by filling up community colleges. That's a problem only if you were thinking of using the community colleges for anything else, such as retraining people from the timber industry.

All in all, there can't be many graduates anywhere as relieved to escape from their institutions as you are today. And as you head for the exits—don't run; the board won't actually meet for a few weeks—carry with you the greatest lesson the state of Oregon has been able to teach you:

Timing is everything.

(Music: "Burning Down the House.")

THE OREGONIAN, JUNE 30, 1992

Higher Education Quietly Getting Lower

Mike Lowry, in his new job as governor of Washington, will have the full-time equivalent of 15,000 professors working for him.

He's not willing to spare one.

"Beyond that level, I will talk about taxes," he said earlier this month. "I think that cutting that back is so bad for the economic vitality of the state that beyond that I will talk about taxes."

This is the kind of Washington attitude, not unique to Lowry, that makes you wonder how the Columbia River got so wide.

Washington State, facing its own budget problems, is persisting in a higher-education expansion plan that is adding two new University of Washington campuses and four new Washington State campuses, including WSU-Vancouver. Oregon, as seen in Gov. Barbara Roberts' proposed budget, is struggling to keep its current campuses open, and by 1995 will have cut its 1991 enrollment by about 12 percent.

It's hard to say that higher education is taking a worse beating than K-12 education or health and welfare funding. But it's certainly taking the least-noticed beating; several thousand Oregon students are being dropped down the memory hole, and the reaction is quieter than a campus library on Christmas.

State higher-education systems across the country are taking financial hits at the moment. But most of them, according to Dr. Edward R. Hines at the Center for Higher Education at Illinois State, are holding stable; not many are into absolute enrollment cuts. Especially not many where the student demand is running so sharply in the opposite direction.

In 1991, the number of high-school graduates in Oregon, declining through the late '80s, bottomed out at 25,635. It will rise through the '90s, reaching 33,875 in 2000.

In 1991, the Oregon State System of Higher Education had 62,571 students. In the first, "painless" round of cuts, enrollment dropped by 3,000. In the coming round, according to this budget, the system will drop another 4,400, to 55,000—with another round of cuts to come.

By 2000, admission to the system could be through the Oregon Lottery.

"This doesn't make much sense in terms of the direction where the state has to go," says higher-education Chancellor Thomas Bartlett. "There's going to be an additional amount of demand for which there'll be no supply."

In fact, there'll be less supply than there is now, less than the demand that already exists, 12 percent less than there was in 1991.

For the students who do make it into the system, it won't be quite the same system. The budget calls for a 15 percent increase in faculty productivity, but nobody's sure what that means: Teaching 15 percent more classes? Increasing the size of existing classes by 15 percent? Having faculty spend 15 percent more time doing administrative work formerly done by now-vanished administrators?

In contrast to Lowry's commitment to preserving his professors, Oregon plans to cut its higher-education employment by 800-plus, including large hunks of its non-tenured faculty. The cuts are coming from what was not exactly a fat system in the first place—one difference from other states now facing squeezes on their systems.

"If you start at a high enough base, you can do a lot of cutting before it matters," says Bartlett. "California's average salary is maybe twice ours, their expenditures per student are at least 50 percent greater. One person's disaster is another person's prosperity."

California, facing its own relative budget disaster, has slowed plans for expanding its systems, but is not cutting its overall enrollment. Still, Californians worry that they're contradicting their own statements on the importance of education.

"Students and families are reacting to those messages, doing exactly what we told them to do and, lo and behold, there's no room at the inn," says Kirk Knutsen, senior policy analyst at the California Post-Secondary Education Commission. "Even if you maintain current enrollment, it's the same as declining enrollment, because the pressure is increasing drastically."

And if, like Oregon, you're actually cutting enrollment, you're almost tearing down the inn. There are various groups emerging who want to make it financially possible for any Oregon high-school graduate to go to college; nobody seems to be asking, "Where?"

Well, there is the state north of us, which seems to see these things differently.

"It would be a mistake to go off our time line for developing campuses," Mike Lowry says firmly. "I think that cutting back from that plan would be the biggest mistake for our economic future. I think that a highly educated work force is the biggest part of our economic future."

Of course, as people often tell me, it's not fair to make these kinds of comparisons between Oregon and Washington. Washington, after all, is more prosperous, is growing faster and has a more diverse economy.

Guess why.

THE OREGONIAN, DECEMBER 20, 1992

"It'll Be Like a T-Shirt That Says USSR"

Since 1990, when Brian Clem first came up to Oregon State from Coos Bay, he has seen his tuition nearly double, while the education he was buying shrank like a sawmill payroll.

If the state of Oregon were regulated by the Better Business Bureau, he'd have a good case.

"I had a professor my freshman year who said this place was going to be hurting," remembers Clem. "No one believed him, no students understood.

"Now, if I'd just had one more French class, I'd be at the University of Washington now and probably stay in Washington the rest of my life."

The sharpest analysis of what's happening to Oregon's higher-education system comes from its consumers, who view their new situation with the cold eye of a jeweler scanning a zircon. With a shrewdness that at least speaks well for the university's admissions staff, they see themselves investing four or five years and increasing amounts of money to buy diminished degrees.

"If you get it in agriculture or forestry, it will always be a good degree," calculates Evelyn Grant, a Spanish major who came up from the Bay area because both of her parents went to Oregon State. "In business, in education, in communications, in fine arts, I don't think that it's going to mean a thing."

Asked what her Oregon State diploma will be worth in 10 years, senior Maggie Lang guesses, "Maybe it'll be like a T-shirt reading 'USSR.'"

Beaver unbelievers feel this way not just because of the cuts that they've already seen, but because of what they know is coming down Interstate 5 at them. "People say, 'Take this class, it's really good,'" says Amy Berg, a sophomore in psychology. "It may not be here next term, but it's really good."

This uncertainty, students say, has rearranged schedules and planning. Some students who can't fit into a jammed class that they need try to pick it up at Linn-Benton Community College—which is pretty crowded itself. In principle, college students are supposed to take broad introductory courses first, and specialize in their majors later. But if you're not sure how much longer the major will be around, the process can get reversed.

"The goal is to take what you need and get out," explains Dave Herman of Oregon City, who graduated last June. "You can't count on the class being there two years in the future."

Increasingly, the students aren't counting on themselves being around in the future. "People will leave to go out of state, they'll go to other places and stay there," says Herman. "I see that as a problem."

Graduates needing more training, say the students, clearly expect to go somewhere else. "People coming through here wouldn't think about returning for graduate school," says Bryan Curb, a senior from Corvallis. "There's a little bit of anger, a little bit of fear."

Grant sees herself as ending up in Arizona; Berg figures she'll be going back to California. Brian Clem is trying to do something about the situation; he works for a student lobbying group, telling legislators what's happening to Oregon State, about the sharp decrease he's seen in students from places such as Coos County. Clem, says one administrator, will cheerfully go into a state legislator's office with a list of OSU students from that district and explain that the lobbying group will be getting in touch with all of them.

But he doesn't expect to be doing it here permanently.

"I'll probably go to Washington," he figures. "I could never raise a family here, with the situation in higher ed, in public safety, even in what's going to happen in K-through-12. The things that government is supposed to do won't be here."

And the places where government promises to do it are withering.

Oregon State is not, of course, the only state institution with these problems, and it's probably not even the worst-off. Portland State not only has fewer resources to start with, but Nancy Tang, PSU vice provost, noted recently that PSU's largely part-time student body is more expensive to serve and faces an even harder hit.

Talk for a while to some of the students populating Oregon State, and it will occur to you that we're doing something wrong. These are smart, shrewd, thoughtful kids; we should be hiring out-of-work East German border guards to keep them from leaving the state.

Instead, we're telling them to get lost.

Jimmy Breslin once wrote, in a slightly different context, that New York City was spilling its future across the floor of the criminal courts building. We're spilling ours across the desks of abandoned college classrooms.

But even with reduced programs, more crowded classrooms and disappearing faculty, the students are still learning something.

They're learning their future is someplace else.

THE OREGONIAN, FEBRUARY 17, 1993

Washington Invests

Once again, it became clear last week that the leaders of Washington State just don't understand life in the 1990s.

Unless, of course, they've got it right—and Oregon's got it wrong.

Last week, the Washington Legislature passed its state budget, while the Oregon Legislature passeth all understanding. After facing a $1.5 billion shortfall, and cutting away at various parts of government, the Legislature managed to continue the expansion of the state's higher-education system.

The Washington budget will increase capacity by about 10,000 students—about half of those special community college spots for retraining laid-off workers, the rest divided between community colleges and the university system. It includes $554 million for new higher-education construction, including $100 million for the new campuses of the University of Washington and Washington State University—especially the one in Vancouver, which may one day be called Portland Metro U.

Meanwhile, Oregon's higher-education system is getting cut back like a blackberry vine. The last budget cut out 2,500 students; the current one projects another cut of 4,000, although a bill from Senate Democrats would add back $27 million, reducing the cuts to 1,200 students.

The House leaders are against it.

Moreover, a growing number of the remaining slots will be filled by out-of-state students, who are willing to pay more for the college seats than the Legislature will pay to keep Oregon students in them.

All of this raises the obvious question:

What's wrong with those people north of the Columbia?

"If you look at the executive, the Senate, the House, they all agreed that higher education was a priority," explains Anne Fennessy, a spokeswoman for Washington Gov. Mike Lowry. "One of the ways you strengthen and diversify your economy is by strengthening higher education."

Strangely enough, that might even be true. Thursday, the Corporation for Enterprise Development in the other Washington released its annual "Development Report Card for the States," on how states are doing in creating and attracting high-paying jobs. At the top of the list, along with Maryland, Colorado and Utah, is Washington.

Since 1989, Washington has consistently received A's in Development Capacity: human resources, technology resources, infrastructure and capital. Several of the criteria in that area—levels of college education, numbers of science and technology graduate students, university research and development—get filled on campuses.

"The states with the top grades in development capacity," said Daphne Clones, a policy analyst at the CED, "also won the top grades in earning capacity."

Oregon received a B in development capacity, with a C in technology capacity.

And while Washington is buying in the higher-education market, Oregon is selling.

Traditionally, Southern Oregon State College in Ashland drew around 8 percent of its students from outside Oregon. Since the passage of Measure 5, SOSC has been recruiting out-of-state, seeking to replace state money with out-of-state tuition dollars. Now, out-of-state enrollment is 19 percent; next fall the total will be 25 percent to 30 percent. By 1997, especially if cuts continue, it could be more than 50 percent.

"We're preserving capacity—which is my primary task—we're preserving the faculty, we're preserving the library," says SOSC President Joseph W. Cox. "Is this a good thing for Oregon? That's another question. It's hard to argue that this is in Oregon's long-term best interest."

Cox decided his college was faced with two futures: It could be a gutted institution of about 2,000 students, almost all from Oregon, or a strong institution of more than twice that many, largely from out of state. What it could not be was what it was intended to be: a strong institution of nearly 5,000 students, almost all from Oregon.

This is what you might call the neutron bomb approach to higher education: It preserves the institution, but eliminates the Oregon students.

Southern Oregon is just the most extreme case; other institutions, especially the University of Oregon, are finding that their best chance for financial survival is educating Californians. It turns out that the Oregon higher-education system is a state service that people from other places will pay a premium to use.

To get some perspective on this, ask yourself if any other state would pay to use our legislators.

What many Oregonians thought was a higher-education double bind—more high school graduates, fewer college spaces—is actually a triple bind: more high school graduates, fewer college spaces, more of those spaces sold to out-of-state students.

But it would be wrong to think that Oregon has no long-term higher-education policy.

The plan is called the Interstate Bridge.

THE OREGONIAN, MAY 9, 1993

59

On Higher Ed, Not Quite High Enough

In the spirit of the season, the House Republican leadership last week produced a small graduation gift for the state higher-education system. House Speaker Larry Campbell and House Appropriations chairman John Minnis proposed an education package that provides $10 million more for higher education than Gov. Barbara Roberts could find.

As with all gifts, it's the thought that counts, and some vital rethinking—and greater understanding—went into this. But the Legislature doesn't graduate with honors just yet.

The House's graduation gift isn't quite the size of the Senate's, and the House has attached a card that brings some problems of its own.

The Senate, in a heavy bipartisan vote, passed a $27 million increase, intended to ransom 2,800 of the 4,000 students who would have disappeared under the governor's plan. The House leaders, for their $10 million—still a higher-ed budget cut of about $76 million—want them all to stay.

That's a lot of names to fit on a card.

Probably, the final line will be somewhere in between. But higher-education Chancellor Thomas Bartlett has been talking for years about a university downsizing program that would not "thin the soup," that would not pretend that Oregon was spending more on higher education than it really was. There might be fewer students and fewer programs, but the students and programs left would be reasonably maintained.

The House proposal has the faint gurgle of soup being thinned.

And the louder crunch of fewer classes packing in more bodies.

One of the ways that the House proposal achieves this is by cutting administration in the chancellor's office by 25 percent and on each campus by 20 percent, and providing $17 million from the lottery for computerization to make that work. As Campbell pointed out Thursday, this figure is in line with an outside audit recently done of the system, and the cuts are already in the works.

But the speaker also wrote on the card a requirement that the system start programs to deal with retention, to try to increase the number of entering students who actually hang around, maybe even graduate. This is a major problem in the Oregon system, and Campbell was shrewd to face it.

The problem is that campus administration doesn't just include vice presidents having lunch with deans, it also means academic counselors and student-affairs people—the kind of folks who might actually help students hang around and graduate. One reason the Senate bill took more money to support fewer students was that it included more student services.

If you want systems that offer, as Minnis rightly suggested Thursday, "a clearer path to getting degrees," you need some people answering questions—and usually explaining to students which questions they need to get answered.

Judith Ramaley, president of Portland State University, thinks that campuses can address retention with smaller staffs and more focus, and says that PSU has already made some progress. But it means losing other things, which can come around to undercut your efforts to keep your students.

"Your retention is affected by how long it takes to know whether you'll have financial aid next year," points out Ramaley. "If you don't know whether a class will show up where it needs to be, it means you may not be in college that term."

In approved bureaucratic form, campuses could face the retention issue—and meet the mandate—by forming high-level committees and issuing regular reassuring reports. But if they actually want to affect retention—as Campbell appropriately wants—it will take more than mirrors.

When the House works out its final grade on higher education—and when it gets averaged in with the Senate's—all these elements need to be considered, along with a realistic view of the House's conflicting wishes. And the outcome will connect with the desire of the House—and the governor—for virtually untouched financing of the state's corrections programs.

There's an interesting number that somebody might note about that.

In the budget for 1985-87—the last budget of Gov. Vic Atiyeh, the last governor with much interest in higher education—the general fund provided $515,920,000 for higher education. In Gov. Roberts' proposal for 1993-95, higher ed gets $663,604,000—an increase of 28 percent over eight years, or in real dollars, a decrease.

In that same 1985-87 budget, corrections received $151,127,000, now rising to $343,371,000—a rise of 126 percent. At this rate, just after 2000, Oregon will be spending more on prisons than colleges.

It's hard to deny that the state prison system needed some expansion.

But it's also hard to deny that in terms of state attention, it's been a lot better to be a felon than a freshman.

Trying writing that on a graduation card.

THE OREGONIAN, MAY 30, 1993

U of O President Won't Duck the Future

In late October, three weeks before the sales tax got less support than legalizing marijuana, University of Oregon President Myles Brand told his faculty, "We've got to find a way to stand on our own two feet."

The alternative was being cut off at the knees.

In 1990, notes Brand, the state of Oregon paid 40 percent of the costs of running the university. The figure is now around 22 percent. By 1997 it will be about 15 percent, and by the end of the century, Brand predicts the number will be in single digits.

There is no mystery about where the replacement money comes from. As a recent newspaper study of Virginia's higher-education system began, "It comes down to tuition or taxes. Either way you pay."

So far, the University of Oregon has maximized its tuition income skillfully. While losing $12 million per year from the state, it has brought in $11 million in out-of-state tuition, with a freshman class that is now 48 percent out-of-state. At Eugene, what some colleges call Public Relations is now the Office of Communications and Marketing.

"If you go to another university to read a paper," Brand told the faculty, "ask if you can speak to some 17- and 18-year-olds. At $10,000, a hundred students is a million dollars. A hundred students is not a lot of students. A million dollars is a lot of money."

Academics are not as deep in the ivory tower as you might think.

So far, the strategy has worked, with the university cutting some programs and reducing enrollment but staying basically intact. But with more cuts coming, Brand has a new strategy.

Higher tuition rates—and more students paying them.

After the next round of cuts, Brand predicted Wednesday, "the public should expect a hefty tuition increase again." Since 1990, in-state tuition is up by about 60 percent. To the next system wide increase, Brand wants to add an annual $360 surcharge—about another 10 percent—just for students at the U of O, and to increase enrollment closer to the pre-Measure 5 level.

With the extra money, he says, the university could improve undergraduate education and retention—with strategies similar to what's now being planned at Portland State—and also have enough scholarship money to keep students from being priced out.

The new tuition would be among the highest for Western public universities, but not the highest—especially not with California's soaring rates.

"The danger is excluding people on the margins, and the state will have to re-examine our financial aid systems," says Brand. "But the price is still within the market. It's still less expensive to get a full college education than to buy a Honda."

In both cases, of course, there are also questions about accessories. For students, that means living expenses.

Higher-education system Chancellor Thomas Bartlett, whose office would eventually have to approve Brand's proposals, calls them "interesting ideas." He notes that there is a close relationship between price and interest, and asks, "Are the students there at that price, in-state or out of state?"

Brand is certain that the university can find them, and also that it has no choice.

"We can do this," he says. "This is not a problem. We do not expect new revenues from the state, probably not in our lifetime."

And Brand is scheduled to teach a freshman seminar on "Immortality."

The market impact of tuition pricing is direct. While sharply increasing out-of-state enrollment, Brand points out, the university has still admitted every qualified Oregon student who applies. But with the sizable increases in tuition, the number of Oregon applicants has dropped.

The U of O used to enroll 8½ percent of all Oregon high school graduates; now the number is below 7 percent and dropping, while 70 percent of applications are from out of state.

In terms of how the higher-education system will be able to serve the state's needs, Bartlett has his own judgment: "Success consists of lowering your expectations."

But trying to run a public university by driving up tuition income brings up some direct questions about those needs.

People might be asking about less wealthy students losing access to the system, especially students who may not be poor enough to qualify for financial aid.

There are still questions about just how the state's colleges and universities will respond to the huge approaching increase in high school graduates.

And then there's a basic uncertainty about whether the system will be strong enough to support the state in a future economy that will run on information.

Brand thinks, logically, that those questions have been answered by the Legislature and the voters. His job is just to preserve a University of Oregon.

Or rather, a university in Oregon.

THE OREGONIAN, DECEMBER 12, 1993

Portland State Ventures Into Portland

Normally, people don't rejoice when they get a letter from the audi-tor. Frequently, it causes them to start checking the airline schedules to Rio.

But a recent assessment from an outside auditor to the management of Portland State University was different.

"We at the Pappas Consulting Group," wrote the New York consul-tants, part of the Big Six accounting corporation KPMG Peat Marwick, "believe that Portland State University will emerge as the model for the urban/metropolitan university in the United States."

And that's even without raising football to Division I-A level.

Four years ago, Judith Ramaley became president of Portland State and started talking about something called an "urban grant" university, a downtown equivalent of the nation's land grant universities. For a uni-versity that spent several decades wandering in an institutional identity crisis—PSU has been billed as everything from a third research univer-sity to a commuter convenience—the idea of being defined by more than its address was encouraging.

"For a long time, Portland State didn't think of itself as part of the national movement to create an urban university," points out higher-education Chancellor Thomas Bartlett. "It thought of itself as a university that happened to be in Portland."

In a major overhaul of the undergraduate program that starts this fall, there's a greater prominence to the Portland part—and some new ideas about the university part. Peat Marwick, whose study was part of a statewide audit of the entire state higher-education system, isn't the only outsider who has noticed.

This fall, entering freshmen at Portland State will study in 25 interdisciplinary seminars, each with five faculty members from different areas and with upper-division student mentors. One seminar is "Values and Politics," which includes a political scientist, a chemist, a physicist, an ethics specialist and an English professor. Besides the course material, the students will work on writing, presentation and high-tech data acquisition.

Maybe just as importantly, it might do something about Portland State's student retention rate, among the lowest in the country. PSU's strongest connection to the city was how quickly many of its students went back into it.

What's important to change the retention rate, says Ramaley, "is that the student feels that someone sees him as a person and cares what his experience is like. With this, the majority of students, within their first weeks here, will have some positive experience."

Sophomore and upper-division courses, still being designed, will keep the focus on interdisciplinary styles. The conclusion, in the senior year, will be the Capstone Experience—admittedly, it sounds like a mutual fund—in which teams of seniors, from different areas of study, will go out to do major projects in the community and use what they've learned.

"We've been consistently told by people in the community," explains Charles White, a political scientist who chaired the redesign committee, "that a major weakness of college graduates is being unable to work in teams. And this provides a way to connect the university and the community."

To Ramaley, this is the program's core.

"The urban mission is different from the traditional university mission," she declares. "Most community service, although appreciated, is peripheral to the institution. What we're doing is changing the ground rules, taking community service into the heart of the institution.

"This is what convinced Peat Marwick that we were doing something interesting."

So far, the model has been a three-year program by several sets of PSU students to study and project the growth of Gresham.

Portland State has reason to think that the world is interested. "The response from the community has been very positive," says White. "There are people just waiting for us to get up and going."

Those numbers include people from around the country, watching the Portland State overhaul as an urban university model. The committee report outlining the new curriculum, in somewhat revised form, will be published next month in the *Journal of General Education*.

"Judith is very verbal, and she's gotten the attention of the rest of the country on this," says Bartlett. "I've tried to find a little money for it—darned little, but some."

For three years, while planning this, Portland State has been squeezed more and more tightly by the state, throwing other programs overboard while trying to set up something new. Like the rest of the system, it has responded to a mandate to rethink itself.

If Portland and Oregon want a vital university system, it may be time for voters to do some rethinking, too.

THE OREGONIAN, JUNE 10, 1994

Oregon's Rising Role:
Collegiate Colony

More than 40 years ago, Tom Bartlett was raking it in, part of an Oregon economy with no entrance requirements. As a foreman in a cannery, as a summer worker in the woods, he made more money than he would make for years after joining the Foreign Service.

Bartlett just finished spending five years as chancellor of the Oregon State System of Higher Education, in a completely different Oregon economy. He's not sure that enough people have noticed the difference.

At a time when 63 percent of Oregon's high school graduates go directly on to some kind of further education—a time when 18-year-olds would look a long time for high-paying woods or cannery jobs—Bartlett thinks Oregonians still consider higher education basically a private matter.

And getting more private all the time, as Oregonians consider initiatives to protect elementary and secondary education partly at the expensive of their universities.

"We say, up through 12th grade, we'll pay it all," says Bartlett. "Then you go to 13th, and you're on your own. What's the difference between the 12th and 13th years? We say in one case there is a compelling public interest, in the other, a compelling private interest. But if you look at our economy, there is no difference."

Anyone who doubts that position is free to go looking for those cannery jobs.

What Bartlett says he's learned from his experience is that all education has to fit together. What he sees is an attitude that treats different levels of education as different worlds—and different political forces.

He came to Oregon in 1989 from running the University of Alabama campuses, recruited by Gov. Neil Goldschmidt to strengthen the Oregon system as part of his economic development strategy. Instead, Bartlett was greeted by the passage of Measure 5, and he got to spend his tenure playing defense.

Over the last four years, Oregon's higher-education system has dealt with deepening cutbacks by paring enrollment, raising tuition and increasing the number of high-tuition students from out of state. "It's a way to salvage the institutions," says Bartlett, "but it doesn't salvage the Oregonians who wanted to go there."

And it doesn't really suggest that Oregon has any broader interest in Oregonians going to college.

As Dave Frohnmayer, former attorney general and new interim president of the University of Oregon, pointed out recently, every major center of high-tech economic activity—Route 128 near Boston, Silicon Valley in California, the Research Triangle in North Carolina, the Microsoft metropolis—is closely connected to powerful university resources.

"There's been an attitude on the part of some of our political leaders that the real folks are the ones who go no further than community college," says Bartlett. Yet, "It's clear that if we want to go to the kind of high-value-added society we want, people can't stop at community college—unless we want to import our talent.

"We can do that, and imperceptibly colonize ourselves. It's efficient, socially, to get someone else to pay the bill, but it's not necessarily good policy if you're growing up here."

Already, according to studies of new settlers, the average new arrival in Oregon is better-educated than the average native. Traditionally, Oregon has been an economic colony; becoming an educational colony could fit right into the pattern.

After five years, Bartlett still isn't quite sure why Oregon's leadership hasn't seen a connection that other places' powers have perceived.

"Leadership is a puzzle. This is a state based on lots of small enterprises, and very mixed cultures," he notes. "I don't understand why the business leaders of this state don't understand how important higher education is to them. It just didn't happen here the way it happened all around us," in Washington and California.

Now, the state's system faces the possibility of new, tighter crunches. From this fall's initiative menu, Oregonians could decide to increase their prison needs sharply, strip the Legislature of the power to raise any taxes, and insist that elementary and secondary schools not be hurt by any of this.

If you're interested in higher education—or in human services, or in the state police—this could squeeze things considerably. Especially since after four years, as Bartlett notes, "We're running out of tricks."

But the world economy has no plans to get any simpler.

"To say that we're going to hold part of education harmless and eviscerate the other part, as though that was a consistent policy," says Bartlett, "flies in the face of everything we're learning about the need for lifelong learning."

And it pretends that right after high school, there'll always be a cannery job.

THE OREGONIAN, JULY 31, 1994

71

State Colleges:
Onward and Downward

Once again, Oregon is setting a bold new path for the rest of the country, sending its higher-education system in a whole different direction from the path chosen by the rest of the states.

The direction is down.

Over the last two years, according to figures published recently by the *Chronicle of Higher Education*, Oregon cut its state support for higher education by more than any other state—10.5 percent. It was an impressive leap—it couldn't have been done without the help of thousands of out-of-state-tuition-paying Californians—but Oregon did have some competition for the title; eight other states cut their state support by lower percentages.

In fact, Montana, at 8 percent, made a real run.

But in the next round, Oregon has no competition. According to a breakdown in the *Chronicle* last month, only one state in the country is proposing to cut its support for higher education again this year.

In terms of national recognition for state universities, this is a much bigger deal than the Rose Bowl. Lots of states sent teams to bowl games; only one state was cutting the university while the team was gone.

In Gov. John Kitzhaber's current budget proposal, state support for higher education would drop by 14.4 percent—beating even Oregon's record of last time. Meanwhile, virtually every other state legislature received proposals to increase state spending on colleges and universities.

Many of the proposals probably won't be funded in full; provosts propose, legislators dispose. But just about all other state university systems see a chance for some increases in their present budgets.

Even Montana plans to be up by 2 percent.

Actually, it's not entirely accurate to say that every other state was proposing to increase spending. In one state—Virginia—the governor offered a higher-education budget that the *Chronicle* calculated as no change and that some people calculated as a cut. In Virginia, as in Oregon, higher education has been cut back steadily since 1990.

But at the beginning of this month, the darndest thing happened in Virginia.

A 36-member Virginia Business-Higher Education Council protested the cuts, with one member noting, "Once Virginia gets a reputation as having a public higher-education system that is a perpetually easy mark for budget cutters, gifted educators, scientists and students will go elsewhere, as will business and industry."

Three former governors, two Republicans and a Democrat, declared that the state's fiscal policy had traditionally reflected "integrity, foresight, frugality and the courage to make investments for the long run. Now is the time to make critical new investments in Virginia's future," and the place to start was higher education.

The two houses of the Virginia General Assembly then passed budgets providing $50 million more for higher education than the governor had proposed. So Oregon's title as the only state preparing to undermine its universities seems secure.

Virginia might even end up doing better than Montana.

"We have to ask ourselves, what do the other states know that we don't know?" says Joseph W. Cox, chancellor of the Oregon State System of Higher Education. "Why are they beginning to reinvest, and we're continuing to disinvest?"

For a while, the Oregon Legislature thought it knew something other places didn't: that the people running the system were overpaid and inefficient. But since then, both the system's Chancellor Thomas Bartlett and University of Oregon President Myles Brand have been hired by other states for considerably more money to run much larger operations.

So far, there have been no outside offers for the Legislature.

The issue here isn't what other states know that Oregon doesn't. It's what everybody knows, and Oregon doesn't want to admit.

It's that states are not going to function in a 21st-century economy without a 21st-century higher-education system, and that you're not going to get one by constantly hacking away at it. There's also a general feeling—general except in Oregon—that you're not doing much for your state's kids when you have 5,000 fewer students in your higher-education system in 1995 than you had in 1980.

And probably 10,000 fewer students from Oregon.

This idea—that the route to the future does not run through higher education—doesn't seem to be shared by other states. So while it's not quite clear where Oregon's low-investment strategy of dismissing the role of universities is going, it will certainly be our very own path.

Maybe we'll call it the Oregon Trail.

THE OREGONIAN, FEBRUARY 12, 1995

The Future Is Exciting—
Next Door

It was an exciting week in higher education in the Northwest, with developments showing how public universities can pay back the state's investment and fuel the future.

The developments weren't in Oregon, of course, but we're still allowed to watch.

The University of Washington medical school lured from Berkeley Mary-Claire King, an internationally known genetics researcher now specializing in breast cancer. King joins recent top-level UW recruits from Cal Tech, Stanford and Stockholm.

"This is somewhat unusual in seeing so many capable people coming together in one place," Paul Ramsey, chairman of the UW's department of medicine, told the Associated Press. "It's a snowball effect. We have one of the largest, best groups in the world."

UW's medical school is in a position to recruit this kind of talent because of a $12-million donation from Microsoft's Bill Gates. Like most major high-tech operations, Microsoft grew up near a research university. In this particular case, it was across the lake from . . . but you guessed.

This, in an unusually dramatic and simplified way, is how higher education and economic development feed off each other. Nobody can say for certain how this particular cycle will continue, but in a future where biotechnology will be a major job creator, it probably won't hurt to be the university—and the city—that produces a major breast cancer breakthrough.

And maybe the head of the Puget Sound-area company that makes several billion dollars from that breakthrough then gives some money to the University of Washington—as well as producing a large amount of taxes that get to the university as well.

This is not a complicated cycle to imagine—at least not a complicated cycle for many places to imagine.

"In Washington, there doesn't seem to be any big controversy to say that 'Higher education fuels our economy.' It's accepted there," says Jim Craven, government affairs manager for the American Electronics Association of Oregon. "Here, when higher-ed folks are cutting 8 percent instead of 15 percent, that's a great victory.

"We're still concerned about this state's historic inattention to higher education. I just heard last week from a senator who asked, why is higher ed wasting time on research? Why not just teach?"

In Washington, of course, people are also complaining about their higher-education system. Often, what they're complaining about is that there isn't enough of it.

"Today our new, emerging industries are only as strong as the higher-education system that feeds them talent," wrote Kelso Gillenwater, publisher of the *Tacoma News Tribune*, recently. Gillenwater warned that Washington was doing much too little to increase access to higher education, and that "our ability as a state to recruit and sustain industries that require college-educated people will suffer."

In Oregon, of course, the question isn't increasing access, but watching it get reduced. Currently, as the system is facing a 14.4 percent cut in real dollars, the Legislature is busily setting up an independent corporation status for the state's higher-ed system. The approach, which is estimated to save about $20 million of the $100 million cut the system faces, is a good idea, but it sums up Oregon's loftiest aspiration for its higher-education system:

To be mediocre more cheaply.

Besides, people argue, Oregon can get into the high-tech world even with half-hearted higher education; look at all the high-tech companies rushing to come here. But as Jim Barnett and Rob Eure reported in the *Oregonian* recently, Oregon is developing a particular kind of high-tech identity.

Aside from Intel, companies aren't setting up research and development operations here; Oregon is mostly the place where products designed elsewhere are manufactured and shipped. Still, even those kinds of operations require significant numbers of highly trained engineers and specialists—which the companies usually have to bring in from other states.

We're not exactly a Silicon Forest; we're more a stop on a Silicon Assembly Line.

Craven points out, legitimately, that decent-paying assembly jobs are not to be dismissed, and that a local venture capital shortage is also a key problem. But, he notes, even if a company can get around a local higher-ed shortfall by importing its upper levels, it's still stymied if it can't rely on local continuing education resources.

Even without vital higher-ed support, of course, Oregon still has a high-tech future—but maybe not the kind that produces Microsofts and large, highly-paid workforces and opportunities for local kids and $12 million gifts to higher education.

So our model might not be Seattle.

More like a highly livable Sri Lanka.

THE OREGONIAN, FEBRUARY 26, 1995

Llamas Carry the Load for Higher Ed

Thursday was Llama Day at the state capitol. This is yet another of these unique Oregon political traditions that enrich our political culture but can be so hard to explain to outsiders.

Other examples include lawn signs and the Oregon Citizens Alliance.

In the last legislative session and in this one, the governor and the state's higher-education leaders looked at the system's financial problem and proposed saving $8 million by closing down the Oregon State University veterinary school. In 1993, the school's supporters responded by attending the committee hearing in full force—meaning with llamas.

The vet school was saved, and months later, a high-ranking aide to the governor was still unnerved by the experience. "Llamas," she would mumble, with a look in her eyes from an unknown area code. "They brought in llamas."

They brought the llamas in again Thursday, and an education subcommittee, enthralled by constituents bred to carry heavy burdens and not talk about it, unanimously voted for the vet school. The llamas themselves did not testify in the hearing room, although there was an appearance by a pygmy goat, who behaved with due respect for the legislators and the rug.

The followers of the llamas did the actual talking, explaining that there was a strong connection between the vet school and the Oregon economy, that it brought jobs into the state, that the new technological world demanded more and not less training, that the quality of the education was strong, and that if legislators hacked at it, it would make Oregon students more dependent on space available in other states. It was a wide-ranging and persuasive argument of the importance of higher education for llamas.

Of course, it's also all true for the state's investing in lliberal arts.

Not to mention llanguages, llogic and the llaw school.

There are reasons, naturally, why the vet school has emerged as the High Llama of higher-education funding in Oregon. Aside from its products being more cuddly than those of some of the other institutions, the connection between education and effect is more direct—especially in a Legislature now dominated by rural interests.

But in a broader sense, the argument for the full higher-education system closely resembles the llama argument. In fact, you could call it the spitting image.

And in this session—as the state's colleges and universities, having taken the nation's largest percentage hit in state support last time, and having increased their tuition 66 percent, face another 14 percent real-dollar cut in the governor's budget—a growing number of legislators are seeing the connection.

"If things go the way I'd like, they'll do better," says House Majority Leader Ray Baum, R-La Grande, about higher ed's prospects. "I want to look at doing something there, and doing better than the governor would be a goal of mine."

Oregon's colleges and universities, several members have noticed, have taken considerable financial hits over a long period of time. While some of the state's general fund money has been replaced by higher tuition (especially higher tuition from lots more out-of-state students) you can't do that forever—or Oregon students' access shrinks to the size of a pygmy goat.

"I think it has to be a priority, when you consider that we're in the bottom 20 percent of the United States," says Sen. Eugene Timms, R-Burns, co-chairman of the Joint Ways and Means Committee. "We will do something about the 14 percent cut."

Partly, as Rep. John Minnis, R-Troutdale, notes, there's a greater understanding in the Legislature of higher ed's situation. There's also a feeling, widely expressed, that acting Chancellor Joseph Cox and University of Oregon President Dave Frohnmayer are making a clear, persuasive case—a sense that higher ed is llearning to llobby.

None of this may matter, of course, unless the Legislature can find the money. And the most likely source, the greater-than-predicted tax revenues to be returned to taxpayers in the personal and corporate kickers, is not now a popular place to look. Oregon business leaders are telling the Legislature to support higher ed—but also that they want the corporate kicker money back.

Of course, nobody would suggest taking money from the llamas, which have higher education's strongest ability to kick back.

"It's an investment, that's what makes it so hard," says Rep. Del Parks, R-Klamath Falls, who'd keep both kickers, for higher ed and other needs. "When someone makes a higher income because of college, the state takes 10 percent off the top. For every extra $1,000 they make, the state gets another $100. It doesn't come back for 15 years, but then it comes back big-time."

On Llama Day, that's an argument that could sway a llama.

Or even a llegislator.

THE OREGONIAN, MARCH 19, 1995

Higher Ed:
A Motto to Match Its Money

The motto of the University of Oregon is "Mens Agitat Molem," or "Minds Move Matter." The motto of Portland State University is "Doctrina Urbi Serviat," or "Let Knowledge Serve the City."

And last week, as the Legislature pottered toward a finish on its budget, the air was full of the unofficial motto of the entire Oregon State System of Higher Education:

"Well, It Could Be Worse."

And, of course, it will be.

As of now, Oregon's higher-education system is indeed doing a bit better than it would have under the governor's first budget, which took a 14 percent whack at the system's state support. But it's still on track to take its third consecutive sizable state budget cut, another kick at a system whose enrollment is now down about 5,000 from the number of students it had in 1989.

This situation even alarms some leaders of the Legislature, who are looking hard to find a way to get the system's budget a little closer to where it was after the last session's cutbacks.

Considering the rising impact of the cuts at the state's colleges and universities, they should look hard.

They could find some inspiration north of the Columbia, where the residents of Washington State keep insisting on this curious idea that more higher education is better than less. When their legislature ground to a halt last week, it had produced an expansion of the state's higher-education system, with projected enrollment increases throughout its system and especially in its six new campuses. The budget plans continued growth at the Washington State University-Vancouver campus—the one that may someday be known as Portland Out-of-State University.

With the motto, "Let Knowledge Cross the I-205 Bridge."

In total, Washington plans an increase in higher-education enrollment of 5,258 more students.

Of course, as we say in Oregon: 5,000 more students, 5,000 fewer students, what's the difference?

As the higher-education appropriation bill passed the Oregon Legislature last week, the system did indeed dodge some bullets—but it also got hit by some.

At the governor's urging, the Legislature produced money to get the system's proposed 9-percent-a-year tuition increases down to 4 percent annually. Legislators added back money for the Oregon State veterinary school and statewide services such as agricultural extension, and found some more money for faculty salaries—which, after two years with no increase, were bumping along even closer to the national bottom than usual. The Legislature is also cutting the system loose from some state requirements, which will save it some money.

But as of now, the system is still taking a hit of about 10 percent in its state support—in real dollars. The overall budget is going up, but lots of the other money doesn't do much for students; a federal grant for advanced energy planning is nice, but you can't use the money to reach freshmen.

(Actually, you can, but it tends to get you indicted.)

So Portland State, for example, out of an instructional budget of $75 million, faces a cut of about $4.5 million. It is not the kind of number you can hide in the on-campus parking budget. It means, as PSU President Judith Ramaley puts it, "major program impact."

Another word for "impact," of course, is "crash."

Senate President Gordon Smith, R-Pendleton, has been saying since the start of the session that higher education needs more than another kick. Now, he's trying to find some way to cushion the blow.

"There's been a recognition all along, especially in the Senate, that we'd like to do better by higher ed," says Smith's spokesman, Dan Lavey. "Smith and Senator (Greg) Walden (R-Hood River) are trying to push an idea to try to capture higher-than-expected revenues for higher education."

The idea could inch things a bit closer to livability—to the 5 percent cut that higher-education people suggest they could manage.

It doesn't get us near the Washington plan, of course, but then they have strange ideas over there. The chairman of the Washington House Higher Education Committee, Don Carlson, R-Vancouver, actually told the Associated Press that Washington should be planning for the 50,000 new higher-education slots it will need in the next decade as its number of 18-year-olds rises sharply.

Oregon's number of high school graduates will rise by about 33,000, but we're going to let them worry about it themselves—and to tell them, "Well, It Could Be Worse."

But at least we could try to avoid the motto, "Minds Don't Matter."

THE OREGONIAN, MAY 28, 1995

Oregon Offers Breaks Instead of Brains

Outside Austin, Texas, the neighborhood is hot and hilly. You're a thousand miles from a salmon, the heat and humidity make you an involuntary contestant in a daily wet T-shirt contest, and the land doesn't exactly flow with half-decaf raspberry lattes.

Why, Oregonians ask, would anybody want to put a high-tech factory there? Moreover, why does Oregon have to offer tax breaks to attract companies away from a place low on the minimal amenities needed to support intelligent Northwestern life?

The answer, of course, is what Austin has. It starts with a U, and goes on for quite a while.

The University of Texas is a major research university. Unsurprisingly, the national high-tech high points—Silicon Valley; Massachusetts' Route 128; Redmond, Wash.—all seem to be located near one, or near more than one.

"In Silicon Valley, we have Stanford, San Jose State and the University of Santa Clara," explained Wilfred Corrigan, CEO of LSI Logic, when he came by to talk about the new plant he's building in Gresham. In Austin, he notes, the university made an investment in the semiconductor field "which then draws the industry funding, and the whole thing approaches critical mass."

And then there's Oregon, which has water, and lattes, and tax breaks— as partial compensation for what we don't have.

"The main concern about coming to Oregon would be the educational institutions," said Corrigan. "What we do on this site in the future is going to be determined by the flow of educated people. If it's not available, this will just be a manufacturing site."

In other words, without a steady supply of highly educated locals, we won't be talking Silicon Gorge; we'll be talking four acres of people making $8 an hour.

This summer, while Oregon is enforcing another set of higher-education cutbacks, states across the nation are seeing the connection between higher ed and their future. In Connecticut, a conservative Republican governor, cutting most of the rest of the state budget, joined with legislative leaders to put through a $1 billion university expansion program, UConn 2000. After years of cutting away, the university will be upgrading its main campus—including a biotechnology facility and expansion of the Technology Quadrant—as well as expanding another one, and starting a whole new branch in suburban Fairfield County.

"In order to be truly competitive in the new, higher-technology economy, I believe that Connecticut must have a state-of-the-art, distinguished university system," said Gov. John Rowland. "Now is the time to abandon the quick-fix approach and engage in fundamental revitalization."

Here we'd be lucky to get to quick-fix.

Last year in Virginia, 37 state business leaders and the presidents of Virginia's 15 public colleges formed the Virginia Business Higher Education Council and managed to defeat another round of deep cuts. Last month, they called for a significantly increased investment in the state's system.

Lately, Virginia hasn't done badly in attracting high-tech development—which is having its own effect on the debate.

"It's reinforcing the push to investment in higher education," explained Karen Washabau, the council's executive director, last week. "Part of the incentive to bring Motorola here was a promise that the state will put significant resources into engineering at Virginia Commonwealth University here in Richmond."

That's one way of attracting high-tech industry—but why bother, when you can just do tax breaks?

Across the river in Washington—where the difference in outlook can't possibly be attributed to latte deprivation—August marked the first meeting of a task force named by Gov. Mike Lowry to find a way to produce the 50,000 additional higher-education slots Washington will need by 2010. The task force includes eight legislators, including the chairmen of the higher-education committees from the Senate (Democratic) and the House (Republican).

"There's overall agreement that higher ed is a key priority," said Lowry spokesman Martin Munguia Tuesday. "The state needs to have a well-educated work force to deal with the international market. We might even attract some more employers like Microsoft and Boeing, companies that want a more educated work force."

Naming the task force on the problem, of course, is the easy step. But it's a step ahead of Oregon, whose high-school graduates are also increasing sharply, while its higher-education spaces are shrinking slowly.

The possibility of Oregon doing anything about that is unlikely to come up soon. So while other states invest in their work force, to the advantage of both their citizens and their companies, we just offer high-tech companies what we know the 21st century will really be about:

Cut-rate property taxes.

And all the latte they can drink. Take that, Austin.

THE OREGONIAN, AUGUST 23, 1995

The Eyes of Texas
Are on Research

The September 1995 *Austin Fact Book*, published by the Economic Development Division of the Greater Austin Chamber of Commerce, has a lovely color photo of a proud skyline rising over the green banks of the Colorado River. Austin, it coos, is "an oasis city of dazzling lakes and dramatic terrain."

But it doesn't take too long to get to the point.

"Perhaps the key to Austin's cutting-edge competitiveness is the emphasis on education, springing from the University of Texas at Austin. With 50,000 students, a growing research reputation and top-ranked departments, students and faculty, the University is a magnet for the best and brightest people, ideas and companies."

After that, the report just dribbles off into a lot of boring stuff about all the new companies arriving and the local ones expanding.

Some people from the Austin Chamber of Commerce were in Portland last week, following up a selling trip through California with a stop at one of Austin's recruitment rivals. Understandably, they weren't giving away any secrets—but they didn't consider their strategy a secret.

"For us, the University of Texas is economic development, and economic development is the University of Texas," explained Angelos Angelou, the Austin chamber's vice president for—guess what?—economic development. "Our bread and butter is education. It's what we've built our marketing programs on for the last 20 years.

"They've put us on the map."

In Oregon, of course, we have—dazzling lakes and dramatic terrain.

After spending years listening to Oregon's assurances that we don't need to invest in higher education because we're so attractive, it's fascinating to watch the marketing of a place that's figured out that you can be both smart and pretty. The University of Texas is as prominent in the Austin promotional material as it used to be in the Cotton Bowl.

The UT Longhorns' football slogan is "Hook 'em, 'Horns." Austin is out to hook some things itself.

In its passage on "Why Companies Choose Austin," the first two items are "a well-educated work force" and "the presence of a world-class research university." Austin boasts "the most highly educated work force of cities with 250,000+ population: over 34 percent of adults have a college degree (QUALITY). The 7 area colleges & universities graduate over 16,000 students each year (QUANTITY)."

In fact, the report includes a helpful "Comparison to Selected U.S. Cities"—namely, seven metropolitan areas prominent in the high-tech business—showing percentage of population with bachelor's degrees. No prizes for guessing who's first.

There are also no prizes for guessing who comes in last—after Austin, Seattle, San Jose, Boston, Raleigh-Durham and Colorado Springs. It's Portland, at 23.3 percent.

But did we tell you about our river?

After a lot more chatter about the University of Texas—by now, the message would be clear to even someone from SMU, although possibly not to someone from the Oregon Legislature—the package explains, "Since 1984, more than 40 $1-million endowed chairs have been created at UT to recruit internationally recognized faculty in order to accelerate research programs in engineering and science."

Oregon has nice mountains.

Partly because of this attitude, UT is also prominent in another big book that appeared last week: *Research-Doctorate Programs in the United States*, a National Research Council survey. In it, UT was eighth in aerospace engineering, 10th in chemical engineering and tied for 10th in ecology.

And seventh in computer sciences.

In that area, reported the Eugene *Register-Guard*, the University of Oregon was 64th, Oregon State University 70th and the Oregon Graduate Institute 42nd.

Obviously, Oregon universities aren't going to compete straight-up with UT.

But the state does have to be in the game.

The Oregon university rankings in the survey may not be disastrous. Frequently, though, they're down notably from the last time the survey was taken, in 1982.

At the U of O, physics is now 60th; in 1982, it was 50th. Mathematics is 47th instead of 41st. Chemistry is down from 29th to 41st.

At Oregon State, chemical engineering now ranks 77th among 93 programs in the nation; in 1982, it was 28th. Mechanical engineering has gone from 58th to 81st and civil engineering from 40th to 52nd.

Some distinctions may not be vast, and some departments went up a bit. But the overall direction is not encouraging. When we happily announce that our universities aren't losing much ground, we forget that other places keep gaining some.

Of course, we don't have to compete with Austin for research and design jobs.

We can just concentrate on assembly line jobs—and compete with Sri Lanka.

On the other hand, that's also a pretty place.

THE OREGONIAN, SEPTEMBER 17, 1995

Starved Colleges
Turn on Each Other

When Judith Ramaley first arrived from Kansas State to become president of Portland State University, she remarked that she'd never been anyplace where people spent so much time and energy on structures and organizations.

Four years later, people are still talking about it. The state higher-education system may have shortcomings in other ways—coming off five years of being top-ranked in budget cuts—but it's a national leader in the production of flow charts.

This Friday, the state Board of Higher Education will meet to decide how to come up with an overhaul proposal, to be presented to the governor and the 1997 Legislature. Just like fight songs and parking policies, every institution in the system seems to have its own proposal.

In the past, talking about restructuring has been a way to avoid talking about the system's real problems: increasing demand and diminishing resources. And in a time when there's no new money around, restructuring is the only way for one institution to gain—if only by cannibalizing others.

Already, it seems that University of Oregon President Dave

Frohnmayer is just about ready to come into the Portland State president's office and measure the drapes.

The people who are talking about restructuring, notably Chancellor Joseph Cox, insist that avoidance is not what's going on.

Not this time, anyway.

"The whole point of the conversations has not been structure. Structure is a means to an end," says Cox. "We're on a disinvestment slide that doesn't seem to be stopping. Old answers won't work if we go into the legislative session with the status quo."

Among the new answers floating around are a single-university system, in which everything becomes a branch of the University of Oregon; a two-university system, which splits things with Oregon State; a three-university system; and any other administrative structure that can be drawn in Magic Marker and shown with an overhead projector.

The biggest buzz followed the U of O-everywhere outline, and Frohnmayer was soon talking enthusiastically about U of O-Portland, U of O-Ashland, and even U of O-Bend, and touting the tightly centrally controlled Penn State system as the model. The core, he explained, was "a single standard for peer review and admissions."

The problem, objects PSU President Ramaley, is that Frohnmayer ignores the different nature of her university.

"It would be forcing our faculty to use a U of O syllabus designed for young adults in a residential environment," says Ramaley. "Ours is a community-based, age-differentiated, largely part-time and working student body. This would take down a second viable model and replace it with a program used in Eugene."

Worse, to her mind, is that people are redesigning Portland State without talking to anybody at Portland State.

"I'm professionally offended, but I also see this as dirty politics," says Ramaley. "It feels, whether it is or not, like a hostile takeover. I'm waiting for the lawyers to show up and tell me they're buying all our stock."

To Ramaley's objections, Cox responds delicately, "I think there is some legitimate criticism. Part of it stems from the fact that this activity is still at the thinking stage."

Restructuring is not, he insists, a Frohnmayer plot to expand the sway of the University of Oregon—although "I think it's fair to say that Dave resonated to the idea."

And the resonating is getting pretty loud.

Basically, it hardly seems to matter whether there's a Portland State University, or a University of Oregon-Portland, or whether the entire system becomes Portland State, with branches at Eugene and Corvallis. In fact, the best strategic move might be for PSU to secede from the system entirely and become the University of Washington at Portland—joining a system that's weak on imaginative renaming but stronger on commitment to the future.

What's important is that institutional maneuvering and self-delusion don't lead us to a New Letterhead Theory of Higher Education—an idea that by simply crossing out "Portland State" and writing in another name, the metropolitan area will suddenly have another university.

"As far as I'm concerned," says President John Byrne of Oregon State, currently heading toward retirement with no regrets at all, "they're proposing a solution before they've identified the problem. The name change should be the last thing that you come to."

Except that this is Oregon, where we like to talk about structures.

"This is not about moving boxes around here," says Ramaley. "All you're doing is taking a bunch of underfunded institutions and putting them together to share our poverty."

Now there's a name for the system: U of O-Shortfall.

THE OREGONIAN, OCTOBER 18, 1995

A Prayer, and a Wing, for Higher Ed

Considering how serious the situation is, it made sense that Washington's higher-education task force hearing at Sea-Tac airport was near the meditation and prayer chapel.

Considering what will be landing on the state's higher-education system in the next 15 years, maybe it should have been near the air traffic control center.

Just from 1995 to 2002, the number of graduates of Washington's high schools will be up by 100,000, as the baby-boom echo booms across the land. Monday afternoon, right behind the Delta ticket booths, Gov. Mike Lowry's task force to find them some college seats held its next-to-last session.

Its grade is still incomplete, but at least it's studying the right subject. By its count, Washington needs to find another 84,000 spaces in its higher-education system by 2010.

"We are not dealing with an ordinary set of facts," pointed out Ann Daley, deputy state treasurer and University of Washington regent, during the session. "We are dealing with extraordinary pressures from two directions."

Not only is the number of high school graduates soaring, but the percentage planning to go on to higher education keeps rising, as education looks like the only life raft in an economic downpour.

"There's no question," notes Daley, "that there will be a demand for better-educated workers. Hopefully, some will be our residents, and not imports from other states."

Washington, of course, is not the only state in the Northwest with this problem; the number of Oregon's high school graduates will increase by 35 percent from 1990 to 2005, and they're heading for a higher-education system that's frozen if not shrinking. Recently, new Oregon State University President Paul Risser said he was "haunted" by the situation, and he picked the right word: In Oregon, the issue is treated like a ghost.

In Washington, or at least in a conference room at Sea-Tac, people are trying to address it. Monday, the task force was discussing a proposal from its chairman, former state House Speaker Joe King of Vancouver, that would dedicate some state revenues—possibly from the business and operations tax or the utility tax—to higher education. This would provide some protection to a system that's been getting a steadily shrinking piece of the state budget, losing ground to prisons and health care.

Lowry, who has attended every meeting of the task force, strongly supports the dedicated-funding idea.

"The facts are simply there," he said during a break from the hearing. "Increased funding for higher education simply can't be done in competition with the existing 601 limitations," referring to Washington's initiative-passed expenditure limits. "The Legislature simply needs to enact it as a dedicated fund."

Of course, any legislature afterwards could change it—but, says Lowry with a knowing grin, no legislature would want to be the one that took down the wall protecting higher education.

Several task force members—including several key Republican legislators—are not on board. "If they want my signature," House Appropriations Chairman Tom Huff says of the task force report, "it will not have dedicated funding."

Instead, Huff supports tax credits for business contributions to some higher-education programs. But he also points out that in the current Republican-dominated Legislature, higher ed did well, expanding by 8,400 students. If that pace continues until 2010, he notes, the system can get where it needs to go.

"We've looked at the budgeting process," he says, "with higher education as a very high priority."

King insists that, "At this point, the idea of dedicated funding for higher education has legs of its own." Others on the task force suggest that the final proposal—due this summer, and aimed at stirring conversation in this year's election campaign—will likely be a mix of several ideas.

But the members agree that the students are coming, and the demand is there already. After all, as Rep. Helen Sommars, D-Seattle, pointed out, "Boeing is already going out of state for engineers, and Microsoft goes worldwide." Her point was met with the reverence that mention of the two always stirs in Washington politics.

In Oregon, U.S. Senate candidate Tom Bruggere, a founder of Mentor Graphics, also points out that Mentor and other Oregon high-tech firms have to recruit educated labor outside the state. Here, it's considered reason to be pleased about Oregon's ability to attract other people's children.

So far, trying to match a booming demand for higher education with an inadequate state supply, the Washington task force doesn't have the answer. But up near the Sea-Tac chapel, it's asking the question.

Oregon, by contrast, doesn't even have a process.

Or a prayer.

THE OREGONIAN, MAY 8, 1996

Oregon Higher Ed:
Last Known Address

Good afternoon, and it's nice to have you all here at the 1996 Commencement of the Oregon State System of Higher Education—or, as we sometimes call it, OOPS. We're pleased to have a nice day for it; fortunately, that did not require help from the Legislature.

We'll get to our program as soon as all you graduates put down your calculators and stop figuring the interest on your student loans.

We were going to get a commencement speaker to tell you about the challenges of making your own way in the world, but Steve Forbes was busy. Then we thought we'd get someone to talk to you about the exciting prospects for the future, but it turns out that Bill Gates has all that copyrighted.

So instead of urging you on to new accomplishments, we decided to bring in someone to tell you how much you've already achieved. So welcome this year's commencement speaker, John Hammang, director of state and campus relations for the American Association of State Colleges and Universities, who brings you an inspiring message:

You made it through with less support from your state than the graduates of just about any other state university system.

Give yourselves a hand—possibly the one Oregon's had in your wallet.

According to Hammang's most recent figures, which he explained Tuesday on National Public Radio's *All Things Considered,* Oregon now provides just 22 percent of the revenue of its higher-education system, around the bottom of the state rankings. That puts it at the other end of the spectrum from Hawaii, where the state covers around 64 percent, and Texas, which springs for 63 percent.

Texas, of course, even has the tackiness to boast about its higher-education commitment—and Austin's highly college-educated workforce—in its economic-development materials. Those Texans are so gauche—a term that more of you would understand if we hadn't also cut back on our foreign-language programs.

But that's the glory of your achievement. In a place like Texas, where there's more support and access to higher education, lots of people graduate from the state system. Here there's you: the few, the proud, the deeply in debt.

So in a sense, your degrees are really worth more than Texas degrees—or at least, they cost you more.

We're putting a small note to that effect on your diplomas. It's the least we can do.

"Back in 1991, you were around the middle of the pack," said Hammang Thursday morning; that now means just over 40 percent from the state. Vermont, he says, may actually be lower than Oregon in percentage, but northeastern states can count on a much greater private role in higher education. Oregon, notes Hammang, is a particular standout among its neighboring states: "Out West, the difference is really stark."

Back in 1993-94, when Oregon was providing around 31 percent of the cost of higher education, California was covering 47 percent of the costs of its program, Washington 43 percent and Idaho 42 percent.

That was, of course, around the middle of your college careers. When you look back at your graduation, you may see the date not as 1996, but as "just in time."

At least you get a unique chance to study different commencement styles. Princeton got President Clinton, declaring that "Higher education is the key to the growth we need to lift our country. . .and the key to a successful future in the 21st century," and proposing a range of new approaches to make it financially more accessible.

You get to hear officials of a state that has been going steadily—and sharply—in the other direction. One reason that Oregon, just since 1993-94, has gone from low-level to bottom-level is that not only has Oregon cut its funding, but states that were below Oregon have increased theirs.

As a consolation, you can have a second graduation speaker, writer and social commentator Nicholas Lemann, who writes about the issue in the current *Time*—and I've noticed some of you sneaking peaks at it when you should have been listening to the remarks from the chancellor.

Noting the sharp increases in tuition at state universities intended to provide easy access—a topic that could have put Oregon on the magazine's cover—Lemann writes, "Across-the-board increases at state schools amount to a major change in government policy, yet they remain mysteriously under-discussed . . . It gives a distinctive feeling to this country if, unlike the rest of the world, we offer education at all levels in an open and unrestricted way to everyone who qualifies. This unique and precious national commitment is now diminishing."

So to those of you who have just made it through the Oregon system, especially warm greetings. And we are proud to offer the hand of fellowship and congratulations.

With our other hand, we're accepting spare change.

THE OREGONIAN, JUNE 9, 1996

Higher Ed:
Washington's Got a Secret

To an Oregonian, seeing Washington state's ideas about higher education can be like looking at a Victoria's Secret catalogue.

There's the same powerful sense of allure and unattainability—and it's always impressive to look at the figures.

At least until it's time to return to the shapeless higher-ed debate in Oregon.

Which is why, before turning to the solemn consideration of how dramatically Oregon's situation would be improved by giving the PSU engineering department a new name, it's worth spending some relaxing moments with *The Final Report of the Governor's Task Force on Higher Education*.

The governor of Washington, of course.

The report projects that, just at current participation rates, Washington will need another 84,000 higher-education spaces in 2010. At current inflation levels, that means that state support for higher ed would have to double by then. To get there, the report proposes dedicating part of the state's revenues to higher ed—as well as an intriguing idea of giving businesses a full tax credit for donations to state college and university programs.

The proposal may not be enacted quite like that—three Republican legislators on the commission filed a minority report opposing the dedicated-revenue idea. But a big part of their argument was that the Washington Legislature understands the need to beef up the state system, was already doing it and would keep on doing it.

In other words, Washington has Republicans and Democrats arguing over who's the stronger and more effective supporter of strengthening the state's higher-ed system.

You won't find a pose like that anywhere in the Victoria's Secret catalogue—or anywhere in Oregon.

What you'll find in Oregon, of course, is a constant effort to improve our colleges by changing their names.

The current idea—now described as a proposal, although a little while ago it was supposed to be a policy—is to have Oregon State take over Portland State's engineering school, which would then presumably become the Oregon State University School of Engineering, Portland (OSUSEP). There's also a plan to rename the state colleges, making them Oregon state universities, but not Oregon State University.

This should not be confused with last year's plan to divide up the whole system between the University of Oregon and Oregon State. And it certainly can't compare with the most imaginative proposal, from a few years back, to merge Portland State and the Health Sciences University and then declare the result a major national research center.

Seeing how much time everybody around here spends thinking about structure, maybe we could just rename the whole system the Oregon School of Architecture.

"What I don't see is, what's the point of merging the two schools?" wonders Jim Craven, lobbyist for the Oregon Council of the American Electronics Association, a consistent voice for higher education's interests in Salem. "It seems that at the same meeting of the higher-education board, they went directly from objective to solution, without taking a breath."

Doing that, says Craven, the planners may have missed the key objective: producing lots more engineers—something that the same facilities and faculty would have trouble doing, whatever the name on the wall.

"Ten years ago, it was a quality issue. Now, it's mostly a quantity issue; people are relatively pleased with what they're getting from Oregon State and Portland State," although improvements would also help.

What's most important to local electronics firms, says Craven, is getting more local engineers produced.

Oddly, Washington arrived at the same objective—but a different way of getting there.

In Oregon, business groups have joined to produce a brief report, *The Need for Customer-Driven Higher Education*, giving the system something local business has always been generous with: free advice. With hardly a number in sight, the report offers suggestions such as a top-10 ranked school of electrical engineering in the Portland area.

Together, Oregon State and Portland State now spend around $16 million a year on engineering. The University of Washington spends $81.8 million—and as PSU President Judith Ramaley points out, the UW is ranked only 24th.

Maybe the key is to merge the OSU and PSU schools, and rename the result "A Top Ten Ranked School of Engineering."

In the Northwest, as elsewhere, there is a rapidly rising need for high-quality higher education. Filling it will take more than changing names or stern exhortation.

That wouldn't seem too hard to figure out, but somehow Washington has realized it much faster than Oregon has.

You might call it Olympia's Secret.

THE OREGONIAN, JULY 19, 1996

Billing Our Children

Typically, a shiny new graduate of the University of Oregon has a broad education, a promising future and one of America's last tie-dyed wardrobes. Lately, there's a good chance he's also carrying something else.

A debt of just under $20,000.

This figure has, of course, drawn a lot of interest—although not as much as the graduate will pay. Widely, people argue that there's something uncomfortable about that number:

It's not big enough.

As Oregon's support of its higher-education system recedes like a thirtysomething hairline, there are multiple suggestions about where the system should get the money. Many of these suggestions have come up with the same idea:

Students.

Over the past decade, Oregon has been rapidly transferring college costs to students, raising tuition and cutting the state's share, cutting its investment as if the future had turned into an unpromising land deal.

In 1989-90, full-time in-state tuition at the University of Oregon was $1,338; this year, it's $3,540. Seven years ago, tuition paid 36.4 percent of undergraduate education costs, up from about 25 percent earlier in the decade. This year, tuition is covering—with the help of lots more out-of-state students—51 percent.

And increasingly, the full graduation uniform includes cap, gown and loan coupon book—often for a loan greater than what the graduate will probably be earning his first year out.

For this year's budget, Gov. John Kitzhaber has proposed a two-year tuition freeze, on the grounds that the state has shrugged off enough responsibility for now. For Oregon's college students, he points out, the situation has already gotten pretty chilly.

This idea is opposed by the argument that tuition is an endless gold mine, since the system is selling something of major financial value. So sending students deeper into debt—or even, according to one proposal, taking a percentage of their income for the next 30 years—is still a shrewd deal for them, and a way for the state to save even more money.

On the other hand, even the tuition golden goose is not unkillable. As prices rise, demand drops—or at least gets scared off, especially if you're part of the rapidly rising percentage of older students not living off regular checks from home.

"There is a question of sticker shock," says the state system's Chancellor Joe Cox. "The independent student, the middle-class student who's not entitled to a lot of aid, is getting crushed."

And a major tuition jackpot, Californians willing to pay more than $11,000 a year to attend Oregon's schools, may be dwindling—as Southern Oregon State College has found. It seems that—unconvinced by nifty arguments about how this can be done much cheaper—California is reinvesting in its higher-education system, and more Californians are staying home.

Increasingly, that golden goose will be staying in the Golden State.

But there is another idea, that the generation in power has a responsibility to prepare its children for the future, instead of cleverly devising ways to bill them for it. People have believed this since, say, the Bronze Age, and it's remarkable how recently people actually believed it in Oregon.

In 1987-1989, Oregon spent $626 million on its higher-education system, spending 15.4 percent of the state general fund on it. (In 1991-1993, the number went to $732 million.) This time, 1995-1997, the number is $603 million—or about $450 million in 1987 dollars—and it's 8.2 percent of the general fund.

It's possible, of course, that the Oregonians of the last decade just had lots more money to throw around—but it's not true. Back then, the state was coming out of a recession, and Oregon's median income was only about 90 percent of the national level. Now, we've got one of our hottest economies ever, and the state median income is more like 95 percent of the nation's.

We've also got an economy in which a college degree is even more important, and pays out more to the state later.

What earlier Oregonians had wasn't more money; just some idea that they had some responsibility to build a state and a future.

What saps.

With just a little foresight, every Oregon kid coming to college could have been offered his own co-signer.

THE OREGONIAN, JANUARY 31, 1997

3. Average debt at graduation per borrower

Rank per borrower, Public 4-yearr, Class of 2007	State	Average debt at graduation
1	Alaska	$27,043
2	Iowa	$26,175
3	Vermont	$24,368
4	New Hampshire	$24,272
5	Pennsylvania	$23,294
6	Minnesota	$21,988
7	Idaho	$21,816
8	North Dakota	$21,569
9	Ohio	$21,458
10	South Dakota	$21,321
11	Michigan	$21,258
12	Alabama	$21,176
13	Rhode Island	$21,125
14	Maine	$20,823
15	Indiana	$20,700
16	South Carolina	$20,549
17	New Jersey	$20,017
18	Tennessee	$19,393
19	Oregon	$19,093
20	Louisiana	$19,077
21	Nebraska	$18,563
	United States	$18,482
22	Colorado	$18,417
23	Missouri	$18,394
24	Virginia	$18,056
25	Kansas	$18,012

Rank per borrower, Public 4-year, Class of 2007	State	Average debt at graduation
26	Arkansas	$17,495
27	Texas	$17,267
28	Delaware	$17,200
29	Oklahoma	$17,186
30	Montana	$17,179
31	New York	$17,157
32	Arizona	$17,143
33	Wisconsin	$17,094
34	Kentucky	$17,059
35	Connecticut	$16,846
36	Illinois	$16,786
37	Florida	$16,755
38	Washington	$16,562
39	Maryland	$16,452
40	Nevada	$16,422
41	Mississippi	$16,195
42	Massachusetts	$16,031
43	Wyoming	$16,005
44	West Virginia	$15,846
45	Georgia	$15,636
46	North Carolina	$15,547
47	New Mexico	$15,467
48	California	$13,975
49	Utah	$13,046
50	Hawaii	$12,583

SOURCE: Calculations by the Project on Student Debt on student debt data from Petersons's Undergraduate Financial Database, copyright 2007, 2008 Peterson's, a Nelnet company.

The average debt at graduation of students who required aid while in school at public 4-year universities.

Viking Queen Sets Sail

In the Portland State University president's office, for years a castle of cuts and crises, the mood now feels a bit different. A couple of months before departing to the top job at the University of Vermont—and a couple of months after winning the battle to keep an independent engineering department at PSU—Judith Ramaley is as mellow as maple syrup.

It's not just the prospect of switching from Viking to Vermont—which must feel like checking into a ski lodge after years in an ice storm. Also thawing Ramaley's mood is the fact that Oregon higher education actually shows signs of spring.

Inspired by the University of Oregon mascot, the state government's traditional response to the challenge of funding the Oregon university system has been to duck it.

"This is the first time in the seven years I've seen it, and it may go back much further than that," says Ramaley, "when higher education is treated as a part of education, and an actual investment goal for the state.

"Up to now, there's been an underlying assumption that higher education is a cost, an underlying expense, and we've gotten what's left when the important things are taken care of. Now, we're considered not just an expense; we're an investment."

According to higher-education Chancellor Joe Cox, this is the first higher-education budget since 1989 that doesn't lose more ground. Admittedly, lots has already been evacuated; one estimate is that the Oregon higher-education system now enrolls 7,000 fewer Oregonians than it did back then.

But this year, at least the drop stops—with the Legislature's clear support. The difference, says Ramaley, has to do with increasing understanding of how the state's new economy works and with the people involved.

"Since the late 1980s," she explains, "there's a new business leadership that's less likely to feel, 'I don't need to support public universities, I'll send my kid to Princeton.'

"The change is in the nature of the businesses, in a generational shift, and that a much larger proportion of the new civic leadership didn't grow up here. People from elsewhere are more used to public/private partnerships, and they're more used to a strong public university system."

The engineering situation—partly about control, largely about resources—shows all of the elements of Oregon's higher-education condition. There's a new set of business leaders with a new set of expectations, a belated understanding and effort to deal with the need, and a nagging concern that the state's response may still be too little and too late.

"Currently," says Donald R. VanLuvanee, president of Electro Scientific Industries Inc., "we're producing a tenth of the graduates we expect to need."

VanLuvanee is a leader of the higher-ed system's industry task force to upgrade the state's engineering programs. The original plan called for a investment of $25 million; the governor's final proposal was $9 million; so far, the Legislature is prepared to spend $5 million.

How does the task force feel about that number?

"Our group was excited about the first proposal," VanLuvanee says. "Practically, if the funding stays at this level, we would have people who'd say, we've been here before."

Still, Ramaley is encouraged—and not just because she's leaving. There is, she thinks, a change in "the assumptions that have shaped what went on here in this state for a decade, as we let higher education slip through our fingers. This may be our last chance, because other states are now starting to invest in their higher-education infrastructure."

The past weeks have shown examples of that, as both houses of the Washington Legislature—both Republican—have adopted budgets increasing both investment and capacity in the Washington system. California, after a bad fiscal battering in the first half of the decade, is now planning small increases in both the University of California and the California State University system.

And the Golden State is considering further expansion. There's planning for a new state college in fast-growing Ventura County, northwest of Los Angeles, and now the thinking focuses on the evacuated grounds of Camarillo State Hospital.

Oregon, coincidentally enough, is also planning the future of a former state hospital, Dammasch in Wilsonville. The difference, of course, is that Oregon is thinking of using the space for a prison.

At least that way, some Oregonians won't think of escaping to Vermont.

THE OREGONIAN, MARCH 30, 1997

Degrees of Deeper Debt

"I'm lucky," Benjamin Unger, newly elected vice president of the University of Oregon student body, explained to his closely listening audience.

"I had the chance to be a student."

"And all it's cost me so far is $25,000 in loans, and all I have is one year to go."

As a Duck debtor, Unger has lots of company. Of the new U of O alumni who graduated Saturday, estimates student financial aid director Edmond Vignoul, about half are in debt, with an average load of around $18,000. Many of Saturday's graduates from Portland State and Sunday's from Oregon State will have similarly hefty loan coupon books balanced unsteadily on their new mortarboards.

In college today, the biggest three-letter fraternity is IOU.

Unger was one of several student speakers last week at the University of Montana's second Q-A-C (quality, access, cost) conference on higher education, drawing from all over the West. But concerns about the rising debt levels of college students came from conference participants a long way from their last midterm.

In fact, three of the people collecting the money that students are borrowing—state legislators—expressed some of the strongest worries about a trend that's increasingly sending students out into the world deep in the hole.

"The pressure that we're putting on students to borrow the money to continue their education is something we need to think about," said state Sen. John Hansen, R-Idaho. "The likelihood of their getting a job that would pay them enough to service that debt is not strong. There's a big disconnect there."

Increasingly, the rising levels of college loan debt are constricting opportunities, just when possibilities are supposed to be widest.

"When a lot of these people get out of schools owing vast sums of money,"what sort of future do they have?" asked state Sen. Greg Jergeson, D-Mont. "The average level of debt for a student from Montana is about $20,000. That's caused a lot of families to self-select themselves out of accessing the state university system."

A few states are even trying to do something about it. Washington's Legislature, in this year's session, increased its commitment to higher education, and it increased its student aid. But cutting against national trends, it put its additional aid money into grants and work-study programs, not loans.

"We think our students are already in debt too much," explained Rep. Don Carlson, a Republican from Vancouver who chairs Washington's House higher-education committee.

"And if the loan level is a burden for those of us who are white Anglo-Saxon Protestants, let me suggest that minorities are particularly affected."

The trail that led to many twentysomethings now owing twenty-something is easy to trace. For the last decade, legislatures have been cutting away their support of state colleges and universities, leading to sharp, steady tuition raises that shift the burden onto students' families.

"It's part of government instincts to find the path of least resistance," explained Montana Gov. Marc Racicot, a second-term Republican. "The path of least resistance has been tuition increases."

And since multi-thousand-dollar state university tuition outruns many family incomes, the answer has been borrowing. And at the same time, many government aid programs, at the federal and state level, have switched from scholarships to loans.

So now, a large part of a rising generation starts out deeply in debt—compared with their elders, who've had a long romance with credit cards that let them work up to it.

Looking back over 40 years of experience in higher education, President Lattie F. Coor of Arizona State University mused, "The single most significant thing that's changed is that we now expect the students to pay for it."

And increasingly, we expect them to pay for virtually all of it.

Historically, legislatures and voters have been prepared to pick up a hefty piece of the tab, on the grounds that there was a considerable public benefit to increasing access to higher education. By all economic and social experience, that has become even more true, but the willingness to pay for it has faded—especially compared to the exciting opportunity to pay for more and more prisons.

So every year, we expect more from our public higher-education systems, and we invest less in them.

And every June, we produce a new debtor class.

THE OREGONIAN, JUNE 15, 1997

Irate PSU Alumni Report

From the viewpoint of departed Portland State president Judith Ramaley, it seems only a sensible precaution that her new job as president of the University of Vermont is a full 3,000 miles from the Oregon State System of Higher Education.

"The system," she explained, "is about to blow up."

Not only is the Oregon higher-education system embarrassingly short of money, but in her view, it's at least as short on leadership.

"The system is in total chaos," Ramaley declared on her last official day in the president's office. "Decisions are being made in strange ways without any logic.

"Oregon is a national laughingstock in the higher-education community because of its system, its disinvestment in higher education and what it's doing to its higher-education system."

During her seven years as PSU president, Ramaley was often at odds with the state system's leadership—especially during the last year, when it supported and she successfully resisted restructurings that Ramaley thought would undermine Portland State. To many PSU observers, those disputes—and the state leadership's frequent wish for a "team player" at Portland State—led to this month's surprise choice of Ramaley's successor, against the preferences and expectations of much of the campus community.

To Ramaley, the higher-education board meeting announcing the decision reflected the board's lack of understanding both of Portland State and of higher education's challenges. The selection was revealed in an offhand, by-the-way manner; it produced gasps from PSU faculty, and the board chairman then asked if he was facing a mob.

"What we've got here is a board that's lacking in grace, courtesy, and respect for a campus community that's made enormous progress," said Ramaley, still angry a week after the event. "The choice of a new president at a place like Portland State should be a moment of major ceremony and transition, and they didn't know it. This is a group of people who have never understood their role.

"What's wrong is the attitude of the board, which is clearly to view this institution with disdain."

To Ramaley, the limitations of the board—and of Oregon's higher-education leadership and philosophy—also keep it from dealing with the problems of the state's other universities.

She warned that the system runs on "a '30s philosophy" assuming that "in perpetuity, all institutions will grow and new money will follow the growth. Neither of those is true any more."

So now, "OIT (Oregon Institute of Technology) is on life support. Oregon State is in very serious trouble," and the board can't find a way to respond.

Last week, declining enrollments led to announcements of sharp budget cuts at both institutions. For 1996-1997, Oregon Tech had its lowest enrollment since 1978-1979, and Oregon State its lowest since 1967-68—when the entire system was considerably smaller. In head-count statistics, Oregon State's enrollment has now, for the first time, dipped significantly below Portland State's numbers.

"If they look at productivity and quality," said Ramaley, "money will come to Portland State at the expense of Oregon State and OIT, but that's politically unacceptable."

By contrast, Ramaley sees the University of Oregon's problems as more financial—but equally hard to avoid.

"The problem is that the University of Oregon, compared with the institutions it competes with, pays the least," noted Ramaley. "Faculty can usually go from Oregon to any other reasonably funded system and do at least a third better. Oregon's institutions are in the bottom of the bottom quartile, and have been for years."

This situation was particularly noticeable last week, when the U of O announced that 10 tenured professors—a historically high number—had accepted better-paying positions in other states.

But to Ramaley, neither of the older universities, or the system in general, have gone through the restructuring and redefinition process that PSU has experienced. She feels that the governor has provided little direction or guidance—and the state's higher-education leadership not only hasn't helped, but probably can't.

"We should see contemporary management put in place," she said, "but there's now no one who could do that in the state of Oregon.

"Most of these folks mean well, but they don't know what they're doing. It's like watching a bunch of kids playing with dangerous chemicals."

And from her perspective, the place to watch that from is Vermont.

THE OREGONIAN, JUNE 22, 1997

Making a University

Stephen J. Reno has now been a university president for a more than a year. He wasn't the one who showed up last year; the university did.

Last April, Southern Oregon State College—along with Western Oregon in Monmouth and Eastern Oregon in La Grande—became a university, promoted by a Legislature ready to do anything for higher education that didn't cost money.

By now, the effect of Oregon claiming six universities has begun to settle in; as Reno noted Thursday morning, "We've just about used up all the old stationery."

For SOU, the year also has marked closer connections with the Southern Oregon community, a rising sense that a campus gets its identity not from the Legislature, but from its surroundings. Like Judith Ramaley's efforts at Portland State, Reno's direction at Southern has been to move not just upward, but outward.

Last week produced another success for the strategy, as Reno announced a gift of $165,000 from the Jeld-Wen Foundation of Klamath

Falls for the university's new Center for the Visual Arts. Together with $150,000 from the Bear Creek company, it's the largest local contribution ever brought in by Southern Oregon University.

Or by Southern Oregon State College, for that matter.

Thursday, as Reno discussed the new university status at a very Ashland cafe called Morning Glory—Portobello-mushroom burgers with smoked mozzarella aren't standard in Monmouth or La Grande— he spoke first of its effect in the neighborhood.

"People in the community say, 'the university,' with a slight stiffening of the spine," he reported. "A little pride doesn't hurt."

And with the pride, says Reno, comes a new seriousness: "There's a feeling that the university is clearly a partner in regional economic development."

Other effects go as far afield as Asia and Europe, where SOU develops exchange programs; "university" sounds better than "college" in translation.

But Reno declares that a powerful impact has been internal: "As Southern has gone through a wrenching strategic planning effort over the last six months, it's been very helpful to have the name."

Southern Oregon University isn't the only local higher-education institution with a recent theme change. Rogue Community College has expanded into Jackson County, home of Medford and Ashland, and the two institutions are seeking to adjust to each other.

Southern has cut its off-campus lower-division offerings, in the hope that more students will try out higher education at the community college level, and SOU can concentrate more on upper-division offerings and specialties, notably in the arts.

For the last two years, it hopes to attract more RCC graduates.

For those freshmen who do start at Southern, the university now has freshmen seminars—also adapted from a PSU model—to try to connect them to the campus and to one professor, who both teaches the seminar and serves as academic adviser.

"If this is what we're going to do, let's try to do it extremely well," says Reno about the university's tighter focus. "There's going to be more competition among institutions for students, a challenge to say what is the value-added for a student coming to Southern."

In planning its future, Southern has not only turned to its local resources; it's been thrown upon them. Along with the University of Oregon, Southern managed to fend off some of the Measure 5 pressure by sharply increasing enrollment of non-Oregon students, Californians bearing rich out-of-state tans and paying rich out-of-state tuition.

At a time when California was in recession, and its higher-education system closer to depression, parents and students stampeded to the pleasant campus in a pleasant town with a California-close climate.

Oregon's higher-education Chancellor Joe Cox, then president of Southern, told of a wave of telephoning parents asking a single question: Could their kids graduate in four years? Compared with what seemed almost a dissolving California system, Oregon could at least offer that.

Now, with California's powerfully reviving economy and universities, the wave is waning. Southern's out-of-state enrollment, which went from 11 percent to 22 percent from 1989-90 to 1992-93, is now closing to 17 percent.

"We took a fairly large cut in budget when we didn't continue on that upward slope," admits Reno. "We've adapted our spending accordingly."

Spending cuts, of course, have been the steady diet of Oregon state universities during the decade. Looking for strength and balance, Southern, like Portland State, is reaching out more into its community constituency.

Next, Reno is looking to draw from Southern's 36-member regional advisory board, and the board of its university foundation, to set up a smaller local group that would be more closely involved in the campus, something like a private university's board of trustees. In charting the direction and future of Southern Oregon University, "university" turns out to be a key phrase.

So does "Southern Oregon."

THE OREGONIAN, JULY 5, 1998

The Future Is Sighted Elsewhere:
Newsweek's Hottest Tech Cities All Boast Higher-Ed Engines— and Guess Who Didn't Qualify

For Oregon, the sign of the future is the sign that was missing.

The now-famous *Newsweek* cover of Nov. 9, "The Hottest Tech Cities," directed the future toward Seattle; Austin, Texas; Salt Lake City; Washington, D.C.; Boise; and Boston. After more than a decade of boosterish booming of Oregon's "Silicon Forest," it seems that to the rest of the world, we're on line to be the place back of Boise.

Surprisingly—and this may be where we made our mistake—*Newsweek*'s calculation of vital ingredients for cybercity status didn't include property tax limits or really good places to get your body pierced.

The No. 1 requirement in *Newsweek*'s recipe—as anybody in the world, or at least in the world outside Salem, would have expected—was "a major research institution." The No. 3 requirement for high-tech city status was "high-tech talent," which is mostly another way of saying the same thing.

In Oregon, of course, it's hardly ever said at all.

Obviously, competing with the powerhouse universities driving most of *Newsweek*'s tomorrow tech towns—the University of Washington, the University of Texas, Stanford and MIT—Oregon is a mouse, and not the high-tech kind. On engineering, the University of Washington spends three times the budget of Oregon State and Portland State combined, and the UW does have this useful corporate neighbor just across Lake Washington.

But as vast as the gap is, it's also widening. Washington Gov. Gary Locke has a proposal in his budget to add $14 million in new high-tech education funding, from information-technology training in high schools to expanding computer science and engineering programs in state universities, expected to draw at least $11 million in additional private funding.

He seems to think it's vital to his state's economic future. To *Newsweek*, Seattle was the top signpost on its high-tech direction center—and the magazine seemed to think that Puget Sound area is the "Silicon Forest."

To Oregon, of course, Seattle and the UW are a different world. But just a bit further down in the magazine's listing of the future is Boise—poised to draw support from a brand-new engineering school at Boise State.

Just opening its doors in 1996, the school has drawn $13 million in private support, including $6 million from Micron Technologies, $2 million for a microfabrication laboratory like only five in the country, and $2 million in equipment from Hewlett-Packard. For that program, H-P received 80 grant applications, and funded two: Stanford and Boise State. In two years, the school's gone from 361 electronics majors to 524.

"It's designed to be very supportive of our local industries," says Larry Burke, Boise State's director of university relations. "So far, it's been very successful."

And it's got a whole future ahead of it.

Washington and Idaho, of course, are hardly the only states to see that the future requires investing in higher education, and that state investments can draw major private support. According to the *Chronicle of Higher Education*, newly elected and re-elected governors from Texas' George W. Bush, a Republican, to Iowa's Tom Vilsack, a Democrat, to Independent Angus King of Maine, ran on increasing state support of technology and research.

Meanwhile, in Oregon, it was considered a higher-education triumph in the last session to get another $5 million for high-tech programs—universally pronounced to be the future of the state.

And nobody—certainly not *Newsweek*—is talking about our higher-education resources driving Oregon to a high-tech pinnacle.

Jim Craven, of Oregon's branch of the American Electronics Association, notes that Oregon has still drawn heavy industry investment, and sees some educational advances. The restructuring of higher-education funding should help, and industry and universities are now gathered into an Engineering Technology Industry Council to set priorities and monitor programs. But even solid priorities need funding.

In Oregon—with the lowest per-capita higher-ed funding in the West—that's always the problem.

The council has proposals for $24 million in high-tech program investment, with about $10 million in matching private support. It wouldn't create a University of Washington—or a Hot High-Tech City—but it would be a considerable increase in Oregon's high-technology funding, at a time when lots of other places are spending lots more.

We have a choice of high-tech futures.

Including one as a suburb of Boise.

THE OREGONIAN, NOVEMBER 22, 1998

Market Rises for Faculty, Not Oregon

Betty Youngblood, president of Western Oregon University, says it's not exactly true that last year the university had nine job searches that failed because the salary offered was so low.

More accurately, she says, three searches failed that way. Then there were the five searches cancelled because "the pool was insufficient, the candidates were not acceptable."

Then there was the search cancelled this year after the administration looked at the salary it was offering and decided not to bother.

"As the years go by," says Youngblood, "this becomes a growing problem, because the salaries just have not kept up."

While Oregon's been squeezing, the academic world has been changing. For years, as the number of would-be faculty greatly exceeded the number of jobs, the professor business was a buyer's market. Even low-paying places like Oregon—although there weren't many low-paying places quite like Oregon—could choose among large numbers of impressive candidates holding signs reading "Will Teach College For Food."

Like anybody who catches a break, Oregon concluded that it was only fair. Teaching here, after all, included the legendary "second paycheck"— you got to live here.

"We used that for years," says Joe Cox, chancellor of the Oregon University System. "We wore it out."

Because now, things look different here—and every place else.

"It's a major change from the mid-'80s," says Edward R. Hines of the Center for Higher Education at Illinois State University. "If you're not competitive, you're going to have trouble filling slots."

There are, Hines points out, several changes working here. The vast armies of professors hired in the huge expansion of the 1960s are finally starting to retire—even though they seemed as permanent as an administration building. Meanwhile, driven by demography and the economy, student enrollments are booming.

Finally, as the rise of the knowledge economy shows the tie between higher education and the future, states have been investing steadily in their university systems.

Well, many states.

In 1990, notes University of Oregon president Dave Frohnmayer, the U of O's salaries were about 90 percent of those of comparable institutions. Now, he estimates, the Oregon level is about 82 percent.

And in 1990, he adds, you could tell candidates with a straight face that housing costs in Portland, Eugene and Corvallis were cheaper than the rest of the country.

"The salary differentials are noticeable, especially at the higher levels," says Frohnmayer—who just lost a senior professor in international studies to the University of Minnesota. "In searches for senior faculty, or senior administrators, we're not competitive."

Frohnmayer and Youngblood, and Portland State president Dan Bernstine, say quickly that their universities have still been able to hire some good people. The situation is different from place to place and from discipline to discipline; it's still easier to pick up a good English professor cheap than it is to stock an engineering department.

But it's getting harder to miss the market's message.

"There is no question that this is an issue whose time has come," says Cox. "You can swim in the Willamette wearing an anchor, but you don't get lots of style points. We've been doing a lot of swimming with anchors."

Thursday and Friday, Cox began meeting with the university presidents and the higher-education board's budget and finance committee to talk about the system's next budget proposals. On top of their list are enrollment growth and faculty salaries.

The hope is to close the salary gap over four years, but there may not be that much time.

"It is serious enough," notes Cox, "that the presidents as a group gave some serious consideration" to making faculty salaries their single priority for the next session.

That choice is a way off, and the political response even further. But the salary issue is now coming up in a new academic reality.

Oregon can always fool itself.

THE OREGONIAN, MARCH 19, 2000

4. Average faculty salaries at public doctoral-granting universities, 2007-08

Rank	State	All-ranks average faculty salaries at public doctoral-granting universities 2007-08 ($ in thousands)
1	California	$104.5
2	New Jersey	$100.7
3	Connecticut	$96.5
4	Maryland	$94.9
5	Delaware	$92.4
6	Minnesota	$91.7
7	New York	$89.9
8	North Carolina	$88.3
9	Massachusetts	$88.0
10	Virginia	$87.2
11	Iowa	$86.2
12	Georgia	$85.8
13	Hawaii	$85.0
14	Arizona	$84.9
14	Nevada	$84.9
16	Michigan	$84.8
17	Washington	$84.4
18	New Hampshire	$84.2
19	Pennsylvania	$83.4
	United States	$82.7
20	Nebraska	$82.2
21	Wisconsin	$81.5
22	Texas	$81.0
23	Alabama	$80.6
23	Illinois	$80.6
25	Colorado	$80.1

Rank	State	All-ranks average faculty salaries at public doctoral-granting universities 2007-08 ($ in thousands)
26	Indiana	$79.0
27	Rhode Island	$77.7
28	Kentucky	$77.4
29	South Carolina	$77.0
30	Ohio	$76.5
31	Kansas	$76.2
32	Arkansas	$76.0
32	Florida	$76.0
34	Missouri	$75.6
35	Utah	$74.8
36	Tennessee	$74.7
37	Oklahoma	$74.3
38	Maine	$73.5
39	Vermont	$72.3
40	Wyoming	$72.2
41	West Virginia	$71.6
42	New Mexico	$71.2
43	Louisiana	$70.8
44	Idaho	$68.3
45	Mississippi	$67.0
46	Oregon	$66.5
47	Alaska	$64.2
48	North Dakota	$63.3
49	Montana	$62.3
50	South Dakota	$60.4

SOURCE: *AAUP Faculty Compensation Survey, 2007-08*. NOTE: In calculating an institution's average salary, the distribution of faculty was not standardized by rank. New Hampshire imputed.

Chart indicates Oregon professors at public universities granting doctorates were paid 5th lowest in the country in 2007-2008.

Trying to Catch Up with Old Wash Tech

Offhand, Oregon's drive to have a Top 25 engineering program—the universally endorsed effort to exalt Oregon State from its current national level somewhere in the top 75—might have only a couple of problems.

The first is that, being Oregon, we don't seem ready to spend anything close to the money that it would take.

The second problem is the 74 engineering programs ahead of us—which aren't just waiting around for us to make a move.

In fact, some of them are moving faster than we are.

In other words, it's not just a matter of looking up at places like the University of Washington. Now, we can start worrying about Washington Institute of Technology—good old Wash Tech, or just WIT.

In his new budget, Washington Gov. Gary Locke—who already has a Top 25 engineering program—is proposing significant increases in his state's high-tech higher-education effort, including the start of a new Washington Institute of Technology at the University of Washington-Tacoma.

"In a decade, we hope for 1,000 bachelor's and master's graduates a year," explained Rich Nafziger, Locke's policy adviser for higher education, Friday. "That would make it one of the largest engineering schools in the country."

In a decade, Oregon will probably be just perfecting its strategy.

"It's a tough budget year," said Nafziger apologetically. "We have $52 million in enhancements" for addressing Washington's high-tech higher-ed needs. Besides the seed money for WIT, that includes $23 million in high-tech capacity expansion on other campuses and $10 million for keeping and attracting faculty.

"We think it's like *Field of Dreams*," explained Nafziger: "If you build it, they will come. In the tech economy, it's all people."

Washington doesn't want to be left short of them.

Meanwhile in Oregon, aiming at a quantum leap upward in its engineering programs, the state board of higher education requested $40 million in "enhancements," and the governor's budget proposes $20 million.

This money—actually, part of this money, plus Oregon State's private fund-raising—is supposed to fuel take-off for the OSU program from Top 75 status to Top 25 ranking.

"I don't think there's any question," said Oregon University System spokesman Bob Bruce, "that we have a pretty substantial mountain to climb."

Especially when people already ahead of us are climbing faster.

Certainly, it's a tough budget year here, too, without a lot of loose money floating around and not a lot of fat budgets that could spare money for higher-ed high-tech. And maybe Washington is the exception, and lots of the other engineering programs ahead of Oregon State aren't investing to strengthen themselves, and will be easy to overtake—although somehow, that seems unlikely.

Being Oregon, home of the bottle bill, we always figure that when we come up with an idea, we got it first. But in seeing higher-education investment as driving the economy, we're a lot closer to last.

If this budget is all we can afford, that's one thing. But we might go easy on the self-congratulation about our explosive drive toward Top 25 status.

"We have this sense in Oregon," says Bruce, "that when we propose something, just by talking about it, it's accomplished."

For example, there was the Oregon Education Act for the 21st Century, which we celebrated for a decade without mentioning that we weren't actually funding it.

Other states invest in their kids.

In Oregon, we just kid ourselves.

Still, any improvement helps, and there is increasing private support—although there is increasing private support in other places, too. And maybe the state can find some more money later.

Maybe, despite everything, we could actually end up with a Top 25 engineering program.

Or maybe, being Oregon, we'll just end up with a half WIT.

THE OREGONIAN, JANUARY 14, 2001

Again Oregon Tries the Old College Trash

We've been here before.

Friday, the higher-education system was thinking about the Oregon Institute of Technology going private.

In 1991, at the start of Oregon's last budget crunch, the thinking was about sending the University of Oregon, and maybe Southern Oregon, off on their own. In the early '80s, in the state's worst recession, the talk was about shutting Eastern Oregon down, or turning Western Oregon into something useful like a prison.

In the last two Oregon fiscal crises, higher education ended up as the hardest hit of state programs. Now there's another crunch, and the prospect of Oregon's universities getting slapped backward for the third time in a generation.

In Gov. John Kitzhaber's preliminary all-cuts budget, higher education goes down particularly sharply.

"If you look at our position on the list, I don't think that there's anybody with a higher percentage of cuts," says higher-education chancellor Joe Cox.

"We are prepared to, and expect to, do our fair share. What we ask is that that's all it should be."

That hasn't been the typical pattern.

Especially in the years after the passage of Measure 5 in 1990, higher education took bigger hits than K-12 or human services. Corrections, of course, has been booming.

To make up some of the difference, the university system took other steps.

"In 1991, we raised tuition 38 percent, and we lost 5,000 kids," says Cox. "I don't know what happened to them. When we raise tuition $100, we lose some. When we're pushed to the wall, we're going to raise tuition, and I know the effect that will have."

As Oregon student enrollment dropped, the University of Oregon stayed afloat on out-of-state tuition, becoming known as the University of California, Eugene. Maybe we can still find the sweatshirts.

"We were a decade recovering from Measure 5," recalls Cox. "My sense of the Legislature's collective memory is that they remember that, and they don't want it to happen again."

Higher education did well in the 2001 legislative session, and the legislative leadership budget released Thursday treated it a bit more evenly than the governor's all-cuts budget.

Still, as a proportion of its state funding, higher ed would lose more than the other major budget parts. That may be inevitable, but it has a cost.

The universal saying in Oregon—which figured it out just a while after most other states—is that high tech and higher education are the future. But deep cuts erode our path to it.

Oregon's goal of a Top 25 engineering program—always something that required the rest of the country to freeze in place—won't be helped by cuts in the efforts to strengthen the program. The next wave, the biotechnology that's so central to metro Portland's economic planning, won't be getting much of a ride, either.

"Biotech? That's all going to have to be private money," calculates Cox. "Is that going to make us competitive with the Texases?"

Well, no.

Right now, the state's universities are relatively strong, largely because students figured out their importance before Salem did. Enrollment is booming, especially on the three big campuses (helped by limiting tuition increases), and entering student profiles are high; freshmen at Oregon State average a 3.5 high school grade-point.

We won't even mention the last two Fiesta Bowls.

And there is a feeling of foreboding.

"There is a sort of fatalism, of 'here we go again,'" says Cox.

"I spend a lot of time on the campuses, and I'm worried about morale. This is a pretty resilient bunch, they've been through floods and locusts, and it does begin to wear you down."

Within the lifetime of an average Oregon student today, in fact, the universities have been worn down twice. This time, the dangers of going through another higher-education free-fall are even more obvious.

As they could tell you at the Oregon State College of Oceanography—or in the high-tech world—there is such a thing as going down for the third time.

THE OREGONIAN, JANUARY 20, 2002

Salem Needs Some Higher Education

Last Friday, the U.S. Postal Service dropped off three bulging sacks to the University of Oregon. At the deadline for fall admission, the U of O—along with the rest of the state higher-education system—was swamped with applications, while its lecture halls are already bulging at the windows.

The problem is what the Legislature will be dropping at the university's door today.

"We're trying," says University of Oregon president Dave Frohnmayer, "to avoid the catastrophe of an all-cuts budget."

And to live with the likely hit of a many-cuts budget. At a time when Oregonians are stampeding into the higher-education system, just as they've been instructed by their elders—rotten kids, always do what you tell them—we're cutting away at it. Just as we're declaiming about the vital nature of higher education in Oregon's economic future, we're about to hack away at its research support.

Lots of parts of state government, of course, are going to hurt in this process, and what happens to higher education—bad or much worse—

will reflect what happens to other programs. Gov. John Kitzhaber proposes to cut higher ed by 4.8 percent, but he protects undergraduate programs. Legislative efforts are focusing on a 7.6 percent cut—at a time when freshman applications to Portland State are up 30 percent, the University of Oregon is seeing 25 percent growth and Oregon State is up 15 percent.

"Every indication is good except the state budget," says Frohnmayer. "How can you cut back when you have increased demand?"

The Legislature's general recommendation has been to spend less on each student, to let the universities keep their tuition revenue while the promised state support diminishes. As Frohnmayer notes, "The Legislature and the public don't want to tell people they can't come."

It's easier just to weaken what they're coming to.

The Legislature has also been reluctant to let the universities deal with the problems by adjusting their own tuition, something that might let some of the campuses get a little closer to balance. In theory, the Legislature gave up its power to set tuition; in practice, it gave up nothing—but seems unlikely to give the universities much.

So far, in fact, the Legislature is approaching its budget-rebalancing responsibilities like a dysfunctional family approaching Thanksgiving. Frohnmayer, a former legislator and attorney general, has some ideas about what's missing—besides money.

"The big difference now is term limits," he says. "There really is no institutional memory of how to handle anything but relative prosperity."

And no idea of what to do when increased revenue forecasts or video poker receipts don't fall out of the sky to keep your schools going.

"The other piece that's noticeably different is a much greater reliance on caucus politics, for both Democrats and Republicans. Individual legislators have less breathing room to pick their own positions. In those days, you owed the leadership your vote on organizing, but in nine out of 10 votes, you were a free agent."

Now there's more pressure: "People say, 'How can we campaign on no new taxes when the other side can point to five of our members who voted for new taxes?' The idea is, you have to find a message for your caucus."

And we have a Legislature more polarized than an ice flow. The legislative leadership plan both cuts away at K-12 and higher education, and borrows against future revenues. The effect not only cheats the future, it sends it the bill.

We also have a state government that can lose sight of its most basic duties. Taking down a volume on Oregon constitutional law, Frohnmayer points out that when the state was admitted to the union, it was required to make "only two promises of any substance: that we would provide public education and that we would establish a state university."

At any time now, we may revert to territorial status.

By the end of the special session, we'll see what else the Legislature stuffs into a sack.

THE OREGONIAN, FEBRUARY 8, 2002

World-Class Universities, Discounted

Every spring, just around the last date to drop classes to avoid graduating, comes another landmark of the college year: the American Association of University Professors' annual *Report on the Economic Status of the Profession.*

It's kind of a highlight of the higher-education calendar:

After March Madness comes the April Accounting.

This past year, says the AAUP, overall salaries rose against inflation, as many legislatures increased their investment in their higher-education systems. Overall, it was a good year for professors.

Oregon, as always, keeps its own books.

According to the report's state-by-state breakdowns, the pay scale at Oregon's three research universities is at the bottom of any bell curve. In fact, it seems to be under the bell.

Nationally, the University of Oregon is in the fourth, or next-to-lowest, quintile of pay for full professors; it's in the bottom quintile for associates and assistants. Oregon State deftly reverses the pattern; it's in the bottom quintile for full professors, fourth for lower ranks. Portland State is the most consistent: It's in the bottom quintile for all ranks.

As John Curtis, the AAUP's research director, notes, "When your salaries are at the bottom—and these are at the very bottom—it becomes hard to attract new people and even hard to keep the ones you have."

Or, as Joe Cox, Oregon's higher-education chancellor, puts it, "It's not encouraging. I wish I could say it was.

"Faculty come to Oregon, and they stick, but if you work hard enough, you can dislodge them."

Oregon's faculty pay has been around this level, of course, for quite a while. These days, however, politicians and businessmen like to pound their chests and declare that Oregon State will be a "top-tier" engineering school—at the same time that it's in the bottom tier of senior-professor pay.

You can't be, at the same time, at the bottom and the top.

It's a basic principle of engineering—and of everything else.

There are, points out Curtis, 157 doctorate-granting universities in the group with Oregon, Oregon State and PSU, meaning "These three universities are in the bottom 30 to 35. They're at rank 120 and down."

To calculate the distance from that to "top-tier," you need a slide rule—or maybe a telescope.

Politicians have a general idea that in the 21st century, this is a problem. Monday in Eugene, at a forum for candidates for governor, Democratic hopeful Jim Hill declared, "At the end of my first term, Oregon's universities will stand shoulder to shoulder-to-shoulder with other world-class institutions of higher learning, trailblazing in scientific development and reaping the financial benefits of their efforts."

It would be quite a leap. Right now, according to the AAUP study, we're standing about shoulder-to-knee.

To consider where Oregon is, forget the entire state of California and the private universities that dominate the top parts of the salary scale. The University of Washington is in the third quintile, and its full professors average $90,100 compared with $76,700 at Oregon and $76,100 at Oregon State. (They're closer to Washington State, at $79,300.) The University of Arizona averages $87,700, Arizona State $88,300; the University of Colorado $89,700.

It's a central Oregon belief, of course, that none of this matters—that people will take less to work here because they get to live here. We are certain of this, and when it turns out not to be true—as in senior science research professors, or school superintendents—we're not only surprised, we're insulted.

"There's a certain element of people who will come because of life-style," says Curtis—who worked in Montana, which tells itself the same thing—"but that only covers you so far."

About as far as the bottom quintile.

Still, in this year's campaign and next year's Legislature, the discussion of Oregon universities will make wide use of the words "top-tier" and "world-class." And the people who use them will be right about one thing: Oregon is in a lovely setting.

Just a little northwest of reality.

THE OREGONIAN, APRIL 17, 2002

Oregon's Newest Varsity Letter Is an F

Last week, when the National Center for Public Policy and Higher Education released its bleak assessment of the Oregon system, new chancellor Richard Jarvis was asked if the situation hadn't actually gotten worse since the numbers were collected.

"Well," said Jarvis, "on affordability, you can't get worse than F."

This is what passes for good news in the Oregon higher-education system: We've bottomed out.

For Oregon, the big news in the annual report was indeed the Affordability grade dropping from D- to F, largely because "Oregon invests even less in financial aid for low-income families than reported in 2000." And by comparison, other states are doing better in reducing the share of income needed to attend a public institution.

We're being graded on a curve, and as usual in higher education, we're behind the curve. And, hard as it is to fall below F, Oregon is falling. Not only is the higher-education budget dropping in every special session, but the educational endowment fund that legislators and voters dipped into was previously used to pay for scholarships. Half that money has now gone to K-12, and if the income tax surcharge is rejected by voters next January, Republican candidate for governor Kevin Mannix proposes to take the other half. At the same time, state universities are planning for a tuition increase.

Maybe you can get worse than F.

Things are, of course, tough all over, and every part of Oregon and Oregon government is taking some hits. But while politicians around the state are pledging to bring the state's economy back, it seems Oregonians are still running behind other states in figuring out how much economic growth has to do with higher education.

On the total National Center for Public Policy and Higher Education report card, Oregon gets a B, two Cs, a D and an F. Washington gets an A, two Bs and two Cs. California gets a straight A in affordability, the best grade in the country.

In higher education, we're what's known as a coastal depression.

And the NCPPHE isn't the only place that's noticed. You might say the word is all over the Web.

The Center for Higher Education and Public Finance at Illinois State University, which keeps track of state appropriations, reports that Oregon's "state tax funds for operating expenses of higher education" plunged from $680 million in 2001-02 to a projected $604 million in 2002-03. (The state's own figures are slightly different, and some cuts would be restored if the tax surcharge passes in January.)

Meanwhile, Washington, with an economy just as bad, somehow held the line, going from $1.370 billion to $1.375 billion.

In futures, you get what you pay for.

Washington is, of course, a bigger state, and should have a bigger system. But at Illinois State, they also keep track of each state's level of financial commitment.

In fiscal year 2002—the year before Oregon's state higher-ed budget went down $72 million, or 10.6 percent—Oregon was spending

$205.83 per capita on higher education, 33rd in the country. Washington spends $229.44 per capita, and is 24th. California lays out $274.43 per Californian, in 11th place nationally.

Even when we think we're gaining, other states are leaving us behind. From fiscal 2000 to fiscal 2002, according to Illinois State's numbers, Oregon increased its higher-ed spending by 8.9 percent. (The jubilation and self-congratulation in the Legislature is easily remembered.) But among states, Oregon's rate of increase was 34th—the same two-thirds of the way down the ladder. At that rate, Oregon would catch up with other states . . . never.

Oregon, a fairly small state, is never going to have a UCLA or a UW. But it's hard to claim a rosy future in technology, trade and biotech when your higher-ed investment and affordability is below average—if not below passing.

And while it might be hard to get worse than F, you probably wouldn't want to find out.

THE OREGONIAN, OCTOBER 6, 2002

Oregon's Idea of a Research University

You have to love the idea of merging Portland State and Oregon Health & Science University to create a comprehensive research university.

It's not that it's such a good idea.

But it's such an Oregon idea.

For decades, after all, it's been the Oregon belief that higher education should be built not the way other states did, by investing in it—we were too smart for that—but by shrewd organizational restructuring. What other places did with stronger programs and faculty recruitment, Oregon could do with new letterheads.

In Oregon terms, merging OHSU and PSU could be the biggest advance in state higher education since we changed the names of our state colleges to universities.

As former Portland State President Judith Ramaley once said, arriving here after a well-traveled academic career, "I've never seen any place that had such faith in moving around boxes."

Even if, as in the case of a PSU-OHSU merger, the boxes might have to be connected by tram.

Rep. Mitch Greenlick, D-Portland, has been on the faculty of both institutions and co-sponsors the bill with Rep. Linda Flores, R-Clackamas. He says that he has the votes to get it out of the House Education Committee, but is trying to build some more support, especially at the institutions.

"I have achieved, probably for the first time in memory, complete consensus between the presidents of the two universities," says Greenlick. "If they're both unhappy, it must be the right idea."

Of course, he has other arguments.

"Right now, a corporation looks at Portland, and it's not like Seattle, San Diego, Austin or Boston," places with sizable research university firepower. "Linking the two, you have a sizable university with 20,000 students. Symbolically, you've almost instantly created a university with twice the research of Washington State or Oregon State."

Except you've reached that number not with a comprehensive research university, but by combining Portland State's $38 million in annual research with almost 10 times that amount from OHSU. In PSU President Dan Bernstine's view, you haven't created a research university; you've created a university with a hospital.

"It's an attempt to create a University of Washington without putting a dime into it," Bernstine says about the idea, neatly summing up half a century of Oregon higher-education policy. "The University of Washington didn't get to be what it is by just putting things together."

Greenlick has considerable experience with both PSU and OHSU, and points out areas where the two might fit into each other. He also argues that OHSU should "get into the context of a university," which he thinks would clarify its educational mission.

Still, he admits, "We're not going to have a University of Washington. The University of Washington has $1 billion of research a year. They also have the fact that the state has invested about twice the per capita investment that Oregon has."

So maybe the way to have a research university is to actually invest in a research university?

"If you have a suggestion for that," he says, "I'd be happy to drop this in an instant."

Of course, nobody has a suggestion for that, and so we have this Oregon-style approach. When we paper over a higher-education problem, we do it literally; we cover it with new stationery.

Clearly, even if we combine Portland State and OHSU, Portland won't be able to offer corporations the research firepower of Seattle—let alone Boston or Austin. But Greenlick also mentions San Diego, and suggests that maybe the new institution might be the equivalent of, say, San Diego State.

Well, that's one ambition. SDSU, with 33,000 students, would still be bigger than the new entity, and while its research of $122 million a year dwarfs PSU's current level, the new entity's combined total would be much bigger. But SDSU isn't San Diego's research engine; as SDSU spokesman Jason Foster admits, "UC San Diego is the big kid on the block," with more than $500 million in research a year.

So we wouldn't be San Diego, either.

Greenlick isn't kidding himself about any of this; his idea is, he admits, a "catch-as-catch-can" solution. You play the cards you're dealt, and on higher education, Oregon hasn't dealt itself much.

The temptation of this idea is that we could sum up decades of Oregon's approach to its universities by seizing the moment to create a new PSU.

We could call it Pretend State University.

Education Funding:
At Least We Should Savor Oregon's Comic Aspects

Looking at the highlights of the Oregon year so far—lacking the rarefied diversion of a gathering of the Legislature—we start with a fundamental question:

How does someone get through an Oregon Business Summit without laughing?

If you're a summiteer, that is.

If you're a student, you might miss out on the entertainment value of it all.

Every so often—sometimes under this title, sometimes under another—members of the Oregon business community gather and conclude, after careful and rigorous consideration, that education is important. They hear experts on the subject, discuss evidence and pass ringing resolutions on the issue.

After which, they depart, and Oregon education deteriorates a little more until it's time for them to meet again.

In this sense, a business summit is a lot like a session of the

Legislature, and its presence does indeed help compensate for the even-numbered-year emptiness at the state capitol. (This is not to be confused with the odd-numbered-year emptiness at the state capitol, which is the Legislature.)

The main risk in listening to a summit is that, when you hear about education's being at the center of the state's future, that Oregon's first priority must be to fix its education financing, and that there's no route through the 21st century without a powerful university research capacity, you can't tell whether the words just came from the current speaker—or whether they've been bouncing around the space/time continuum since somebody said them in 1993.

The ricochets from the echoes can be dangerous.

This time, according to the *Oregonian*'s coverage, the agreement that education was a good thing was thunderous, and even high-tech. Using hand-held clickers, more than 80 percent of those present at the Portland gathering agreed that education was the most important element in Oregon's future prosperity, that Oregon kids need to learn at higher levels than they do now, and that the state's education system is not currently good enough to support its economic future.

Moreover, Michael Porter, a Harvard Business School professor appearing on teleconference—OK, maybe that wouldn't have happened in 1993—told the group that the shortcomings of Oregon's current higher-education system "is a show stopper" for the state's future competitiveness.

Everybody agreed—in a state that several years ago cut its higher-education spending faster than any other state in the country, and that now has one of the lowest higher-ed spending rates per capita in the country—that Porter had a good point.

Meanwhile, at the same time Oregon was carrying out its performance-art approach to education planning, the state's neighbors—not to say competitors—were following other strategies.

In Washington Gov. Christine Gregoire's State of the State message this month, she declared, "We made education our number one invest-ment in 2005," citing advances in teacher pay, reducing class sizes and adding 8,000 spaces in higher education.

Moreover, she proposed a new Cabinet-level Department of Early Childhood Learning—focusing on an issue that Oregon leaders have been mumbling about for 20 years. The idea emerged from a planning committee including representatives of businesses, including Boeing—which isn't even based in Washington any more.

California Gov. Arnold Schwarzenegger announced what the *Sacramento Bee* called "his proposal to dump an astounding amount of new money on the public schools," and proposed enough money for the state's higher-education systems to raise enrollment and buy back sched-uled tuition and fee increases.

In educational commitment, Oregon doesn't quite have the vision of Conan the Barbarian.

Not only are we not making up ground on other states, but they may be putting some more distance between us.

Still, we shouldn't lose sight of the entertainment component of a business summit. In 2003, Gov. Ted Kulongoski used it to unveil our new slogan, "Oregon: We Love Dreamers."

After all, our educational strategizing seems to consist largely of dreaming.

At least we could be laughing.

THE OREGONIAN, JANUARY 22, 2006

5. A snapshot of state subsidy patterns for education and related expenses in the public research sector

Student share of costs

← Net tuition portion of E&R → ← Average subsidy portion of E&R →

State	Net tuition portion of E&R	Average subsidy portion of E&R	Student share of costs
MN	$10,522	$13,616	44%
WA	$9,037	$14,002	42%
VT	$16,847	$6,148	73%
CA	$7,654	$14,835	37%
NY	$5,272	$16,551	26%
AK	$4,842	$16,869	22%
DE	$12,814	$8,429	60%
CT	$8,696	$11,772	42%
PA	$13,405	$6,388	68%
HI	$5,707	$14,025	29%
AL	$7,427	$11,938	48%
NC	$5,966	$12,076	35%
MA	$9,827	$8,018	55%
NJ	$11,602	$6,000	67%
NV	$6,113	$11,414	36%
KY	$7,811	$9,550	46%
WY	$4,025	$13,131	23%
TN	$6,373	$10,773	38%
IN	$8,949	$8,134	52%
IL	$8,749	$7,533	55%
VA	$8,873	$7,201	55%
MI	$9,744	$6,141	64%
MO	$8,272	$7,440	54%
OH	$9,909	$5,751	64%

0   $2,500 $5,000 $7,500 $10,000 $12,500 $15,000 $17,500 $20,000 $22,500

State			
U.S.	$7,563	$8,055	51% ← NATIONAL AVERAGE
AZ	$7,206	$8,262	46%
IA	$7,591	$7,746	50%
SC	$10,311	$5,013	67%
MD	$7,136	$8,072	46%
CO	$11,115	$3,719	80%
RI	$11,116	$3,367	77%
UT	$4,817	$9,030	34%
WI	$7,335	$6,396	55%
NH	$10,869	$2,631	81%
ID	$4,843	$8,582	36%
KS	$6,892	$6,299	52%
ND	$7,441	$5,670	60%
ME	$7,229	$5,709	56%
GA	$6,059	$6,647	47%
OK	$6,457	$5,987	52%
WV	$8,620	$3,599	71%
TX	$6,882	$5,336	58%
NE	$4,115	$7,890	34%
OR	$7,951	$3,849	67% ← OREGON
MS	$5,591	$6,140	48%
LA	$4,556	$7,142	41%
FL	$4,375	$7,277	39%
SD	$5,234	$6,236	47%
NM	$4,474	$6,994	40%
AR	$4,994	$5,709	47%
MT	$7,267	$3,305	69%

University budgets
by state at public
research institutions.

SOURCE: Delta Cost Project IPEDS
state database 2003-2008.

0   $2,500 $5,000 $7,500 $10,000 $12,500 $15,000 $17,500 $20,000 $22,500

The Legislature:
On Higher Ed, No Reasonable Offer Received

Since the last session of the Oregon Legislature ended without any professors being pushed off a cliff, state leaders like to congratulate themselves on how well the higher-education system is doing.

Imagine the surprise when, at this month's meeting of the State Board of Higher Education, the vice chairman suggested that the system's condition is so desperate it should think about selling a campus.

It's always so rude for reality to show up during an election year.

"At a certain point, we've got to say, 'We can't do this any more,' " said Kirby Dyess last week. "That's my position, and also the position of the rest of the board. We're at a point where we have to do something significant to catch up."

That's not, of course, the public position of Gov. Ted Kulongoski, who appointed Dyess two years ago, and who's currently running for re-election on the slogan "Do Nothing and We'll Be Fine."

For higher education, as well as K-12, that means proposing increases of 10 percent in state funding for each two-year budget period, and promising that it will bolster the health of the university system.

Except, considering the realities of where higher education is and where Oregon is, it won't.

Which is why Dyess is talking about turning someplace like Western Oregon University in Monmouth into condos.

It won't get Oregon where it wants to go, says Dyess, to "take the budget up 10 percent when expenses are going up 14 percent—especially after 10 years of system underspending.

"When you look at our history, at what we've been doing to our university system, you have to ask how long it's going to take us to catch up."

Actually, you don't have to ask.

By all indications, we're not going to catch up.

In fact, considering the investments other states are making, we're likely to keep losing ground.

According to the Center for the Study of Education Policy, over the past decade the average state increased its general fund spending for higher education by 50.1 percent. California increased by 85.5 percent, Washington by 53.5 percent.

Oregon's rose just 33.3 percent.

Just over the past five years, with hard budget times for many states, the average state increase was 9.9 percent. California rose 7.9 percent, Washington by 14.9 percent. Oregon dropped 8 percent.

On per capita spending for higher education, the average state spends $225 a citizen. Our southern neighbor spends $266 per Californian, and our northern neighbor spends $243 per Washingtonian. We spend $168 per Oregonian—43rd among 50 states.

Increasing at 10 percent a biennium, with states already ahead of us also increasing, Oregon will catch up about the time Idaho plays in the Rose Bowl.

Over the last decade, notes Dyess, the state's share of the higher-education budget has dropped, while the system's weak national position on faculty salaries has gotten weaker. During that time, she points out, faculty were included in a state salary freeze.

"There's no other state," says Dyess, "that freezes faculty salaries in this time of competitiveness. When you offer professors 20 to 40 percent below market level, they just look at you."

Dyess, a retired Intel executive, says she's been impressed by the universities' innovations in education and teaching, and how they've adapted to repeated cuts. But, she warns, that doesn't go on forever.

"I had 23 years in a company that invented the concept of doing more with less," she says. "But at a certain point, you can't go beyond that."

Last week, the provost of Oregon State announced the university had to cut $13 million to $14 million, or 5.5 percent of its budget, for next year. According to the Corvallis *Gazette-Times*, faculty members suggested that OSU may be trying to do too much with the money it gets.

It's the kind of thing that makes Dyess think that the Oregon University System's only option is to price a campus to move.

For example, we could sell Eastern Oregon University in La Grande to Washington—transferring it from a state that doesn't want to pay for college to one that does.

From Washington, EOU is only about 50 miles off.

And a world away.

THE OREGONIAN, MARCH 12, 2006

School Systems Worlds Apart:

Standing on the Wrong Side of the Entrance to the Future

Thursday morning in downtown Portland, it seemed as if one of those transdimensional time warps had opened up. Within blocks of each other, as in a video game or a digitized special effects movie, there yawned forth both a portal to the future and a passage to nowhere.

You almost looked around for Keanu Reeves.

Looking toward the rest of the century, Washington Gov. Christine Gregoire came to Portland to talk about investments and preparations her state was making for the future, emphasizing the idea that in a globalized world, "We must have a world-class education system. If not, we'll fall behind."

For her, that means expanding the Washington education system, from a new Department of Early Learning to investments in K-12 education to considerably expanding the spaces in Washington's higher-education system. Although, she said, almost apologetically, in the near future she envisions only one additional University of Washington campus.

She talked about an overhauled high school system based on a new three R's—Rigor, Relationships, Relevance; about attacking the dropout rate by assigning each entering ninth-grader a teacher who stays connected to the student through high school; and about the Washington Legislature putting $30 million into a program to help high school students meet graduation standards.

Washington isn't competing, she said, with the schools of other states, but with the schools of Europe and Asia.

Over here, on the other side of the time portal, Portland's schools aren't competing with schools in other states, either.

They're competing with each other, to try to stay open.

Just a few blocks away from Gregoire, Portland schools were holding one of their regular—at least regular during the past 15 years—events to mark the warding off of absolute disaster. In the City Council chambers, an array of city, county, school district and business leaders talked triumphantly about an emergency package that would, for the second consecutive year, cut the system's budget by about 7 percent.

Around here, that's a school funding victory.

That's how the school district's motto went from "The last great urban school district" to "Hey, it could've been worse."

So the first question around here isn't how to strengthen our district, but which schools to close.

And Portland isn't a different place from the rest of Oregon; in its school problems, it's just a little ahead of other places. It seems that Washington and Oregon aren't just on different sides of the Columbia, but on different planets.

Or on different ends of the time warp.

In the Portland City Council chambers, Mayor Tom Potter—in yet another instance of a Portland mayor going beyond the job description to ward off a school disaster—tried to be positive about the day and the agreement. But a little earlier, in a forum with Gregoire, he said flatly, "Our funding mechanism in education is in a state of failure."

A bad state to inhabit, in Oregon or Washington.

The school district talks about the new opportunities in its newest trip up the downsizing staircase, but talking to the *Oregonian,* board co-chairwoman Bobbie Regan was direct: "I don't know what choice we have . . . This is our reality."

Even this could be only another temporary reality, depending on all the pieces actually falling together, and subsequent efforts by legislators and voters. Everybody could easily be back in the City Council chamber again next year.

It's not only that Oregon doesn't have the money. It's that we like to pretend Oregon doesn't have a problem.

Or that somehow, in our own vision of the future, the problem will just go away.

When Gregoire talks with companies thinking about Washington, she relates, "The single Number One issue discussed without fail is education. They ask, 'Do you have a K-12 system that will meet the needs of my workforce?'

On this side of the transdimensional time warp, we have our own answer to that question:

Don't ask.

THE OREGONIAN, MARCH 19, 2006

Oregon's Universities:
In Politics, Higher Ed Rarely Comes Up, As It Goes Down

CORVALLIS—Oregon State University, and most of the rest of the state higher-education system, may be conducting one more round of tightening a belt already a notch past strangle, but its president explains that the process is always worth something.

"I'm an economist," Ed Ray says. "I understand scarcity and tradeoffs.

"If there are three people in a rowboat and only two can live, you still have choices to be made."

As the motto of the Oregon University System declares: Glub.

Higher education is one of the four major pieces of the state budget, but it was the one that somehow never showed up in the months of two primary campaigns for governor. Candidates not only orated on K-12 education, human services and public safety, but used the issues to attack each other. In Oregon politics, you're nothing unless you can be used as an example of an opponent's waste or indifference.

But higher education came up in this spring's primary campaign about as often as Oregon State appears in the Rose Bowl.

156

It didn't come up much, even though in the past five years, Oregon has cut its higher-ed budget while virtually every other state was raising its spending, and Oregon is now 46th in the country in state spending per student.

It didn't come up after the March meeting of the Board of Higher Education, when the vice chairman of the board pointed out that the system could not go on in its present situation and suggested selling one of the campuses.

It didn't come up after the April meeting, when the board found that six of the seven campuses would have to cut some more to get through the coming year, and that nobody in the political world particularly noticed.

"I know K-12 has needs," board member Gretchen Schuette said rather plaintively, "but we have needs, too."

If higher ed hadn't been a way to raise the subject of Neil Goldschmidt, it might never have been mentioned in the campaign at all.

This leaves the problem to the higher-ed board and the campuses— such as Oregon State, where Ray is leading an effort to cut programs to try to find some money for faculty salaries—to try to get a little closer to comparable universities in other states.

"We can't keep thinning the soup," Ray says. "The only thing that makes sense if we're serious about quality is to narrow the menu."

This is, of course, only another in Oregon's endless series of higher-ed Band-Aids. The only real change would be for the state's leadership to somehow take higher education seriously.

"We need to do that as a state," Ray says, "if we have any hope for higher ed to be the engine of economic development and social advance here that it is in other states.

"It's a subject that I wish had been discussed more in the primary, but I think it will be in the autumn."

After all, football sometimes reminds even Oregon's leadership about the state's universities. But the only solid indication of a funding discussion is the governor's Educational Enterprise plan, which promises steady 10 percent increases for all of education—as long as the economy does even better than that.

But in national terms, the higher-ed system is in an even deeper hole than K-12. So while the governor's plan offers a clear schedule for raising K-12, it's vaguer on the prospects of the university system.

"Since Measure 5, in post-secondary, we have divested from those programs in our state," James Sager, education adviser to Gov. Ted Kulongoski, admits.

"We are beginning to reinvest," he says. "Are we reinvesting at a fast pace? No. But what we don't want to see is a continued decline."

As battle cries go, or even battle plans, it's not exactly stirring. But at least the people on the campuses understand the reality.

When Ray first explained his plan to the faculty senate, he recalls, "One guy said, 'Well, you're just asking us to do more with less.' I said, 'No. I'm asking you to do less with less.'"

Which is one economic strategy to run a university.

As a strategy for running a state university system, amid a knowledge economy, it may have some limits.

THE OREGONIAN, MAY 28, 2006

An Assignment for Higher Ed

Looking over the committees and subcommittees of the Oregon Legislature—a pastime for either a calculating lobbyist or an unimaginably bored citizen—you can survey education, health, justice and commerce, all the great concerns of the public servants of Oregon.

With one exception.

In both House and Senate, higher education is the kid who didn't show up for the yearbook photo, there but not really there. Higher education floats around every legislative session as an afterthought to education committees far more absorbed by the problems of K-12.

And like the kid who misses the yearbook photo, it seems to fade from people's thinking.

From 2001 to 2006, the average state appropriation for higher ed rose 9.9 percent nationally. Washington's rose 14.9 percent. Oregon's Legislature actually spent 8 percent less.

Higher education has plummeted, stonelike, from 12.2 percent of the general fund budget in 1987-89 to 6.3 percent now. Oregon now ranks

46th in the country in per-student higher-education funding, while Washington is 21st and California 24th.

Lately—as politicians orate about an information society and "seamless" education funding—fewer Oregon students are actually going on to college.

The situation might deserve some official legislative attention.

"I think we have disinvested in this state in the past 20 years," says George Pernsteiner, chancellor of the Oregon University System. "Our young people are not attending college at the rate they did 10 or 20 years ago. We've been going the wrong way."

Having a higher-education committee or subcommittee wouldn't change all that and wouldn't reinvent the state's economic realities. But lots of other states—states that do better in maintaining their higher-education system than Oregon, although that's not much of a distinction—seem to find it useful to have specific legislators charged with thinking about, or even arguing for, higher ed.

Eighteen states have higher-education committees in one or both of their legislative houses, not counting many others with higher-education subcommittees. Connecticut has a joint legislative committee, Minnesota has a committee specifically on Higher Education Finance, and the Wisconsin Senate has a committee on Higher Education and Tourism—which sounds like a strange mixture, but probably has something to do with cheese.

All of Oregon's fellow Pac-10 states—Washington, California and Arizona—have a higher-education committee. They seem to find it useful.

"I think it's just a must," says Rep. Phyllis Kenney, D-Seattle, chairwoman of the Higher Education and Work Force Education Committee in the Washington House.

"You can't focus on everything if you have it in one large (education) committee. Everything gets lost in K-12."

The Washington Senate has recently gone to a single Education Committee, with what Vancouver Sen. Craig Pridemore, vice chairman for higher education, calls "mixed results . . . The K-12 system has really dominated. I will say that over the past two years higher education has not gotten the attention that it needs and deserves in the Senate."

Oregon knows the feeling.

Oregon has seven state universities, but every legislator has elementary schools in his district. And faculty members and accounting majors don't storm the capitol in busloads demanding support for higher education.

"I do believe, by unscientific opinion, that we come out better when a legislative committee is devoted to higher ed," says Jim Sulton, executive director of the Washington Higher Education Consulting Board. Legislators "get more introspective, they devote more time to it, they concentrate on higher education.

"We'd get a better shake on the budget, better understanding of what we do, more intensive focus on access and quality." Washington, he notes, "has placed a more serious focus on this than many other states."

A higher-education committee or subcommittee might move some legislators to look at realities that seem to float around the state capitol without landing anywhere in particular.

Since 1991, most states have seen a decline in real per-student state spending on higher education. But Oregon's spending has dropped the most in the country. The average state decline has been 13.5 percent; Oregon's support has fallen 41.4 percent.

In 1987-89, higher education received 12.2 percent of the state general fund budget. This budget period, it gets 6.3 percent. Twenty years ago, tuition and fees covered 29 percent of the higher-ed budget; now it's 61 percent, and Oregonian students graduate with five-figure debts.

Over the past few years, the state university system has gotten a little bigger. But that's because of a rise in revenue-producing out-of-state and international students; the number of Oregonians attending has actually dropped.

The situation is worst for the regional universities. As Oregon's legislators gathered last week to elect next session's leaders, the president of

161

Southern Oregon University in Ashland formally announced consider-ation of a state of emergency, which would allow the university to abolish programs and fire tenured faculty.

Nobody expects this incoming Legislature to fix 20 years of neglect. But it might not hurt to have some legislators responsible for thinking about it.

"It seems to me that this is an idea well worth considering," says Rep. Jeff Merkley, D-Portland, elected last week by his fellow Democrats to be speaker of the next House. "One thing I've been looking at is an Education Committee with a higher-education subcommittee."

Senate President Peter Courtney, D-Salem, also thinks, "Maybe a sub-committee of Education would be the best option," although he argues the Senate Education Committee has focused on some higher-education issues. But, Courtney admits, when funding questions get to the edu-cation subcommittee of the Ways and Means Committee, "There's no question that the 10,000-pound penguin in the middle of the room is K-12. That's where it's more pronounced."

That's why Sen. Ginny Burdick, D-Portland, whose district includes Portland State, says, "What you really need to be talking about is a Ways and Means subcommittee." Over the past years, she notes, as costs went up across the budget, "Everything's come out of the hide of higher education."

With no legislator particularly charged to watch its flanks.

Oregonians, says Gov. Ted Kulongoski, consider K-12 a basic right and responsibility but, "They look at higher education differently, and the Legislature reflects that."

Tony Van Vliet spent 17 years in the House as a Republican from Corvallis, most of it on the Ways and Means education subcommittee. Asked whether K-12 issues tended to roll over higher-ed concerns during his time there, he agrees, "They pretty much did."

For the last two years, he's been on the State Board of Higher Educa-tion and thinks something needs to happen differently.

Higher education, says Van Vliet, "really does need some special attention because it's fallen so far back. We've fallen so far behind we really do need a shot in the arm."

Legislators, in campaigns and even in Salem, say all the right things about higher education, about its being central to Oregon's future, about its being the way up for Oregon kids and their chance to get a job that could support a family and let them stay in Oregon. But responsibility for it doesn't land in any particular legislative pocket.

That could be helped by an actual Higher Education Committee, or a subcommittee, or even—in an imaginary Oregon where the state's universities were actually considered a priority and vital to the state's economy—a Ways and Means higher-education subcommittee. Any of them would sharpen the legislature's focus and improve higher education's Salem prospects.

Because the best way to ensure nothing gets done is to give nobody the assignment.

Anyone in education—at any level—could tell you that.

THE OREGONIAN, NOVEMBER 19, 2006

Knowledge Is Power:
Oregon Sees the Light

State Rep. Peter Buckley, D-Ashland, has a job that nobody in Oregon has ever had before.

Buckley is chairman of a new House subcommittee on higher education, a group of legislators focused on the state's universities and the pursuit of a nationally competitive higher-education system.

Oregon's never had one of those, either.

"The goal, I told the committee, is by the end of the session I want everybody involved with higher ed," he says, "the business community and everybody."

That would be a considerable reversal of the direction of higher ed in Oregon over the past two decades. Never a lavishly funded operation—Oregon was, after all, historically a place where people could make a decent living without a diploma, in the woods or the canneries—the university system took two sharp chops. After the passage of Measure 5 in 1990, higher ed took the deepest cuts of any part of state government, and in the recession of 2001-03, Oregon cut its remaining higher-education programs more deeply than any other state.

Now, facing what any politician worth his talking points solemnly calls a knowledge economy, Oregon is 46th in the country in per capita support of higher education; its tuition levels earn it low grades in accessibility; and the number of Oregon students in state universities has actually declined—although an increase in out-of-state students has slightly increased the size of the institutions.

Buckley didn't have to come to Salem to discover this. He talks about visiting an Advanced Placement class at Phoenix High School, and finding only four of 28 students with plans for college. For many of the rest, "It's in their psyche that it's not affordable."

His hometown college, Southern Oregon University, is facing cuts in programs and tenured faculty—and, he points out, even the funding increases in the governor's budget wouldn't change that. A decade ago, SOU was full, bursting with Californians from over the border. Now, its enrollment has dropped, hit by rising tuition costs (and rising Ashland living costs) and by California's major efforts in reinvesting in its own system.

As Oregon battles to catch up, it faces the reality that the states already far ahead in higher ed are busily beefing up their own systems. In universities, Oregon is not only aiming at a moving target, it's also aiming at a target moving away from us.

At least, after repeated sessions of college students getting elbowed aside by the needs of K-12, there's now the beginning of some legislative focus.

"The reason for its existence," Buckley says about the subcommittee, "is (House Speaker) Jeff Merkley felt strongly that there needed to be a higher profile on higher ed, since we've neglected it so long."

"Neglect" about covers it.

Oregon has been badly hit in the resources that underlay its old economy, such as timber and fish. But it's booming in the resource that's key in the new economy, people. In a story that deserved a much bigger headline, United Van Lines recently reported that Oregon was second in the country in the proportion of moving vans coming into the state compared with those leaving it.

"Portland, Bend, Ashland, Eugene, they're all a mecca for (educated) young people," says Sen. Ryan Deckert, D-Beaverton, a higher-education advocate at the other side of the capitol. "We're importing them now, and that's one strategy, but hopefully we can do better.

"I think there's a better understanding and recognition of the influence of higher ed on who we are in Oregon and our ability to compete globally. I think a lot of the new folks coming in are helping people understand these importance of it."

Deckert looks at Gov. Ted Kulongoski's budget, with a considerable increase in the higher-education budget, as a beginning of a change.

"We should show the world that we are serious about reversing the disinvestment in higher ed, to start buying back what was lost in the '90s. That means enrollment growth, and as unsexy as faculty salaries are, they matter."

Kulongoski's budget, among other investments, proposes a faculty salary increase that would raise Oregon's universities from 86 percent to 88 percent of the salaries at comparable universities. Although the benefits package closes the gap a bit, Oregon is still steadily outbid by competitive states.

And they're not standing still, either. Washington Gov. Christine Gregoire's new budget proposes 5 percent increases for faculty in each of the next two years, part of a 10-year university investment plan. We're playing catch-up with states that aren't planning to be caught.

Still, it's a beginning.

"It's not that we're going to rival Washington in terms of their investment per student tomorrow," says Deckert, "but we can get started."

We've got an opportunity with people, and with the possibility of funding. And after a long time, we've got the beginnings of a focus on higher education.

"I talk too fast," Buckley says apologetically after explaining the prospects of his subcommittee. "I get really excited about this stuff."

It's time someone in the Legislature did.

THE OREGONIAN, JANUARY 21, 2007

Funding Higher Ed:
Universities Find a Cheerleader, Still Need a Victory

SALEM—Kari Henningsgaard is broke.

That's what her handmade sign announced Thursday on the front steps of the Oregon state capitol, in the midst of a rally of several hundred students on behalf of higher-education funding. Technically, the sophomore from Astoria, already well in debt after not quite two years at the University of Oregon, is somewhere below broke, but her sign still summed up the occasion.

After all, "I'm Broke" is what the higher-ed system has been saying for decades. The question is whether this time somebody inside the building is listening.

For years, rallies for K-12 funding have occupied the front of the capitol, often several times a session, imploring legislators to support the state's school systems. They've been generally a little larger than this one—though certainly no louder—and drew larger groups from inside the building, as legislators are always eager to appear with second-graders.

On the other hand, Thursday's event featured the mascots from three Oregon universities.

Is your rally more bolstered by the Senate president or Benny Beaver? Tough call.

What Thursday's rally did have was Gov. Ted Kulongoski, who's seeking the largest increases in the university budget, for both capital resources and student access, in memory. It seems about the right beginning for a system that regularly gets F's in affordability, that has a backlog of hundreds of millions of dollars in deferred maintenance, in a state that ranks about 46th in per-capita higher-education support.

"It wasn't that long ago," recalled Kulongoski—before pausing and clarifying, "well, it was a long time ago, that I went to school on the GI Bill."

The first part of fixing our higher-ed system is to get real about the numbers.

"We need you to be in this building, to tell your senators and representatives how important this investment is, not just to you but to the future of our state . . . ," he told the crowd. "We are making an investment in our future, and you are that future."

K-12 rallies may draw larger crowds, but they don't respond by chanting, "Teddy! Teddy!"

As Oregon higher education always has, the crowd was looking hard for something to cheer for, a search reflected in signs reading, "5th largest tuition increases in the country" and "Spare change for college—anything will help."

"I know we're competing with a lot of really needy programs," said Mina Carson, an Oregon State history professor and president of the Interinstitutional Faculty Senate, "but I think we've made the point that they need us."

In 2007, it's clear how closely connected a state's future is to its universities. Still unclear is what this state is prepared to do about it.

Asked how things were looking at Portland State, student Kento Azegami of Tigard explained, "Very sad, to be quite honest," noting that one building was in danger of being seismically condemned, that walking through another made students very nervous, and that the uncertainty of offerings could make it take longer to graduate.

Javier Torres hopes a slowdown in tuition increases might let him increase his course load at Mt. Hood Community College and reduce his 40 hours a week as a custodian at Clackamas High School. Now, he's on track to take five years getting his associate's degree, and his bachelor's when he's about 30.

Kathleen Stuart from Western Oregon University juggled two signs— she wants to go into public relations—while explaining, "We cater to a group of students who are mostly lower-income, the first ones in their family to go to college. For me personally, that's the biggest issue."

Not many capitol rallies finish with the speaker asking the audience to hold their wallets up in the air.

To Kari Henningsgaard, wondering like much of the crowd how much time and debt can go into her own college education, "It's a struggle. We're at a dead end as far as the funds are concerned."

Which is another statement speaking for the whole state university system.

For decades, it's been the height of chin-pulling Salem wisdom to pronounce that if something ain't broke, don't fix it.

But when it is broke, maybe you should.

THE OREGONIAN, FEBRUARY 23, 2007

Losing by Degrees— On Higher-Ed Board, Francesconi Faces Another F

Of all the things people have told Jim Francesconi since he was named the newest member of the state board of higher education, he carries one in particular around with him.

It's a set of grades the U.S. Chamber of Commerce awards each state on education, given him by the folks at a local chamber of commerce. Oregon gets mostly B's and C's, the kind of grades that may not promise much of a future but won't cut off your allowance.

Except for the grade on Postsecondary and Workforce Readiness: F.

The Chamber of Commerce seems to consider it a problem that "only 33% of 9th graders who finish high school in four years go on to college."

On issues of college access, of course, Oregon gets F's more often than a chemistry student who forgot the test was on Tuesday. (Years of underinvestment in the system and increasing overreliance on tuition revenue will do that.) Oregon is now one of the few states where a high school graduate is less likely to go to college today than he was a decade ago, where locals aged 25 to 34 are actually less likely to have a college degree than older residents.

What's Latin for Backward into the Twentieth-First Century?

Even for someone who's survived eight years on the Portland City Council, dealing with the Oregon higher-education system could be draining.

But Friday, Francesconi's first meeting of the higher-education board began with the president of Southern Oregon University talking about closing a swimming pool for financial reasons, and the former parks commissioner thought, "I've been here."

Francesconi is where he is now by appointment of Gov. Ted Kulongoski, with whom he goes way back, back to worker's comp issues 20 years ago. Kulongoski is trying to sharply increase investment in the higher-education system. He also wants to address the access question with a new model of shared responsibility for lower-income students, combining student earnings with family contributions and state support.

The idea is to deal with something else Francesconi has quickly learned in his new job: In the top 25 percent of Oregon income, 75 percent of kids go on to complete a four-year degree. In the bottom 25 percent of income, only 9 percent do.

It's not a good number.

Then again, it's never been much of a priority around here, either.

Higher education has not been a governor's priority for quite a while, and the system took serious financial batterings during the '90s and again at the beginning of this decade. Since 2001, average tuition at Oregon universities has gone up 47 percent, and average costs at community colleges by considerably more.

Even before the recent budget cuts, other states' universities ran ahead of the system in Oregon, a place where for a long time kids could look forward to a decent living without a degree.

"People value higher education, but they think people should pay for it themselves," Francesconi says. "That doesn't work.

"People should contribute. They should have to work. But they can't work 100 hours a week and still learn things."

And people who don't aren't going to be worth as much to their future, or to the state's.

"I think it's the most important issue in Oregon," Francesconi says. The question is, "How are we going to create an awareness in the citizenry of its importance?"

That question presumably has something to do with the governor who appointed him, and who insisted to Francesconi that the issue would stay a priority for him.

"He needs to stay engaged in this," the newest board member says. "When he's engaged, he's tremendous."

Which isn't a bad adjective for the size of the higher-education problem, either.

Meanwhile, at Francesconi's first meeting, the higher-education board discussed—this being Oregon—requests from the Legislature about how it would handle budget cuts of 3 percent, 2 percent or 1 percent.

The board did agree, he says, on one thing: "Raising tuition is not an option."

That's encouraging.

Because there really is no such grade as F-minus.

THE OREGONIAN, MARCH 4, 2007

Higher Education:

How Dumb Can We Get When It Comes to Cutting Budget?

After 15 years of relentlessly cutting higher education faster than any other state in the country—27 percent just from 2001 to 2006—Oregon needs the fingers of 10 different hands to proudly boast, "We're No. 46!"

Even with Gov. Ted Kulongoski's proposed increases, we stay around that level. Seeing the Legislature's Joint Ways and Means co-chairs budget raises a different question:

Can we go below 50th?

Discussing the situation last week, the governor explained evenly, "I believe this is early in the process, and we should not overreact.

"Having said that, I will now overreact."

Actually, that might be hard.

Since 1990, Oregon has disinvested from its universities as if they were selling Enron stock. Kulongoski's budget wouldn't, he admitted, change things much immediately, but if the investment level could be kept up for a few more sessions, the higher-education system might start to look as if it belonged to a 21st-century state.

As Kirby Dyess, vice chairman of the state higher-education board, points out, when it takes you 15 years to dig yourself a hole this deep it could take you 15 years to get out of it.

Except we might not be starting this year.

The governor's budget proposed an increase of about $90 million for higher education, a 12.5 percent rise to $827 million. Kulongoski asked for $594.5 million in capital bonds for universities and community colleges, a historically high level that should be set against the system's $650 million backlog in building maintenance.

The co-chairs marked the higher-ed operating budget down by $35 million, and cut the governor's capital budget by 85 percent. These guys are tough graders—whether or not there's much left to grade.

The State Higher Education Executive Officers group in Colorado shows that even when the ski season ends, Oregon still has its universities on the downhill. On each student, the state now spends two-thirds of—meaning $2,135 less than—the national average. (California and Washington are both just above average level.)

The bar is rising. The executive officers' president, Paul Lingenfelter, notes, "My impression is that in the current year, budgetary prospects in most states are pretty good."

Of course, in Oregon, we're too smart for that.

Does the Legislature understand just how far down the Oregon university system has fallen?

"I don't think they do," muses Kulongoski. "Compared to when I first came in here as a staff member in 1973, these people now are much better educated. But I think the people back in 1973 cared much more about higher education, and I don't know why.

"If you listened to everybody before the session started, they said their first priority was post-secondary education. When the session starts, with the first noise they crumble."

As the higher-education chancellor, George Pernsteiner, points out, Oregon high school graduates are now less likely to go to college than they were 10 years ago, and we're becoming one of the few states where older adults are better educated than younger adults. Dyess, a former Intel executive, notes that Oregon businesses have to hire extensively from out of state.

Facing this situation, the co-chairs' budget removes $35 million from the governor's operations budget. Cuts include $7 million for the state's badly hurting regional universities and $10 million from the proposed $17 million for the Engineering and Technology Industry Council, a joint program of the universities and the high-tech industry to increase high-tech graduates.

Some people think that has something to do with the state's economy.

Community colleges lost $40 million in operating from the governor's budget, and together with universities lost just about all of their capital budget.

Friday, House Majority Leader Dave Hunt, D-Milwaukie, commented, "We were all surprised to see how low community colleges, higher education and Head Start were in the co-chairs' budget."

Hunt, like Kulongoski, insists that the shortfall can be fixed, mostly by looking to an increase in the corporate minimum income tax, which has been $10 since back when hardly anybody went to college, or needed to.

"On a purely political basis," says Kulongoski, "I do not believe that Democrats can leave this building without supporting the university system to the same extent they support the K-12 system."

Supporting the university system to the same extent that other states support theirs—or that the 21st century might seem to require—would be somewhere way down the line.

THE OREGONIAN, APRIL 1, 2007

Oregon's Colleges:

Lincoln Hall's Leaky Roof Is Metaphor for Higher Ed

In a few rare college courses, there's a single moment that grabs your attention and stays with you long after you've closed your books.

For Patrick Beisell, in a class at Portland State on the American novel, it was when the ceiling started leaking.

No literature class anywhere offered a better sense of symbolism.

Beisell's class was in Lincoln Hall, built in 1911, a building that already had structural problems when Vanport College, the ancestor of PSU, inherited it from Portland Public Schools in 1949. Now, it's a relic in need of $36 million in deferred maintenance and seismic upgrades, where 40-year-old acoustic tiles fall off the ceiling, the electrical system is near collapse and, since a 2001 pump failure, a jerry-built array of pipes and wooden slabs holds up the sidewalk.

But Lincoln Hall also contains 12 percent of the instructional area of the highest-enrollment university in Oregon, with classes running from 6 in the morning until 10:30 at night, and it's the home of the PSU arts programs—including a large auditorium that is, in the words of PSU facilities manager Robyn Pierce, "in a seismic event, not a place where you want a large crowd gathering."

You could say that Lincoln Hall is the Walter Reed Army Medical Center Building 18 of the Oregon University System.

Except in real estate terms, you might call the entire system a fixer-upper.

After 30 years of diligent legislative neglect, the state is about $650 million behind in higher-education maintenance. To make a dent, Gov. Ted Kulongoski asked the Legislature for $325 million in capital construction bonds. The Ways and Means co-chairs' budget cut that to $50 million—which, after general maintenance, won't be enough to deal even with Lincoln Hall.

Let alone all the other overburdened, under-maintained buildings at PSU—or on the system's other six campuses.

And the buildings aren't even the system's main problem. The buildings are also—as someone might have said when the rain let up in Patrick Beisell's American Novel class—a metaphor.

For the past 15 years, Oregon cut its higher-education spending faster than any other state. Now, the co-chairs also cut $35 million from the governor's proposed Oregon University System operating budget.

Meanwhile, even under the governor's proposed budget, Portland State needs to cut about $5 million for next year. The university is hoping that a lot of full professors retire.

We tunneled down to this structurally unsound bargain basement by steady disinvesting in our higher-education system, until Oregon now spends $2,400 less per student than the national average. During that time, we have also had the fifth-largest tuition increase in the country, until Oregon universities now get only 85 percent of the national average in revenue but collect 120 percent of the national average in tuition. Just since 1999-2001, the state's funding of the system has fallen from the largest share, around 50 percent, to about 35 percent, while the student share is now approaching 60 percent.

This is why Patrick Beisell, about midway through his college career, is already $11,000 in debt so he can study in classrooms where the ceiling leaks.

The co-chairs' budget does fund the governor's affordability effort. But as Kulongoski told the Portland City Club on Friday afternoon, "Affordability is an empty promise without first-rate faculty, state-of-the-art research facilities, modern buildings and adequate maintenance."

Meaning around here, affordability is close to becoming an empty promise.

In universities, different shortfalls flow into each other. A place where the buildings are decrepit has trouble attracting top faculty, and a place obliged to hope that full professors retire—or maybe get recruited by other universities, which would also save money—has trouble attracting private support.

"These things run on parallel lines," says Robert Daasch, who as professor of electrical and computer engineering at Portland State, and director of the Integrated Circuits Design and Test Laboratory, has a pretty good claim on lab and research space—and yet a shortage of it.

"We are losing ground in terms of competing for the best high school students, we're losing ground in competing for the best faculty, and we're losing infrastructure.

"The dominant thought process is how to build the compromises, not how to exploit the opportunities."

And yet, a higher-education system—and a state's economic future—has to be all about exploiting the opportunities.

And Lincoln Hall isn't the only thing leaking.

THE OREGONIAN, APRIL 8, 2007

Higher Education:
Budget As If the Future Were Coming

For Intel, higher ed is not academic.

It's what drives the company—which, as the state's largest private employer, is a big part of what drives the Oregon economy.

Except our higher-ed system is not exactly driving it on all cylinders.

In 2005, Intel hired 450 PhDs for its programs. Of that number, six came from Oregon universities.

"It's a number we would like to see increase," says Steve Pawlowski, chief technology officer at Intel's digital enterprise group, and one of 10 Intel senior fellows. "The best professors attract the best students, and we like to hire the best."

Oregon should also want to see the number increase.

Not only would that educate more Oregon students, it would also tighten the ties between the high-tech community and the Oregon university system, leading to more support and more opportunities. And when those Intel PhD hires decide to spin off their own companies, it increases the chances they'll do it in Tangent instead of in Tucson.

Oregon scientists are more likely to stay here and strengthen the state and system—a point made by Pawlowski, who grew up in Medford, got degrees from Oregon Institute of Technology and Oregon Graduate Institute, and holds more than 50 patents.

If high tech is important to our state economy, beefing up our higher-ed capacity is vital.

At least, that's how high tech sees it.

This is why Pawlowski represents Intel on the Engineering and Technology Industry Council, set up to support the university system. Over the past several years, it has helped increase faculty and research efforts, especially supporting Oregon State's drive to become a Top 25 engineering university.

For a state whose biggest industry is high tech, it's an understandable goal—except for the several dozen universities, most with bigger faculties and better facilities, who stand in the way. And the goal posts keep moving; over the past few years, Arizona State has increased its engineering faculty by 75 professors.

For this legislative session, the Board of Higher Education tried to budget as if technology—and the future—matters.

That meant endorsing the engineering council's request for $34 million, likely to produce an additional $60 million in private support. Following that pattern for a few sessions would strengthen PSU's engineering school, bolster the University of Oregon's material sciences program and move toward doubling the OSU engineering faculty—which might begin to resemble a Top 25 program.

Gov. Ted Kulongoski backed half the council budget, which kept the industry interested. But then the Ways and Means co-chairs budget slashed it to $7 million, That move deflated everybody's interest and left prospects looking less like Top 25 and more like bottom fishing.

In addition, the co-chairs cut the governor's higher-education capital budget from $400 million to $56 million, ignoring all evidence that technology has anything to do with the future of the state.

For the University of Oregon, that writes off an Integrated Sciences Complex; for Portland State, it drops the rehabilitation of the dilapidated Science 2 building, which runs student laboratory classes at 6 in the morning and at midnight on weekends.

For Oregon State, it zeroes out $31 million for a new chemistry building—OSU had a pretty good idea where to find another $31 million from private sources. It would house offices and labs for the Oregon Nanosciences and Microtechnology Institute; the organic synthesis group, which works on drug synthesizing; and the Linus Pauling Institute, which focuses on health and nutrition; as well as labs for OSU's pre-med, pre-nursing and pre-pharmacy programs.

This matters only if you expect the Oregon economy to operate in the 21st century.

Last week, the Senate Revenue Committee voted overwhelmingly in support of 87 percent of the governor's capital budget. The one vote against was cast by conservative Sen. Gary George, R-Newberg, who said it wasn't enough.

"Somebody," said George, "needs to send a message that this is unacceptable."

That word has already reached John von Schlegell, a Portland venture capitalist and member of the State Board of Higher Education, who has spent most of his time on the board being stunned—baffled by why Oregon never seems to invest in higher education.

"Whether you're a businessman or not," says von Schlegell, "the ROI (return on investment) is pretty commanding.

"Look at Phil Knight or Tim Boyle, and multiply their impact. I don't know anything that has that kind of ROI."

Boyle, head of Columbia Sportswear and an Oregon graduate, seems to agree; Friday he gave the university $5 million. For Knight's contributions to the system, it looks like there is no finish line.

"We'd better make a choice here, because I think we're at a real dangerous fork in the road," says von Schlegell. "The U-Dub (University of

Washington) just carried off a multibillion-dollar campaign that dwarfs anything here, and then there's our neighbors to the south. We don't want to be the state that's the service industry taking care of entrepreneurs from other places."

As the governor and the folks on the engineering council argue, we have ways of avoiding that future. It's a matter of looking at the Oregon University System and seeing the roots of Phil Knight and Tim Boyle and Steve Pawlowski—and a lot of currently missing PhDs in engineering.

But we need to get started.

Because most other places already have.

THE OREGONIAN, APRIL 15, 2007

Oregon Universities:

Bernstine's Exit Underscores the Erosion in Higher Education

Dan Bernstine warmly remembers his first legislative session, in 1999, when a Republican Legislature actually put some more money into higher education.

"That year, we got a bump," recalls the president of Portland State. "I've been cutting budgets ever since."

It seems that after this session, the president of Portland State will be cutting again.

But it won't be Bernstine. This summer, after 10 years, he's leaving, moving to Pennsylvania to take over the company that runs the Law School Admission Test.

"I could say, I'm leaving because I got tired of cutting," Bernstine grins, "but if I was tired of cutting I'd have left a long time ago."

Which doesn't mean that the people staying in the system aren't tired of cutting—and wondering why, with a strong state economy and a Democratic Legislature that says all the right things about higher education, they're likely to be hacking away at themselves one more time.

Bernstine, sitting relaxed in his office wearing a Portland State Vikings windbreaker, has a range of things to be proud of at PSU. He can point to major construction on the campus, an explosion in enrollment that lets PSU call itself (as often as possible) the largest university in Oregon and the rise of something he likes to call "institutional swagger."

But as considerable as Bernstine's achievements are, each of them also points out institutional weakness at the core of the Oregon University System—a weakness that is eating deeper into the state's universities.

For years, people at Portland State regarded themselves as the outsiders of the Oregon system, but according to Bernstine, "they don't think that we're singled out any more. We whine because as a system we're suffering, but we don't cry about the U of O and OSU any more. To me, that's a huge change."

Only in the Oregon University System would it be a breakthrough to think that your situation was no more bleak than anyone else's.

Portland State now has gleaming new engineering and public affairs buildings, and more residential resources creating more of a university community. They're products of the university's first capital fundraising campaign and major efforts by Bernstine.

"If you look at Wisconsin (where he was dean of the law school before coming to PSU), the percentage of state dollars going to institutions is probably less," Bernstine says. "But the state doesn't build buildings here. That's a huge deal. You have to spend a lot of time putting deals together to get basic academic space."

That situation's unlikely to improve with the co-chairs of the Ways and Means Committee shaving Gov. Ted Kulongoski's proposed capital budget from $325 million to $53 million, along with cutting $35 million from his proposed operating budget. Aside from the effect on any new construction, the $53 million also retreats before the system's $640 million in deferred maintenance.

"The public doesn't see that the place is held together by duct tape," Bernstine points out. "Lincoln Hall has been red-tagged by the city, which fortunately has been too busy to come shut it down."

That morning, Kulongoski was inspecting the place, trying to build some support for his capital proposal.

"The governor's up on the roof of Lincoln Hall," notes Bernstine, grinning again. "I told him I wouldn't go up there. It was too dangerous."

Under Bernstine, the head count at PSU has risen sharply, up to 25,000, and more of them are even graduating. But with state support shrinking, each new student puts more pressure on the university's budget, even with rising tuition.

In 1990, the state sent Oregon universities $4,290 per student. In 2006, the state spent $3,858 per student (46th in the country)—which amounts to $2,442 in 1990 dollars, a cut of about 43 percent.

At rapidly growing PSU, and also at Oregon State, even the governor's full budget produces cuts, as the institutions try to absorb more students without enough state support. Not wanting to reduce student access, the co-chairs' budget fully funds the governor's proposed financial aid budget.

The universities appreciate the financial-aid funding, says Jock Mills, director of government relations at Oregon State, but without resources and facilities to deal with the new students, "these funds and efforts are an empty promise."

The Legislature's message to the higher-education system is that while it knows the universities are losing money on every student, they should try to make up the difference on volume.

"As a percentage of fixed costs," notes Bernstine, the state's support "keeps getting smaller."

That's not, he says, why he's leaving.

But it doesn't sound like something he's going to miss.

THE OREGONIAN, APRIL 22, 2007

Subtracting Higher Ed

It was a terrific week for higher education in the Pacific Northwest.

Not in Oregon, of course, but you can't have everything.

The Washington Legislature finished a session of dazzling advances for that state's system. It increased Washington's student capacity by 9,700, including 3,700 high-cost, high-demand engineering and science slots; limited tuition increases; and added $86 million in new scholarship and grant aid.

It also took the next steps to create a fourth University of Washington campus, in the north Puget Sound area, with classes to begin in September 2008. That one took a fight—between people who wanted a UW campus and people who wanted an independent Washington Institute of Technology.

Oregon higher-ed fights are about which campuses and programs we'll have to cut.

"We invested in our research institutions," Washington Gov. Chris Gregoire said Thursday. "We absolutely believe that the U of W and WSU are two of the greatest economic-growth engines in the state."

In addition to operating budgets, the Legislature authorized capital construction bonds for universities and community colleges totaling $1.1 billion. The Oregon Legislature is pondering a higher-ed bonding proposal, from the Ways and Means co-chairs, totalling $57 million.

The University of Washington alone—excluding Washington State; Western, Eastern, Central Washington universities and Evergreen State College; and the entire Washington community college system—is in line for $143 million, almost three times the entire amount in Oregon.

Maybe Portland State could ask to be adopted.

It's not remarkable that Washington and Oregon have different higher-education budgets; they're different states in different situations. What's striking is that Washington and Oregon seem to live in different worlds and different centuries.

Over the past 15 years Washington has established seven new university campuses: three for the University of Washington and four for Washington State, in Spokane, Tri-Cities, Walla Walla and Vancouver. During that time, Oregon has added only the tiny Oregon State University Cascades (enrollment projected at 576 in 2015)—while wondering whether it can continue to support Western, Southern and Eastern Oregon universities.

And, says Washington Gov. Gregoire, in each location there's a strategy for local businesses, state economic development efforts and the local campus to work together. In Walla Walla, that's meant university programs behind the area's growing wine and hospitality industry, and in North Puget Sound an engineering emphasis to support Boeing and its local suppliers. In Clark County, she says, "They want us to invest in WSU Vancouver because they see it as an anchor of a science and research park."

There are also, of course, several departments at the University of Washington with connections to a place across the lake called Microsoft.

You might conclude that in terms of planning and using its higher-education system, Washington is doing algebra while Oregon is doing addition.

Or often, subtraction.

Washington is not just putting money into buildings. The budget includes $184 million for faculty pay increases, in part to raise UW toward the levels of the best national research universities. Currently it's about average for its peer group.

The University of Oregon, in a much smaller peer group, calculates that it's ninth out of nine. The governor's proposed budget included $8 million for faculty pay increases, in a package cut back about 3 percent by the Ways and Means co-chairs.

Of the Washington package, UW President Mark Emmert said happily, "We hope this is the first step in a multiyear plan to close the gap entirely with the global challenge states."

We don't have to worry about that.

Oregon isn't a global challenge state.

Oregon is a globally challenged state.

You can see why Melissa Unger, executive director of the Oregon Student Association, says, "Students are increasingly worried about failed faculty searches, adjunct (part-time) faculty, and getting what they're paying for."

Especially since Oregon university students are now paying more than the state is—which isn't saying much.

In 2006, the state's contribution per student in the Oregon University System was $3,858—down from $4,292 in 1990.

In 2006, Washington's spending on each of its four-year students was $8,164.

Washington students indeed get a better deal.

And Oregon's future might amount taking in Washington's wash.

Admittedly, Oregon doesn't need everything that's in the Washington higher-education budget. This year, Washington's budget includes $30,000 for a state poet laureate.

There's no point to Oregon spending that much on a poet.

Because this year in the Oregon Legislature, nothing about higher education sounds very good.

THE OREGONIAN, APRIL 29, 2007

Higher Education:

Legislature to Students: Let Them Eat Cake (or Cookies)

Monique Teal remembers when she started thinking about a bake sale for higher education.

At Southern Oregon University, where she's a senior, "Our Criminology Club had bake sales, because Taylor Hall was falling in over our heads. Pieces of the roof were coming down."

That must have been distracting.

"You have no idea," she said cheerfully.

Thursday at the capitol, the Oregon Student Association expanded on the idea, setting up its own bake sale just down the marble steps from the House and Senate. It included brownies for the university system, at $875 million; Rice Krispies Treats for the community colleges, at $529 million; cookies for capital construction, at $594 million; and carrot cake for the Shared Responsibility financial aid program, at $47 million.

(The carrot cake, like the public policy of helping kids make it to college, was highly recommended.)

It seemed as promising as any other prospects higher education has had in the building.

As first course, downstairs, a news conference featured a parade of speakers on the desperate condition of the higher-education system, many of them reaching the same conclusion Monique Teal had in Taylor Hall. The group included four legislators—two from each house, two from each party—who differed from the others mainly by looking faintly embarrassed.

The condition of our buildings, pointed out Sen. Frank Morse, R-Albany, creates "actual disruption in classroom service on both the Oregon State and University of Oregon campuses."

It wasn't hard to figure, noted Morse, how we got here: "Just to stay at the watermark level of 1990-91, the higher-education budget is down [by] $169 million."

Rep. Gene Whisnant, R-Sunriver, who doesn't even have a university in his district, was even more direct.

"It's a disgrace, the condition of some of these buildings," he said unhappily. He'd hoped he could help move the Legislature to do something about it, but "today I'm here with my disappointment."

Give that man a cookie.

It seems you don't even have to be a legislator to notice. Wayne Lei, PGE's director of environmental affairs, explained that at a time when business needs ever more sophisticated workers, the state's disinvestment in higher education is having "a dramatic effect," including university buildings that are "frozen in time." He talked about graduates returning to their classrooms and laboratories decades later, and recognizing just about everything.

That's not what most universities mean by alumni outreach.

Throughout the news conference, people kept producing numbers, holding them up as if they didn't quite believe them. Sen. Richard Devlin, D-Tigard, pointed out that in fiscal 2002, the state contributed $321 million to the universities, and students' tuition brought in an equal amount.

By fiscal 2006, the state's share was down to $289 million, and tuition up to $442 million.

People used to talk, he remembered, about a funding system of high tuition and high financial aid: "Oregon has developed a system of higher tuition and lower aid."

We reached this point, said Devlin, even though "no other investment that we make in this building will produce so large a return."

Of course, it turns out that not investing in higher education has an impact, too.

Last week brought the *2007 Benchmark Report* from the Oregon Progress Board, the state's annual, generally burbling, report on its condition. But Oregon lags considerably behind its goals at the higher-education level: With a target of 38 percent of Oregonians over 25 having a four-year degree in 2005, and 45 percent by 2010, only 32.7 percent qualified in 2006. (Oregon runs considerably behind Washington in this measure.)

Oregon also falls far short of its own benchmark in residents over 25 with some college, with 59.7 percent against a goal of 70 percent. The gap between those with some college and those with a degree is wide, suggesting that when Oregon kids make it to college, we don't make it particularly easy for them to finish, either financially or educationally.

Not, for example, if they're looking for professors.

Mark Perlman, philosophy professor at Western Oregon University, talked about the difficulties of all campuses in hiring new faculty to replace those who retire (or flee). His department recently sought an Eastern philosopher, and chose a candidate who was, understandably, a Buddhist.

"Buddhists are not known for monetary interests," said Perlman. "We offered him the job, and he turned us down over money.

"That's how bad it is now. Oregon can't even hire a Buddhist."

Actually, it's even worse. It looks like Oregon can't afford Monique Teal.

Teal is smart, focused, loves Oregon and wants to study and work in a vitally useful area, criminology. States put up barbed wire around their borders to keep kids like this from leaving.

Then there's our approach.

"Originally, I wanted to go to Oregon State," Teal says about graduate study. "But it actually looks cheaper for me to go to the University of Virginia." Going to Oregon State, she fears, "means I would never get out of debt."

But after Virginia, she'd come right back, right?

"I've found a lot of opportunities come because of where I live," Teal says carefully. "If I got involved in politics in Virginia, there's a good chance I'd stay in Virginia. Which is sad, because Oregon is wonderful."

In some ways.

If you're a brownie.

THE OREGONIAN, MAY 6, 2007

Higher Ed:
If You Build it, They'll Help Pay the Bill

Just like the glossy pamphlet says, the Integrative Science Complex is a cutting-edge demonstration of what higher education is supposed to bring to Oregon. On the University of Oregon campus, its centers and laboratories focus on the approaches vital to the next century: nanotechnology, neuroscience, bio- and material sciences. The private contributions to pay half the costs are lined up in the university's sights, and U of O faculty has already attracted federal grants larger than the state's share of the costs.

It would be nice to build it.

But so far, after more than four months of the legislative session, the university would need its electron microscopes to locate the complex's chances.

Gov. Ted Kulongoski's budget called for about $400 million in capital bonds for higher education, including the $30 million to finish the Integrative Science Complex. But the Ways and Means co-chairs' budget slashed that to $50 million, and now the U of O is looking at a "disintegrative science complex."

Across the Oregon University System, administrators gaze hopefully at promising blueprints—and on the other side of the capital budget, at existing buildings crumbling like a decades-old cookie. The system has capital projects that are educationally essential, and now is a good time for the state to borrow the money. In some cases—and this is what breaks university administrators' hearts—fat private wallets are eager to join in partnership with a state playing incomprehensibly hard to get.

For the Integrative Science Complex, the university's new super contributor, Lorry Lokey, stands ready to give $20 million, and the university has a good idea where the other $10 million might be. But it could all end up somewhere besides Eugene.

"I don't want to be," says U of O President Dave Frohnmayer, "in the embarrassing position of going back to the most generous philanthropist in the history of University of Oregon academics and have to give the money back. It's a shocking position to be in."

Because what university presidents hate most—more than parents who can't let go, more than legislators as clueless as Dr. Watson, more even than bad calls on nationally televised football games—is giving large amounts of money back.

And since the university is owned by the people of Oregon, you'd think they wouldn't like it, either.

The people of Oregon have the opportunity to own other, similar buildings. Oregon State has on its drawing board the Linus Pauling/ Chemistry Center, which would house offices and labs for the Oregon Nanosciences and Microtechnology Institute; the organic synthesis group, which works on drug synthesizing; and the Linus Pauling Institute, which researches health and nutrition.

(There is a goal to double the number of health professionals that Oregon produces in the next 10 years, although maybe not if it's going to cost money.)

The chemistry department and the Linus Pauling Institute bring in more than $5 million a year in grants, amounts expected to rise swiftly with the new facility. Chemistry already produces more patents and economic spinoffs than any other part of the OSU College of Science.

Again, Oregon State knows where to get the $31 million in private financing to cover half the center's costs. It's the public funding that seems about to vanish like an unsynthesized molecule.

That could mean another awkward conversation.

"Donors don't make these philanthropic decisions easily," says Mike Goodwin, president of the OSU Foundation. "To reach the point of commitment and then be told that the bond match couldn't be secured, it's hard to imagine the dismay that would cause the people involved in this project, and hard to imagine what we'd say going back to them."

On the other hand, they might not be dismayed long. Somehow, large amounts of money always manage to find more receptive recipients.

The people of Oregon, of course, own all of their state university property. In fact, half the buildings the state owns are part of the university system.

Generally, it's the more dilapidated half. Over the past 15 years, the university system has amassed a total of $640 million in deferred maintenance, which is another reason the governor proposed a serious capital budget—unlike the tiny amounts of past budget periods.

There's also reason to think this is a good time for Oregon to borrow money for higher education. Interest rates are down even from last year, and with the Legislature finally creating a rainy-day fund, the state's credit rating is improving.

"The wind is at our back," says Rob Edmiston, a Portland State alumnus who monitored Oregon's bonds for Standard & Poor's back when the wind was going in the other direction. "It seems we're not taking advantage of what the environment is."

And not planning for what we want our environment to be.

"This is a good time," agrees state Treasurer Randall Edwards, who would actually peddle the bonds. "In higher education and community colleges, infrastructure is really important. If you've got the ability to do this, you should take advantage of it."

For years, Oregon hasn't done that. It hasn't put its money into its higher-education system, with the result that much of its infrastructure is primitive and deteriorating.

And now, with the uncertain prospects of the Integrative Science Complex and the Linus Pauling/Chemistry Center, Oregon is going beyond reluctance to spend its money on higher education.

Now, we even refuse other people's money.

THE OREGONIAN, MAY 13, 2007

Community College Funding: Lower-Income Kids' Access to Higher Ed Sinking

GRESHAM—Before Sean Robinson graduated from Gresham High School in 2000, he took a class at Mt. Hood Community College. Then, thinking he needed some more discipline and wanting to follow a family military tradition, he enlisted before going to college.

Returning to MHCC in 2005—after five years in the Marines, mostly with intelligence, and two tours in Iraq—he saw a difference.

"The first thing I noticed," Robinson recalls, "was the massive increase in price."

In 2000 a MHCC course was $35 a credit. He returned to pay $66.

Which is why he also returned to a campus with considerably fewer students.

In community colleges across Oregon, in what's designed to be the most accessible part of the post-secondary education system, costs have gone up sharply and enrollment has dropped. (MHCC tuition has gone up 107 percent in 10 years.) Robert Jurgen, Portland Community College economist, has shown that every tuition increase immediately

cuts enrollment, an argument strongly supported by a statewide enrollment drop of about 50,000 since 2002.

Robinson also could have noted that students were paying more for
less; MHCC's faculty is down from 174 to 158.

Tuesday, an unexpected boost in the state's revenue projections
brightened community college prospects, which could allow the system
to inch a little further away from the edge of the cliff. But like Oregon's
universities, its community colleges are at the bottom of a decades-long
disinvestment, and this session needs to provide not just a last-minute
rescue but a platform for a long-term recovery.

In the late 1960s, at the beginning of community colleges, Oregon
had one of the best-supported systems in the nation. But as MHCC
President Robert Silverman puts it, "We've been doing a stair step down
for the last 20 years."

At the start of each of the past three decades, community colleges,
like universities, took a beating: in Oregon's crunching recession of the
early '80s, the early '90s Measure 5 funding shortfall and the post-9/11
state budget collapse. In states such as California and Washington, each
downturn was a blip; in Oregon, it was a new bottom. In real dollars,
the governor's proposed community college budget would be 95 percent
of what it got in 1999-2001; the now-abandoned Ways and Means co-
chairmen's budget would have been 88 percent.

Support for higher education in Oregon declined 10 percent in the
1980s, 17 percent in the '90s, and 12 percent so far in the new century.

The burden was largely transferred to Oregon students—the ones who
remained. Enrollment is down, particularly in the professional programs
once central to the community colleges, programs that are expensive to offer
but directly responsive to both student interest and local business needs.

MHCC has the region's only mortuary sciences program, a costly
curriculum but one that can claim a connection to all Oregonians. It has
welding and material sciences programs, and auto-mechanic training
operations co-sponsored by local car dealerships.

Tuesday morning, in the dental hygienist training lab, Mylar balloons rose up from each dental chair: All members of this year's graduating class had passed the national qualifying boards. Considering the college gets more than 100 applications for 18 slots in the program, you can see how that could happen.

Of course, just above one of the chairs is the place where the roof fell in last summer. MHCC, like most community colleges dating from the 1960s and '70s, has a considerable backlog of deferred maintenance and little prospect of passing a local bond issue. The college last passed one in 1980; in 2002, a measure actually got a majority of votes cast but fell short of a majority turnout.

The governor's budget tried to start a state-supported capital construction effort for community colleges but has been derailed in the Legislature.

"Without a significant capital investment," says Michael Wolfe, MHCC's chief operating officer, "our operations and maintenance budget will begin to affect our instructional budget."

Already, Oregon's community colleges are squeezed from several directions, and so are their students—both those in professional programs and those planning to transfer to a four-year school. For students in the lower 40 percent of Oregon incomes, attending a community college full time now costs an average 45 percent of family income. Required classes being offered less frequently often extends the time in school.

Visiting one college recently, says Cam Preus-Bailey, commissioner of the Department of Community Colleges and Workforce Development, "I heard one student say, 'It makes me wonder if it's worth it.' Those are words that mortify me."

When Sean Robinson left the Marines for MHCC and was stunned by the increased prices, he couldn't do anything about tuition. But when he found that books for one quarter came to around $350, he ran successfully for vice president of student government and started a program to buy $5,000 worth of required texts and put them on reserve in the library to try to help pinched students.

He understands part of why costs went up so much; Oregon went through a tough financial stretch. But, Robinson says, "In 2007, the economy's much different. You owe us now.

"Community colleges are your quickest investment in responding to an economic demand. This is the perfect opportunity for people from lower income brackets to have a chance for an education."

Next year Robinson is going to George Washington University in Washington, D.C., to study Eastern European languages; he thinks Vladimir Putin is re-creating the Soviet threat. GWU is the most expensive undergraduate college in the nation, but between scholarships for need and merit, the GI Bill and loans, he thinks he can manage it.

He did consider going to the University of Oregon. But by his calculation, that would have cost him just as much.

THE OREGONIAN, MAY 20, 2007

Higher Education:

We're Losing the Tony Trans As Oregon's Universities Spiral Down

After his junior year at Beaverton High School, Tony Tran started looking carefully at colleges. With a summer volunteering at a muscular dystrophy camp and a weighted GPA of 3.88 ("3.883," he says carefully), he wanted a place to help him become a doctor.

He was impressed by the programs at the University of San Francisco and Whitman College in Walla Walla. Because his guidance counselor told him the University of Oregon was very strong in biology, and because he needed scholarship help and knew how expensive private colleges were, he also applied to the U of O.

But when Tran finished going through his acceptances this spring, Whitman had offered him a scholarship of $100,000, and USF would cover $43,000 of its $46,000 annual total.

And of a projected annual cost of about $17,000, the University of Oregon offered only "a couple of thousand."

So Tony Tran is leaving the state.

And he's not alone.

An Oregon University System study of the high school class of 2005 found only 21.7 percent entering an Oregon public university, the lowest since 1995. On the other hand, the percentage of high achievers (grade point averages above 3.75) leaving the state for college was up, to 27 percent.

This week, the Legislature's Ways and Means Committee focuses on the higher-education budget, at a time when the state's university trends are all going in the wrong direction. The trends can be countered: When an Oregon Legislature last made a significant investment in its universities, in 1999, it produced upsurges in both enrollment and graduation rates—which have only collapsed in the lean times since.

Oregon's historical underinvestment in higher education and tuition's sharp rise during the past five years have landed a double blow on enrollment in its university system. High school graduates have found need barriers harder to hurdle, and enrollment of Oregonians in Oregon public universities has actually declined.

At the same time, a number of Oregon high school graduates, especially high achievers, have found to their general surprise that they could attend private or out-of-state colleges for as much or less than Oregon public universities would cost them.

It's enough to make a graduate throw his *Barron's Complete College Financing Guide* out the window.

Along with his Oregon driver's license.

For Oregon universities, it's harder both to support kids who want to attend, and to recruit the best kids.

"We have students with high GPAs, [Advanced Placement, International Baccalaureate] classes, and they get packages from private schools that make them cheaper than the public universities," says Karen Stabeno, a guidance counselor at Beaverton High School. "Even for our students with 3.8 [averages], the [Oregon University System] scholarships they're able to get aren't that large."

She finds that students look increasingly at Canadian universities. And seniors have other concerns about Oregon universities: "They read the papers."

This year, another Beaverton student found Marquette University in Milwaukee or Miami of Ohio would cost him about as much as Oregon State. He finally decided on the University of Washington.

"It was less expensive for all of my four children to go to private schools out of state than to go in-state, including to Portland State," says Gary Sehorn, in charge of instruction for Beaverton schools. "I don't think there's much to keep kids in state."

University of Oregon President Dave Frohnmayer has heard this before. "I got a letter from a mother," he says, "complaining that her son was able to go to Arizona State cheaper than to U of O."

Frohnmayer points out that Oregon universities, unlike places such as North Carolina State or Georgia Tech, aren't in a position to give sizable tuition rebates to students they really want, let alone to practice the aggressive recruitment of some private schools.

As a result, students leave: "Five years ago, Nevada exported students to Oregon. Now, Oregon exports students to Nevada," Frohnmayer says.

Actually, Oregon has changed from a net regional importer of college students to a net exporter, although so far, not by a huge amount.

Then there are the students with fewer choices.

"The university system keeps getting more and more unaffordable for students," says Sue Brent, principal of Portland's Wilson High School. "They don't have the aspiration to go because they just know they can't afford it."

Even for students who try to make the leap, the prospect is daunting.

"It is really difficult," says Grace Stickney, about to graduate from Portland's Cleveland High School. "It's not hard to get into the U of O as a student. But it's approximately $17,000 a year, and it's difficult."

Stickney has a 3.8 GPA, and belongs to the National Honor Society. She's been a cheerleader and a varsity swimmer, and volunteers at the

Dougy Center, where she went for counseling when her mother died when she was 5. She also has two part-time jobs.

She's gotten some scholarship support from U of O, but still faces borrowing $10,000 a year. The idea of reaching 2011 with a bachelor's degree and $40,000 in debt unnerves her. She heads down to Eugene with no certainty that she can manage all four years there, and might end up coming back.

The Legislature seems to be accepting most of Gov. Ted Kulongoski's Shared Responsibility Plan for easier student access, although it looks like it won't go as far as the governor hoped: Sen. Richard Devlin, D-Tualatin, noted last week, "We can reduce the amount of the grants or reduce who's eligible."

But after years of sinking support, a recent OUS report summed up the situation: "Oregon high school students are choosing to enroll in community colleges, private colleges, out-of-state schools or not participating in postsecondary education at all. Moreover . . . more of Oregon's most talented students are choosing to attend college out of Oregon."

It's not an encouraging trend.

"If you keep a significant proportion of your graduates, you're fueling your economy," says George Pernsteiner, chancellor of the Oregon University System. "About 78 percent of Oregon university graduates stay here. If they go someplace else, perhaps half of them won't come back. I'm a little concerned that we're losing more of the high-achieving students than we were a few years ago."

Tony Tran, looking to spend another summer volunteering at the muscular dystrophy camp, isn't looking too far in the future.

"I've spent my whole life in Oregon," he says. But as for staying in California after college, "If that does happen, I think I'm OK with it."

Which, as the percentage of high-achieving graduates leaving the state for college rises higher, raises another question:

Whether it's OK with Oregon.

THE OREGONIAN, MAY 27, 2007

Higher Ed's Tsunami

In various bowels of the state capitol last week, the Oregon Legislature began to focus on the higher-education budget.

The Legislature being what it is, it was not only looking at the wrong budget, it was in the wrong place.

It should have been in Hangzhou, China, where the Association of Pacific Rim Universities met last week. Not only would the garden spot of China have been a more pleasant place than the Ways and Means Committee room, but legislators would have heard some interesting things.

They'd have heard Paul Chu, president of Hong Kong University of Science and Technology, talk about a 25 percent to 30 percent budget increase and plans to become a global leader in technology and strategic planning.

The president of National Taiwan University explained that universities in his country were working with higher-education budget increases of $1.5 billion a year over the next five years.

They could have heard presidents of the National University of Singapore and Seoul National University—located in what's already the most wired country in the world—explain their plans to become the international leaders in computer technology and stem cell research.

The president of Zhejiang University, one of China's foremost, outlined his university's plans for a massive increase in capacity. It's part of a national expansion that within a decade could mean a higher proportion of college-educated young people in China than in Oregon (where the percentage has been dropping).

Seeking some reassurance in English, legislators could have heard Mark Emmert, president of the University of Washington, express optimism about his university's best budget in decades.

In other words, Oregon legislators might have learned that there is a world outside the capitol's Democratic and Republican caucus rooms. At Hangzhou, University of Oregon President Dave Frohnmayer saw a world where "the pace of new building for higher education is just astonishing. The rapidity of change is breathtaking."

Something nobody has ever said about Salem.

Of course, without ever leaving the borders of this state, people have been trying to explain this to Oregonians for a while.

"We've been beating this drum for a long time," says Jim Craven, public and legislative affairs director for the Oregon branch of the American Electronics Association. "The message is, you've got to get serious. There are no laurels left to rest on. The United States needs to get serious about global competition.

"Ten years ago, people said [about foreign high tech], 'Well, maybe they can produce chips, but they can't write code.' Nobody says that any more. A lot of people are bulking up all around the world."

Earlier this year, the national AEA published a report, *We Are Still Losing the Competitive Advantage*, finding that South Korea now graduates more engineers every year than the United States and that the European Union graduates three times as many we do.

China produces six times as many, and since 1998, its state financing of higher education has doubled and is still rising. Last year, China announced a 15-year plan to boost its technological capacity.

Long-term thinking is vital to build a higher-education system, especially when it's in a long-term hole. Gov. Ted Kulongoski sent the Legislature a proposal to begin a 10-year plan to rebuild the Oregon system, but the legislators are tripping over the first step.

Over the past decade, the state's high-tech capacity has made some progress, notably with the Engineering and Technology Industry Council, a joint university-private effort that brings in almost twice as many private dollars as public ones. The $34 million requested for ETIC by the Oregon State Board of Higher Education was projected to bring in $60 million in private support. So far, the governor and the Legislature have pared that $34 million down to $7 million—and Craven thinks technology is actually doing better than the rest of the university system.

"You can't just build engineering and let the entire infrastructure erode around you," says the American Engineering Association executive. "The trend lines don't look good. At the macro level, we're not stepping up."

Oregon's only Fortune 500 company, Nike, runs a long course through the global market. Don Blair, chief financial officer of Nike, is on the state's board of higher education and tries to connect what he sees in the two places.

"Not only have many manufacturing jobs already left, but we're losing service jobs," Blair says. "Companies are looking for engineering in Eastern Europe. There's an educated labor pool in a lot of places."

To Blair, the issue isn't just a matter of fueling Oregon businesses. There's a saying at Nike, he says: "You can import PhDs, MBAs, anything else you need from other countries or states.

"What we want is the opportunity for our own children to be in that group."

Craven agrees, partly.

"The Intels and Nikes will spend whatever they need to bring in whatever they need. For smaller companies, the local resource is important."

Smaller companies, of course, are where job growth comes from.

"I think the key," says Craven, "is what kind of opportunities we want to give our Oregon kids."

And whether that consists mostly of handling errands for the graduates of Berkeley and Beijing, Seattle and Seoul.

The news of the kind of world we now live in has spread all around the Pacific, to the universities of Chile, Sydney and Tokyo. For almost two years, it's spread to the millions of readers of Thomas L. Friedman's best-seller *The World Is Flat*. It's seeped into Washington, where Congress looks for ways to restimulate American innovation and basic research, and Wall Street, where investment capital swiftly follows jobs offshore.

Any session now, the news might reach Salem.

THE OREGONIAN, JUNE 3, 2007

Higher Education:

Recruiting Difficulties Reflect the Sorry State of Oregon's Colleges

Portland State University is losing a political scientist to an endowed chair at Louisiana State. A Native American Studies professor is heading for the University of California at Santa Barbara, and a young sociologist is off to the University of Alaska.

Oregon Institute of Technology, in Klamath Falls, is losing its admissions director, its library director and its head of counseling.

The University of Oregon math department went out to fill three vacancies and managed to fill just one. These days, finding and hiring someone the department wants and can afford is often a two- or three-year process.

Before the Oregon University System, and Oregon, feel relieved over the Legislature's improvements to the higher-education budget, it's worth being blunt about where the state's universities are and just how far they have to go.

"I think we may have stopped the arterial bleeding," says Rep. Larry Galizio, D-Tigard, a higher-education advocate, "but the patient is still on life support."

Which means, at least, that it's breathing—supported by a last-minute transfusion from a higher-than-expected May revenue forecast.

As of last week, when most of the heavy lifting on the higher-ed budget was done, the system ended up close to or slightly past Gov. Ted Kulongoski's proposals. Overall, the higher-ed budget is up 18 percent over last session.

That's a significant gain. On the other hand, it's no more than the overall increase in this session's general fund budget—and in recent years, higher education has taken the state budget's worst beatings. As Galizio notes, "I don't think it would be accurate to say there was a new strong focus on the university system."

This higher-education budget is far from a windfall. At the end of the budget season, Oregon State and Portland State, with enrollment out-running resources, will still be making cuts for next year—and Portland State and Western Oregon University are planning tuition increases for some students that may be eye-popping.

Still, for Oregon universities, even stopping the bleeding is prog-ress. But getting them to a position where they can compete consistently with universities in other states and countries, and provide an economic engine for the state and accessible opportunity for Oregon kids, is another question.

"We've shifted the burden to students," says Janet Hume-Schwarz, professor of accounting at Eastern Oregon University in La Grande. "In an urban area, students will pay it; in a rural area, they won't. For stu-dents in northeast Oregon, it's cheaper to go to Boise State or Washington State."

One considerable gain in the session was greatly increased funding for the Shared Responsibility Model, intended to help Oregon students cover the steadily increasing costs.

"If I had to rate it," Sen. Richard Devlin, D-Tualatin, says about the higher-education budget, "I'd say it's about a C+. I don't think we're capa-ble of doing much better than a B," given the state's revenue structure.

But in valuing universities, the market doesn't grade on effort. It grades on investment and performance—and it grades over decades.

This budget's chances of moving Oregon universities toward competitiveness get no better grade than Incomplete. The state system competes with universities paying faculty considerably more, and the bidding can be fierce at the highest research levels. The budget provides a total of $10 million for faculty salary increases throughout the state's seven institutions.

"To me, the key is, can we offer a commensurate salary to a scholar we want to bring in, who'll bring in research money and other people," worries Rep. Phil Barnhart, D-Eugene. "Can we find that $30,000?"

We'll still have to look hard for it.

More important, can we find it consistently?

"States that have been successfully using higher ed as an economic engine," points out George Pernsteiner, Oregon's higher-education chancellor, "have made that investment year after year."

That's never been Oregon's style. Instead, about once a decade, a legislative session remembers that Oregon has a higher-education system—in 1985, in 1999 and now in 2007. After that, the following legislatures sent the universities back into higher hibernation.

In the 21st century, we no longer have time to do that.

It's hard to disagree with Devlin's assessment that after weeks when it looked as if this session might flunk higher education, the likely result now looks something like a C+. Maybe that's passing, and graded on a curve against other sessions, it might be a little higher.

But all a C+ means is that you get to try to do better next time.

THE OREGONIAN, JUNE 10, 2007

It's a Wrap

As the end of the legislative session neared, on a warm afternoon close to the end of the school year, Gov. Ted Kulongoski went to talk to students at Beaverton's upscale Jesuit High School. He found himself addressing the entire student body—a hostage situation for students, a mission impossible for a speaker.

After a few minutes, Kulongoski started taking questions. There were a few awkward inquiries on abortion and gay rights, and then a student asked about the governor's choice for president.

It's the kind of question that does not lure Kulongoski to short answers, and he soared through a description of his search for a candidate who spoke to middle-class concerns, to the problems of people seeing their jobs outsourced and their pensions and medical care eroded.

Lately, he noted, they were the people having trouble giving their kids the opportunity for higher education.

And then, he remembers, in a large crowded room of teenagers who wanted to be someplace else, "The kids all stood up and started clapping."

Which caused the governor of Oregon to think that if the students at Jesuit, not exactly an inner-city high school, were themselves concerned about getting squeezed out of the college avenue to a reasonable existence, he could see how the issue had risen to new prominence in Salem.

"I think it had to get on a practical basis," Kulongoski remarked Friday morning, looking back on an unusually academically minded legislative session.

"People had to get to the point of saying, 'I'm going to get screwed.'"

Considering how difficult access to higher education in Oregon had become, and how far Oregon universities had fallen behind institutions in comparable states, you could see how Kulongoski's simple formulation was becoming the state college yell.

Oregon students increasingly faced a choice between getting priced out of their universities and starting life as much as $30,000 or $40,000 in debt.

What happened in this legislative session won't fix all the problems, or even begin to. But it was the first time in quite a while that legislators got to the end of the session thinking about higher education very much at all. This time, legislators considerably increased the universities' operating budget—although no more than the state's overall general fund increase. They doubled financial aid, notably in the governor's Shared Responsibility program. And, at the last minute, $275 million in capital construction bonds reduced the chances of a ceiling falling on a textbook.

The state began to set some different priorities.

This was made considerably easier, of course, by $150 million more falling out of the sky in the May revenue forecast. But the governor insists it would have happened anyway.

"At the beginning," he recalls his message to legislators, "I said, 'You will not go home before July 1 if you underinvest in post-secondary education.'"

For a while, the message didn't seem to sink in. That had been, after all, the pattern in so many previous legislatures, when larger, better-organized forces triumphed over higher education in the final cutting up of the budget.

Kulongoski had seen that before, and understood what was behind it.

"What you want to do is make people like you," he explained, as if walking someone through a long-division problem. "That's what politics is about; you won't want to make them mad at you. They won't vote for you.

"So whatever group had the loudest voice got the funding, to the detriment of others."

And higher education could have been wearing a sweat shirt labeled, "Others."

But this time, pressure came from the governor, who also credits legislators such as Sen. Ryan Deckert, D-Beaverton, and Rep. Larry Galizio, D-Tigard, and from a lot of students and families who saw their chances for a future eroding.

When the conversation started changing, it led to a different conclusion.

Legislators will always listen to the loudest voices, agrees Kulongoski, but, "You have to look at the No. 1 priority, which is not the short term, (but) which is 20 or 30 years, long term. I hope the Legislature continues to look at education as long term."

But the outcomes only change, short or long term, if the politics changes, if people continue to holler for higher education.

Thursday, as the Legislature wound down to an encouragingly early end, one of Kulongoski's aides told him that for the next Legislature he should pick some different priorities.

What the governor had pushed for in this session, the aide noted, were higher education, the high-tech Engineering and Technology Industry Council and improving pay for judges, and there was limited political gratification from the list.

"For all three of these groups, the phrase 'Thank you' is not in their vocabulary," the governor jovially quoted his aide. "They all think they're smarter than you, and whatever they get, they just think they deserve it."

It's indeed useful to know how to say thank you. It's more useful to know how to ask in the first place.

All around the state, from the governor's office to universities to high-tech corporate offices to high school auditoriums, this session saw a greater determination to ask for help for higher ed.

Partly because people had finally realized what was going to happen to them if they didn't.

THE OREGONIAN, JULY 1, 2007

On a Shuttered Library, Words of Caution for Higher Ed

ASHLAND—It's a beautiful library, just about brand-new, right next to downtown Ashland, a temple to literacy in a highly literate (and highly affluent) community. It's a couple of blocks from Bloomsbury Books, one of Oregon's great bookstores, and within a paperback's throw of half-a-dozen specialty bookstores.

Still, some tourists toil up the stone steps, looking for further enlightenment, until they see a printed notice posted on the front door:

"This library (and all other libraries in Jackson County) is closed due to lack of funding."

As Virginia Woolf used to say, back to Bloomsbury.

The disappearance of the Jackson County library system, which checked itself out this spring after federal timber compensation money ended, may be an unsettling reminder to Ashland's other leading institution of enlightenment: Southern Oregon University, just a few blocks down Siskiyou Boulevard.

In Oregon, it turns out, books are no defense.

It's been a bumpy year at SOU as well: the loss of about 10 percent of the teaching staff, a larger proportion of the administration and the end of several departments. For new president Mary Cullinan, just arrived from the California State University system, it was "a difficult year," a baptism of firing.

"I certainly came to Oregon knowing Oregon had been disinvesting in higher education. Everybody in the country knows that," she says. "What I didn't realize, and I don't think anybody realized until we dug into it, was just how precarious we were."

The recent sharp increase in tuition to try to compensate for state cuts was one major problem for SOU, as at several other Oregon campuses. The new prices had the effect of scaring off prospective students, and causing those already enrolled to take fewer classes, which cut university revenues even more.

A large proportion of students at Southern Oregon, and the state's other regional universities, are first-generation college students, who find a big up-front bill daunting and a long-term debt unnerving. As Peg Blake, SOU's director of enrollment management, notes, "They don't come from backgrounds that know how to navigate a university system."

On the other hand, those students are a large part of the point of regional universities. When those institutions price themselves out, and run low on scholarship money, it's harder for them to keep themselves afloat—and to serve their regions.

"Students are dropping in and out, taking longer to graduate, and some are giving up," says Cullinan. "In southern Oregon, a lot of people aren't finishing a college degree."

That's an outcome that doesn't pencil out for anybody.

Last week, as the hillside campus baked in southern Oregon's summer temperatures, hundreds of incoming freshmen wandered the buildings, part of a gradual program to raise enrollment. SOU is overhauling its registration and counseling procedures and building its community connections. It has a strong arts program, drawing about a third of its students, and accounts for about 5 percent of the state system's student body.

Aside from the more specialized Oregon Tech in Klamath Falls, it's also the only state university for about 200 miles.

"Our students cannot pick up and go elsewhere," points out Cullinan. "Our students are highly place-bound."

Earlier this year, Cullinan spent a lot of time in Salem explaining this, working on the problem of being "out of the population area, out of the vision.

"There certainly were people who didn't understand why there were so many universities. I think the message began to get through."

The university system had a relatively good session at the Legislature, and the regionals ultimately got the $9 million that Gov. Ted Kulongoski had proposed and the Ways and Means co-chairs resisted. SOU also hopes to benefit from the governor's Shared Responsibility student support program, although the details are still unclear.

But this was just one session for a university, and a university system, with decades' worth of problems. It will take a while to build SOU's enrollment up and to strengthen programs, and while the session made a dent in its deferred maintenance bill, there's still a long way to go. Its theater building, opened 25 years ago when the program drew 30 students, now teems with an enrollment of 230, and money to expand the building didn't make it through the session.

The university system's overall faculty pay problems have a particular twist in Ashland, where housing prices have exploded over the past 20 years. New junior faculty are now invited to live in the student residence halls.

Building the university, and the Oregon university system, will be a long process, and it's not clear how long the Legislature has signed up for.

"If you're going to build a university system, you need continuity," says Cullinan. "I was in the California State system for 20 years. We weren't rich, but we felt that we would be OK over the next five years. We don't have that feeling in Oregon."

Looking at the past legislative session, says the president of Southern Oregon University, "We're very grateful. But we're not fixed."

And just a few blocks up Siskiyou Boulevard, there's a reminder of how a public institution—even a cherished and vital institution—can one day turn into a printed notice posted on a door.

THE OREGONIAN, JULY 15, 2007

U.S. News Numbers:

Rankings of the Oregon Universities Not Classy

The annual *U.S. News* ratings of "America's Best Colleges" is a kind of higher-education administrator porn.

Everybody disdains it, yet everybody seems to have it tucked away in his sock drawer.

The 2008 edition came out recently, and again, the Oregon public universities aren't exactly the cover girls of the magazine world.

In the *U.S. News* rankings of national universities, the University of Oregon is tied for 112th, right next to the University of Dayton—a ranking that's actually an improvement over last year. Oregon State is down among "third-tier" national universities, the only university in the Pac-10 in that group, while Portland State is "fourth tier," listed next to Oral Roberts University.

Things are no more encouraging among Oregon's regional universities. Among master's degree-granting universities in the West, Southern Oregon and Western Oregon are in the third tier, and Eastern Oregon in the fourth. Strikingly, the best ratings in the system are for Oregon Institute of Technology, ranking as the fourth-best "public baccalaureate college" in the West.

In other words, the Oregon University System has a ways to go.

MANDATORY DISCLAIMERS WHENEVER YOU QUOTE THE *U.S. NEWS* COLLEGE SURVEY RANKINGS:

1. All rankings are subjective and arbitrary, and is something like "alumni giving" really a way to rank a university, even if it's only 5 percent of the formula?
2. It's absurd to say a university is the 112th-best in the country, as opposed to being the 111th or 114th.
3. How important is appearance, anyway? What do we really know about Halle Berry's soul?

SOMETHING TO BEAR IN MIND BEFORE DISMISSING THE *U.S. NEWS* COLLEGE SURVEY RANKINGS:

State legislators, who are fundamentally responsible for higher-ed funding, are hardly the folks to conclude that what people think doesn't matter.

So, as anybody would do with a complaint about a grade, it's worth checking the numbers.

In peer assessment, the University of Oregon actually scores considerably higher than its 112th-place tie would suggest. It also does well in graduation rates. But it gets badly beaten up in the next three categories: faculty resources, student selectivity and financial resources.

"Faculty resources" consists mostly of faculty pay—which Oregon, of course, would rather not discuss at all—and class size. The U of O has a relatively low 39 percent of classes with fewer than 20 students and a relatively high 16 percent of classes of more than 50. It probably also didn't help that only 23 percent of its freshmen were in the top 10 percent of their high school graduating class.

Oregon State shows up worse in all of these categories and faces another complication. The university likes to talk of someday becoming a Top 25 engineering school, but the *U.S. News* Top 70 engineering schools—which does not include OSU—is an intimidating list, particularly heavy on West Coast universities. The list includes Washington (No. 20) and Washington State, plus five University of California campuses.

And even if Oregon State gets the public and private investment to move up, those Top 70 won't be waiting around—not even UC Santa Barbara.

By contrast, the University of Washington (tied for 42nd) has higher freshman retention and graduation rates (which may connect to its impressive 11:1 student faculty ratio) and is ranked a striking No. 29 in financial resources—ahead of places such as UC Berkeley and Georgetown.

Portland State and Oregon's regional universities are weighed down by low peer assessments and low graduation rates; Eastern Oregon's is 29 percent.

Meanwhile, *U.S. News'* list of top public master's-granting universities in the West includes Western Washington at No. 2, Evergreen State College at No. 4, and Central Washington and Eastern Washington tied for No. 12. The rest of the list is mostly a wide selection of California State universities, from Sonoma to Stanislaus.

The exact numbers may be pointless, even if they're going to be all over the universities' recruitment brochures. What matters is the underlying reality, which is that the Oregon universities—and Oregon—are competing nationally and regionally with places of greater reputation and investment, and in most ways we're not winning.

It's true that, like porn, the *U.S. News* assessments provide a somewhat distorted view of reality.

But it's also true that a lot of people watch.

THE OREGONIAN, SEPTEMBER 2, 2007

The Key College Ranking:

How Many Make it to College Oregon Education

For the past few months around here, people talking about college rankings have meant the University of Oregon football team. But every so often, different ways of ranking colleges slip into the news.

And sometimes, they can be just as sad.

"Oregon currently stands ahead of the nation in the percentage of students completing high school," calculated Jobs for the Future, a Boston-based think tank working on expanding educational and workforce opportunities, "but is one of the lowest-performing states in the percentage of recent high school graduates going on to college."

As Duck football fans often said recently: Ouch.

In its recent report, *Adding It Up: State Challenges for Increasing Access and Success*, Jobs for the Future makes a simple calculation: Take a state's percentage of students graduating from high school, multiply it by the percentage of high school graduates going on to higher education within a year, and you get a figure they call "Chance for College."

In the right light, the figure can look a lot like your state's future.

Oregon enters the formula reasonably well, with a 72 percent high school graduation rate, which may not be inspiring but is better than the national average of 68.8 percent. But only 45.5 percent of Oregon's high school graduates—well below the national average of 55.5 percent—immediately go on to further education.

Combining the two Oregon numbers gives the state a "Chance for College" rate of 32.8 percent, well below the national standard of 38.2 percent.

"Today, Oregon ranks on par with the nation in the percentage of adults 25-64 who have a college degree," says the report. "Assuming that current trends in college completion and in-migration of college-educated adults continue, Oregon is expected to fall behind the nation on this measure in 2025."

Oregon would rank even further behind California, and considerably behind Washington, currently and in 2025 a national leader in population percentage with a college degree.

This is the wrong direction to be going.

"When you're trying to attract new industries," says Travis Reindl, program director at Jobs for the Future, "their first question is, 'Do you have a work force ready to go? If we make the decision to locate a major financial group in Eugene or in Portland, will we have staffing problems?'"

States get to strong competitive positions in different ways. Washington and California also have low "Chance for College" rates, but they're the top states in the country in bachelor's degrees produced per 100 students enrolled.

Oregon is above average in that statistic but weighed down by its low high-school-to-college ratio. "You don't want to let higher education off the hook," says Reindl, "but there is a pretty urgent issue here on the handoff from high school to college.

"The research tells us that students who don't go on initially [to a two- or four-year college] face a greater likelihood that they won't ever go—or if they do go, a greater likelihood that they won't finish."

That leaves Oregon in a weaker position against states with more widely degreed populations—and by Reindl's calculations, states will increasingly face a wider competition than each other. His report's 2025 global projections estimate the best-performing nations at that time will have 55 percent of their adult populations with four-year degrees. (The report projects the United States that year at 45.9 percent, and Oregon at 43.8 percent.)

"If any state doesn't ramp up," Reindl says, "they'll find they're not just competing with Washington, they're competing with Ireland and [South] Korea."

During the last legislative session, Oregon made some progress on access with the Shared Responsibility program and some strengthening of its universities. But the state needs to make a major long-term course correction, and societies from Seattle to Seoul are not only ahead of us but moving fast.

Looking at the key college rankings of today—and of 2025—Oregon needs to realize that, just like the University of Oregon football team, it's playing a tough schedule.

And so far, not winning.

THE OREGONIAN, DECEMBER 16, 2007

Investment for a Future:

Commitment to Higher Ed Takes Sharp Bounces

It was a dramatic week, what with a major New York politician emerging from a severe political battering with a bold new theme that actually looks to a future.

No, not that New York politician.

Gov. Eliot Spitzer, who went from Golden Boy honeymoon to Can-this-marriage-be-saved in a New York minute, delivered his second State of the State speech, facing a moment of business and employment uncertainty, especially in the part of the state north of the New York City metropolitan area, and came up with a big-ticket solution:

Higher education.

With numbers sizable even for Wall Street.

Spitzer's speech, on Tuesday, demonstrated the great expectations, and commitment, that many states around the county are now putting into their university systems. "Competition in higher education is fierce, and not just for students," commented the *Boston Globe* about Spitzer's proposals. "States are also chasing first-class status for their public colleges and universities."

Around here, it reminds us again that other states see the opportunities, are way ahead of us and are investing heavily to move faster. Considering the size and wealth of New York, Spitzer's numbers may have no direct relevance to Oregon—although they do remind us that in national terms, the last Legislature's university budget increase amounted to something like a rounding error—but they should remind us how fast the higher-education track has become.

And how high the stakes.

"Higher-education funding should no longer be a budgetary pawn or a yearly battle," Spitzer told his legislators. "It must be a permanent priority."

To him, after a commission's warning that New York was "losing ground in an intensifying global competition for pre-eminence in the knowledge economy," that means hiring 2,000 more faculty for the system, including 250 world-class professors.

"We must create an Innovation Fund for cutting-edge research at New York's public and private colleges, similar to the National Science Foundation and the National Institutes of Health," he proposed. "Supercharging academic cutting-edge research will also supercharge our innovation economy."

To do all this, Spitzer wants a $4 billion endowment for the state system—even if his plan for getting it by rejiggering the state lottery system may be a PhD-level version of three-card monte.

And there's a double objective here: "Made wisely, these investments will also revitalize cities." Specifically, that means expanding the University at Buffalo with a new downtown health sciences campus, "a centerpiece of our strategy to reinvigorate the economy of western New York."

Because it really does work that way.

As the *Boston Globe* said about Spitzer's plan, strong institutions bring in federal research funds, which "translate into jobs and innovation."

Meanwhile, last week, in an economically hurting part of Oregon, Eastern Oregon University announced it would cut $4.1 million over the next three years and drop 17 faculty. Without dismissing the budget calculations involved, it's going to be harder to use the words "EOU" and "economic engine" in the same sentence, in a county that would really like to hear one.

Still, the month did see one world-class manifestation in Oregon higher education: The University of Oregon announced plans for its new $200 million basketball arena, using almost as much state bonding capacity as the entire two-year Oregon University System academic capital budget.

U of O people point out quickly, and rightly, that the two numbers are not comparable, that the Ducks plan to pay off their own state bonds with contributions and big-dollar basketball season tickets, backed by Nike founder Phil Knight's $100 million Duck sports endowment.

The numbers may well pencil out (depending on how often groups like Barenaked Ladies want to play Eugene) and if Duck basketball fans and Knight want to pay for it, that's their lookout—especially since Knight has already been considerably more generous to U of O academics than the Legislature.

And if it does raise some questions about state priorities, maybe it can serve as an encouraging example. After all, according to legend, a former president of the University of Oklahoma once said, "I want a university the football team can be proud of."

Or that won't embarrass the basketball arena.

THE OREGONIAN, JANUARY 13, 2008

Investing in Education and Community:

Public-Private Partnerships Could Help Portland Students

Cities all across America, facing declining school enrollments, loss of families and the need for an educated workforce, are trying a different way to use their public schools: help kids when they get out of them.

Local scholarship programs for a city's high school graduates, drawing from private, public or mixed funding, have appeared from Pittsburgh, Pa., to Hammond, Ind., to Kalamazoo, Mich. A conference on the subject this summer, by the W.E. Upjohn Institute for Employment Research, has 50 communities from 27 states interested so far.

Kalamazoo in summer may not be a destination resort, but maybe Portland should sign up, if only to find out why so many other places are.

The programs come in all shapes and sizes. In the Kalamazoo Promise, anonymous private contributors put up the money to guarantee tuition at Michigan public universities and colleges to the city's graduates. In 2006, the University of Pittsburgh medical school, in fear of ending up alone in the middle of a dying city, pledged $100 million for tuition to any state university for Pittsburgh high school graduates.

Hammond, a Chicago suburb worrying about losing its middle class, committed a quarter of its casino revenues to tuition grants for Indiana public or private colleges for graduates whose families own houses in the city. A tuition aid program now covers three high schools in Denver, and in Greeley, Colo., a local car dealer has started a program to allow all Greeley graduates to attend the local community college.

It's early to assess any effects of what the *Chicago Tribune* calls "a nationwide movement"; many of the programs are barely in place yet. But several signs seem to be surfacing that the programs may approach the goals in mind. Enrollment is up in the public schools involved—up 11 percent in Kalamazoo (the only such growth in any Michigan urban school system), up by 500 students in the three Denver high schools, and increasing in Hammond, where the mayor calls the program "the most positive thing we've ever done." Hardly anything is as powerful an attractor into a school system as a realistic prospect of college.

In Kalamazoo, the proportion of graduates attending college is up considerably, with 60 percent of those getting help from the program returning for their second year in college. In El Dorado, Ark., where a local oil company underwrote a program, the proportion of El Dorado high school graduates going on to college rose from 55 percent to 83 percent.

Consistently, those involved don't see the programs as charity; they see them as economic development efforts. Danette Gerald, assistant director of higher-education policy at the Education Trust in Washington, D.C., told the *Pittsburgh Post-Gazette*, "It's a matter of global competitiveness."

Last week, Parker Hydraulic, a major employer in Kalamazoo, told the *Kalamazoo Gazette* that the Promise made it easier to recruit employees nationally.

It's enough to draw that crowd of 50 communities to the Upjohn Institute conference this summer, which focuses on tuition support as an economic development strategy. "We've gotten a lot of calls, and so have the communities trying to do this," Upjohn's Sarah Klerk says. "Every city has started in a different way."

It should be enough to stir interest in Portland, a city with a healthy economy and a shrinking public school system, in a state where middle-aged Oregonians are more likely to have college educations than young adults, and the projected population growth is among groups with low traditions of higher education.

There might be a particular appeal to a program that would draw kids into the public school system, help more of them to get to college and—because it deals with graduates of local high schools and local colleges—have a strong chance they would stay here after graduation.

It's not like tens of millions of dollars are going to drop out of the sky for a Pittsburgh-style program. But at a time when the city runs budget surpluses and local businesses express extreme concern about higher education and the local workforce, there might be a way to get started.

"I think you could get some support from the business community on this," says Mark Edlen, a partner in Gerding Edlen Development and a higher-education advocate, who says he's been discussing the idea with some other businessmen.

"Could you get $100 million? No. Could you find some seed money to get it started? Probably."

Then there's the city itself, which has both some resources and a rising feeling that its future will seep out of its classrooms.

"I think it's a fantastic idea, and one that I would want to pursue if I were elected," Sam Adams, city commissioner and candidate for mayor, says. Adams would see it as part of a Knowledge City strategy, creating a continuum of educational opportunities and attacking the problem of too few of Portland's eighth-graders ending up graduating from high school. The city should, he argues, also expand routes into skilled trades for graduates wanting to move in that direction.

The strengthening of Portland's educational position, Adams points out, is vital to its economic strategy: "It turns the competitive equation on its head."

The impact of this kind of program on the city's schools could be equally dramatic.

"I think it would be a wonderful motivator," says Barbara K. Rommel, superintendent of the David Douglas school district in East Portland, who finds that many of her students never imagine higher education as an option. "It could be a possibility that would be presented to students at least by middle-school age, when they start to make choices."

Even on a pilot basis, a tuition-support program would create a challenge and opportunities for Portland State University, as well as Portland Community College. PSU, already the largest university in Oregon with an enrollment of 25,000, would find itself with new, unexpected students, as well as the responsibility to help them succeed—a mission that might require a broader PSU role in Portland education.

Western Michigan University, about the same size as PSU, has gotten about a third of Kalamazoo Promise students—more than any institution except Kalamazoo Valley Community College—and has been deeply involved in the program.

"It doesn't work until the university reaches down into the schools," says Lindsay Desrochers, PSU vice president for finance and administration, who worked in a similar operation in California. "We have to get proactive, and the university has to take some responsibility here."

But taking that direction, Desrochers argues, could be a useful PSU investment in itself. PSU is growing now, she points out, but Oregon's population growth is occurring among groups, especially Latinos, now minimally involved in higher education.

Without an effort to face that, she warns, "Ten years from now we're going to be sitting here wondering, 'Where are the students?'"

Besides population shifts, Portland is approaching another historic change. The city's about to get a new mayor, Portland State is about to get a new president, Portland Public Schools has a new superintendent and it could be a moment for a new direction of their common future.

"It's feeling to me like maybe, for the first time in 20 years," Edlen speculates, "we have the sun and moon lined up to block out how we invest back into our community."

At Western Michigan University, Jim Bosco, after decades as an education professor, came out of retirement to oversee the university's involvement, which includes sending nursing and social work students, and mentors and tutors, into Kalamazoo schools, as well as programs for the students who get to WMU. "To get them to college is one thing, but that's not the prize," Bosco says. "The prize is if they're successful in college."

Students and faculty, he says, are drawn into the effort, both out of a sense that "it's the right thing to do" and the scope of what's involved.

"It's not a scholarship program," Bosco says about the Kalamazoo Promise. "It involves a scholarship program, but for those of us involved in it, it's an effort to transform our community."

THE OREGONIAN, JANUARY 27, 2008

Education:

Oregon Could Learn from the Celtic Tiger

Over the last year, Jeff Cogen has taken a long trip and a short trip, but they both took him to the same place:

The certainty that Portland and Oregon need to do a lot more to give their kids a chance to go to college.

Last fall, the Multnomah County commissioner went on a German Marshall Plan trip to Europe, looking at education and work-force development. What he saw seemed a long distance from Oregon.

"It seemed somewhere between amazing and depressing," Cogen recalls, "because they're so much smarter than we are in making investments."

He was particularly struck by Ireland, which some years ago found itself an impoverished outer corner of Europe with a high school dropout rate of 20 percent. (Oregon, with a graduation rate of 71 percent, might be thrilled by that number, but the Irish were alarmed.) After considering various educational investments, says Cogen, "Ireland decided the thing to do was make college free and motivate kids to do well in high school."

As a result, the dropout rate declined, and, combined with some targeted tax breaks, the strategy produced an Irish economy now nicknamed the Celtic Tiger.

The lesson was, notes Cogen, "The ability to view the future with hope affects how you perform at earlier ages."

The lesson was reinforced on another trip, which didn't require a passport or even leaving the city limits. When Mayor Tom Potter moved operations up to Jefferson High School for a week, Cogen went along to talk with some students and remembered talking to one girl in particular.

"I asked, 'Are you thinking about college?' and she said, 'No one from my family has ever gone to college. I wouldn't know how.'"

"We're losing so much by not asking these kids to consider the possibility they can do this," Cogen says. "If there was a sense that there were resources available to get people into college, high schools would work on that."

Now, Cogen has produced a report proposing an Oregon Hope Initiative, to cover tuition costs and raise the number of Oregonians making it into and through college. It's based on programs from 14 other states, notably Georgia and Tennessee, which have set aside money to send more of their kids to college, and from all accounts have benefited from it.

The report notes a couple of interesting points, suggesting that this wouldn't be a bad place for the state to invest some money.

Despite constantly mounting evidence of the importance of college, both for individuals and for local economies, the percentage of Oregon high school graduates heading into the Oregon university system has stayed pretty steady over the past decade, running between 20 percent and 24 percent, now sitting at 20.5 percent. It's not a formula for local economic explosion.

Also, "After a four-year program ramp-up, the ongoing annual cost of a free tuition program—assuming it covered all students going straight from Oregon high schools into Oregon public colleges and universities—

would be $272 million." It's a large number but not an unimaginable one; currently the Oregon Opportunity Grant program goes to $72 million. The difference gets smaller when the program is limited to students with 3.2 GPAs, and/or family incomes less than $60,000—pick your own number. Stanford last week announced it wouldn't charge for tuition or room and board to students from families earning less than $60,000, and wouldn't collect any tuition from families making less than $100,000.

It was a striking week for that announcement. Tuesday, the Brookings Institution and the Pew Charitable Trusts released a report finding that economic mobility was stagnating with college access, that while lower-income and minority students could still raise their prospects through college, getting there was getting harder and harder.

"A growing difference in education levels between income and racial groups, especially in college degrees, implies that mobility will be lower in the future than it is today," Ron Haskins, a former Republican official and welfare expert, told the *New York Times.*

It's not a heartening message for a state, and a city, where population growth will be largely among minorities.

Even low-cost routes to higher education are getting steeper; a report last week from the Institute for College Access and Success found that last year financial aid applications for community colleges rose 37 percent.

To Cogen, changing those numbers in Oregon also would change other local numbers.

"It would spur a stronger local economy. To the extent that we can bring our work force up to a higher level, we have a greater chance of recruiting higher-income jobs," he points out.

"We're never going to be a corporate headquarters city. What we're going to have to be is an entrepreneurial city, creating new jobs."

To the U.S. Census Bureau, the connection between educational level and economic success seems pretty direct. The five cities with the highest proportion of over-25 residents with bachelor degrees have stayed steady for two years: Seattle (52.7 percent); San Francisco (50.1 percent); Raleigh, N.C. (50.1 percent); Washington, D.C., (45.3 percent) and Austin, Texas, (44.1 percent.) They're also all on the list of the top 25 per capita incomes, with San Francisco fourth ($57,496) and Seattle eighth ($49,297).

Portland is 13th in educational level (38.8 percent), trailing not only Seattle and San Francisco but also San Diego and Denver, and trailing all in income ($42,287). There is room for improvement—and from all indications, there is a way to get there.

"If we get up to Seattle levels," says Cogen confidently, "we could see Seattle-level prosperity."

That might be a lot to aim for: Seattle, after all, has Microsoft, Boeing and the University of Washington.

But at least we might get closer to Ireland.

THE OREGONIAN, FEBRUARY 24, 2008

Presidential Politics:
Clinton Gets It: Kids Need Access to College

EUGENE—Over the long history of campaign promises, this one might actually be new.

"I would get rid of the FAFSA," Hillary Clinton declared at South Eugene High School last weekend. "That is the cruelest joke in the world."

FAFSA, which may not be a household word but was immediately recognizable to the Eugene high school/college audience, is the Free Application for Federal Student Aid. It goes on for eight pages, including several sections that might be most successfully filled out by your accountant—although if you have an accountant, you're probably not the typical applicant for financial aid.

High schools run seminars and workshops in how to fill it out, time that could go to SAT prep or algebra homework. Still, unlike the Form 1040 that it closely resembles, the FAFSA lacks the motivation that not quite finishing it can send you to jail.

It's a classic example of how systems set up to provide access turn into barriers themselves.

"Get rid of it," Clinton told the crowd again. "Get a box you can check on your tax form."

This is an idea that makes so much sense that you wonder what it's doing in a presidential campaign. It makes you think, for just a moment, that politics could actually be about solving problems, or at least making them a little more manageable.

"I think we can streamline and simplify the college aid and loan process," Clinton said afterward in an interview. "The FAFSA form is a perfect symbol. My staff calculated people spend 100 million hours a year trying to fill the forms out."

The word that comes to mind here is not "productive." And for a lot of families, the word that comes to mind isn't "successful," either.

"It truly is a daunting task for families to take on," says Roberta Cooper, who is in charge of college counseling at Portland's Madison High School.

"It is a big task, especially for kids in lower socio-economic circumstances, especially when the parents are working two or three jobs and aren't around much. Then it becomes the student's task, and getting family financial information is a horrible task."

And another roadblock in front of kids the system is supposed to be trying to help.

Clinton isn't the only presidential candidate who talks about college access, a situation that has been strikingly stagnant over a decade when the need for it has become steadily more inescapable. But she talks about college, and the way a system providing opportunity ought to work—a lot.

In an interview before she got to Oregon, she talked about the issue as one of her real educational experiences on the campaign trail.

"When I first started out, back in February, March of last year, I was not as aware as I might have been about the depth of feeling concerning college affordability," said Clinton. "It brings people to their feet. They stand up and cheer when I talk about making college affordable, because it is a huge burden on most middle-class and working-class families."

At campaign events in places like Eugene, Clinton often asks the crowd what kind of college-loan interest rates they're paying. She asks who's paying 25 percent, and hands go up. She asks who's paying a rate higher than that, and hands go up again.

"The outrageous interest rates charged by the student loan companies are totally beyond the pale," she says over the phone. "When we have historically low interest rates, it's a ripoff."

In Eugene, Clinton's last question came from a woman high up in the stands, who said at the outset that she didn't need a microphone. She asked about reversing a Reagan-era change in federal rules that changed the age when a student applying for financial aid could declare herself financially independent of her parents.

It's a technical issue—unless you're the student.

Clinton said that it sounded like a reasonable idea, that the whole point of federal college policies should be to give a better chance to "kids who are doing the best they can."

That could be done a lot better than it is.

"So much of what we're doing is steering college attendance toward the wealthy," she told the student up in the bleachers. "You go from campus to campus, and you find that most students are from families making over $100,000."

Which is not an encouraging direction.

But if we think that the system is important, that we're not doing enough to provide college opportunities and get barriers out of the way, that in the 21st century it's going to be a problem that European and some Asian countries are raising their college education levels right past us, it's not a bad thing to talk about during a presidential campaign.

It's even worth talking about the FAFSA form.

After all, it's a lot easier to talk about than fill out.

THE OREGONIAN, APRIL 13, 2008

6. Percentage of income needed to pay for college after aid

Rank	State	Percentage of income needed to pay for college minus financial aid, public 4-yr, 2007-08
1	Pennsylvania	41.1
2	Ohio	39.0
2	Vermont	39.0
4	Delaware	37.1
5	Rhode Island	36.1
6	Oregon	36.0
7	New Hampshire	35.8
8	Maine	35.6
9	Illinois	35.4
10	North Dakota	34.2
11	New Jersey	34.1
12	Alabama	33.7
12	Michigan	33.7
14	Iowa	32.6
15	Massachusetts	32.4
16	Montana	31.5
17	Washington	31.1
18	Colorado	30.3
18	Minnesota	30.3
20	Indiana	30.0
20	Wisconsin	30.0
22	Connecticut	29.4
23	Missouri	28.9
24	Virginia	28.6
25	California	27.9
	United States	27.8

Rank	State	Percentage of income needed to pay for college minus financial aid, public 4-yr, 2007-08
26	Kansas	27.5
26	Kentucky	27.5
28	New York	27.3
29	Hawaii	27.1
30	Nebraska	26.7
30	Nevada	26.7
32	Texas	26.3
33	Maryland	25.3
34	South Carolina	25.2
35	Oklahoma	25.1
36	Alaska	24.9
36	West Virginia	24.9
38	Idaho	24.2
39	Arizona	24.0
40	Mississippi	23.4
41	North Carolina	23.0
42	South Dakota	22.4
43	Utah	20.9
44	New Mexico	20.7
45	Arkansas	19.5
46	Florida	18.3
47	Georgia	14.8
48	Wyoming	14.7
49	Louisiana	13.7
50	Tennessee	12.6

SOURCE: *Measuring Up 2008.*

Percentage of family income needed to pay for college after financial aid has been given; public 4-year institutions, 2005-2006.

E-Board Education:
Facing Another Lowering of Higher Ed

With the uncertainty in the economy, and the difficulty in projecting Oregon state revenues over the next year, you could see why it's a rough time for Oregon to make a real investment in higher education.

Of course, in Oregon, it always is.

You don't get to be 46th in the country in state support of universities by accident.

This month's round of university-squeezing is about higher-ed money overseen by the Emergency Board. The "salary pool" contains $125 million, about $28 million of it bound for higher education. Gov. Ted Kulongoski's office says he will request that the board release the entire amount to agencies, but reports out of Salem say the E-Board is thinking of holding some back.

There are a couple of things the E-Board should bear in mind as it considers excuses not to reach for the wallet when this month's check comes around.

First, this no longer has anything to do with the size of salaries. Universities have to make those calls long before legislative bodies finish mulling. Any higher-ed shortfall at the end of this month ends up cutting programs, not pay raises.

Second, after last year's Legislature, considerable numbers of new students are enrolling in the system, and they might consider program and class cuts to be something of a breach of faith.

The University of Oregon has 800 more freshmen showing up next year than it ever imagined, and it's combing Eugene for places for them to sleep. Meanwhile, with the 2007-08 academic year ending last week, the university doesn't know how much money it will have to teach them in the fall.

"It's a terrible dilemma," says U of O President Dave Frohnmayer, who has declared next year his last one for putting up with these kinds of dilemmas.

"We can't do it without the extra money. Our faculty are very much concerned about this."

Oregon State's projected enrollment for next year is up 2 percent, part of a steady upward curve. But maybe because of the Legislature's new investment in the Shared Responsibility scholarship effort last year, next year's enrollment is up 8 percent among students filing the federal scholarship application form. It's greatly in the interest of Oregon State—and Oregon—to attract and retain such students, and not to be telling them that reduced offerings require them to finance another quarter or two.

Similarly, Portland State projects an enrollment increase of 3.85 percent, with a 9.5 percent increase in freshmen right out of high school.

Darned kids always do what you tell them to do.

Three key members of the Emergency Board cite the uncertainty of the economy, but insist they have higher education's situation in mind.

"There will be no program cuts. There shouldn't be any at all," promises state Sen. Kurt Schrader, D-Canby, co-chair of the Ways and Means Committee and also Democratic nominee for Congress from the district including Oregon State. Moreover, "I'm not asking them to hold positions open. We've identified other savings."

House Speaker (and Democratic U.S. Senate nominee) Jeff Merkley cites the considerable uncertainty of the economy, but says, "I am determined that we do everything possible to maximize what we can give to higher education, but in a fiscally responsible manner . . . If we don't get completely to 100 percent [of higher-ed funding], my hope is we'll complete that the next time."

On the other hand, universities need to complete their budgets July 1.

Says Senate President Peter Courtney, D-Salem, "There is some concern. We've got to watch the economy," and he notes there's two weeks of economy-watching before the E-Board makes its call.

Still, he'll be discussing it this weekend with the governor—at the Western Oregon University commencement.

Nobody knows what's going on with this economy, and higher education isn't the only part of state government with E-Board issues. But last year, legislators made an effort to start to rebuild a system that had fallen far down the national rankings, and it seems that a sizable number of Oregon high school graduates took them seriously.

And just about the first thing you learn in school, way at the beginning of all those years that brought those freshmen to Oregon university campuses, is that E is supposed to stand for Effort.

THE OREGONIAN, JUNE 15, 2008

Thinking Big for Oregon:
Save the Future

CENTRAL POINT—It's a big idea, bigger than you might expect to come out of a small, squat building a block off the main drag in this southern Oregon town. It involves an amount of money, and a number of people, more common to the computerized scorings of Salem than the thinking of Central Point.

But it's no bigger than what the people at the Rogue Valley Council of Governments think their region—and their state—desperately needs.

"Oregon invests in fixing potholes, not in changing paradigms," says Ron Fox, executive director of Southern Oregon Regional Economic Development Inc. "If you think of it, Oregon is West Virginia with a beach. It's a pretty scary future we have in terms of the global market."

So Fox and the other folks represented in this regional council of governments—nonprofits, chambers of commerce, education groups—came up with an idea:

Two years' free tuition at any Oregon public university or community college for any Oregon high school graduate. The state would issue bonds to cover the costs and get its money back when income tax revenues rise because better-educated Oregonians make more money.

In other words, when a young Oregonian becomes a nurse or a welder, or goes on to university instead of setting on a career in fast food, the state will be taking higher income-tax revenues from him or her for the next four decades. The idea is something like urban renewal, except that instead of investing in a piece of geography to produce future tax returns, this play would invest in a generation.

Admittedly, the numbers need running.

"I love the idea," says Rep. Peter Buckley, D-Ashland, chairman of the House Education Committee. "The Legislative Fiscal Office is working to see if it could realistically pencil out. Hopefully, we'll get an idea in July or August and be able to shop it for the 2009 Legislature.

"I explained it to the governor, and his eyes got big, and he said, 'Could we make it work?'"

The people behind the idea admit they don't know that. What they know is that the state needs to do something, something big, before it falls further back in global competitiveness and loses a hunk of another generation.

"Big dreams, big ideas come from southern Oregon," Fox says. "It's that 'state of Jefferson' idea," the 1930s dream of southern Oregon and northernmost California spinning off from their state capital controls and just going off by themselves.

This isn't the kind of thing the group typically thinks about. In the past, the Rogue Valley group has focused on losing kids to drugs, housing that locals could actually afford and work-force preparedness. When they thought about strategies such as getting a little more money for schools, it seemed clear that any little bit they could dig up would just be squeezed from someplace else.

Then they thought about this idea, which could produce a better-prepared work force, one more able to afford housing, and give kids the idea that their lives could actually have a different possibility.

"It just addresses all the issues, and it's market-driven," Fox says. "The money goes not to the universities—the students make the call. It imbues the kids with a different bargaining position.

"If this isn't one of the best investments, long-term, that Oregon could make, I don't know what is."

Maybe because they're close to the state border, they got the funding idea from California, which voted to issue $3 billion in bonds for stem-cell research. If you know the future is coming, you might as well invest to meet it.

They didn't need California to tell them Oregon has a problem. In 1991, the state paid 73.7 percent of the costs of public higher education; families paid 26.3 percent. Now the two percentages are even, and middle-aged Oregonians are more likely to have a degree than Oregonians under 35.

Oregon is below the national average in percentage with a degree, percentage of high school graduates going directly on to college and percentage of college students who graduate in three years (associate degree) or six years (bachelor's). It's also above the national average in percentage of median family income needed to pay for college costs—and outside the Portland metro area, and Benton and Deschutes counties, the disparity gapes even wider.

But Oregon is in the top third of the country in percentage of the work force in high-tech jobs.

The pipeline isn't connecting. And looking around southern Oregon, the group found a lot of other job pipelines weren't connected. By their calculation, it would take at least 65 to 70 percent of high school graduates getting at least a two-year technical degree for Oregon to be globally competitive.

"We thought about a pilot program at the local level," Michael Cavallaro, executive director of the Rogue Valley Council of Governments, says. "Then we decided we can't fool around and should go to the state level."

After all, if you've got a big problem, go big to try to fix it.

But that's a problem in itself, because in Oregon, we don't do big any more. We're too busy admiring the old pictures of us with Tom McCall to remember the last time we tried to do something big to change the nature of the state—maybe the Oregon Health Plan 15 years ago, admittedly not a great reference.

Instead, we try to face major changes with small adjustments, and the gap between who we are and who we hope to be gets steadily wider.

Maybe this is why this idea, whether it pencils out or not, comes from southern Oregon.

Maybe they're too far from Salem to realize we don't do this kind of thing any more.

THE OREGONIAN, JULY 27, 2008

Emerald Opportunity:
Oregon Higher Ed Has Reason to Get Its Irish Up

Nike World Headquarters, built on the power of statistics and the idea that effort equals success, may have been the ideal place to set up the charts. At the Tiger Woods Center on Monday, a poster loomed over the roomful of higher-education executives:

In 1991, Ireland spent $8,360 in U.S. dollars per student in public higher education; Oregon spent $7,086. By 2006, in inflation-adjusted dollars, Ireland was spending nearly twice as much, $15,457, while Oregon was spending more than a third less, $4,615.

That's part of why people call the Irish economy the Celtic Tiger. And why hardly anybody calls Oregon's economy the Soggy Tiger.

The occasion was the fourth meeting of IAHERO, the Irish American Higher Education Research Organization. After gatherings in Dublin, Washington and Galway, it made it this year to Portland, allowing for a comparison of two places about the same size (Ireland, pop. 4.2 million; Oregon, pop. 3.7 million).

Several years ago, Ireland ended college tuition fees. Over the past decades, the country has had a massive increase in its college attendance and graduation rate. Other numbers on display this week showed that 41.8 percent of Irish over 25 have a bachelor's degree, while Oregon's number is 27.5 percent—and as Jim Francesconi of the state Board of Higher Education pointed out, it's only that high because of educated emigres from other states moving here. And our numbers are going in the wrong direction.

"At most OECD [Organization for Economic Cooperation and Development, mostly Europe plus North America, Australia and New Zealand] countries, levels of education are rising, in some cases rapidly," Oregon's higher-education chancellor, George Pernsteiner, said Monday. "Oregon is one of two states in which the education of younger people is lower than their parents, in some cases lower than their grandparents, reversing a thousand-year trend."

It always makes you nervous when Oregon educational trends make you think of Stonehenge.

There are a range of buts involved: Ireland emphasizes access over research, and Oregon is still a better place to get an advanced degree. Oregon's college enrollment has also been rising, and through tuition, philanthropy and federal aid, Oregon's universities are a lot better than their state support would suggest.

Still, there are reasons why Irish eyes—and lots of other European eyes—are smiling.

"There is a very high consensus in Ireland," said Tom Boland, CEO of Ireland's Higher Education Authority, "right across social and economic divisions, about the importance of education, especially higher education."

If this could be exported, it could be way more popular than Guinness. And it does indeed turn out that if you make college education available, people will show up for it. Offer it and they will come.

For Ireland, that has meant a college enrollment virtually doubling since 1990, and a considerable increase from populations not previously well represented in higher education.

As Boland said of the sharp increase, "I'm not sure Ireland did it intentionally"; the system just responded to the turnout. Or, as Philip Nolan, vice president for academic affairs at Trinity College Dublin, explained, working off the culture of the corporate host, "It wasn't that we just did it; it just happened."

And elected leadership can put up more than checks. "Government can never provide enough money for higher education," said Ned Costello of Ireland's Higher Education Authority, "but it can provide certainty."

Which would be the single element most consistently missing from Oregon higher-education planning. For 20 years, the state system has been on a Salem-centered roller coaster, occasionally inching up only to hurtle down, making it difficult for institutions to plan and for students to believe.

But it turns out, from Irish evidence, that making higher education consistently available will cause students to show up, and that the next people to show up will be companies looking to hire them. And when the supporters of higher education are told, as they always are in Salem, that it's not that good an investment, there's now an obvious response:

Put a Cork in it.

THE OREGONIAN, SEPTEMBER 17, 2008

College Track:
Marathon Run for Education

In a time as bleak as a moonscape in March, there is still Ruth Zagorodny.

As it's become inescapable that we've blown the last six years on bad decisions and worse behavior, that we're leaving the next generations a legacy of trillions in debt, a mountain of receipts for the party and vague advice to make something of themselves, Zagorodny sits in Willamette Park, her eyes full of a 15-year-old's intoxication with possibility.

Recent years will be investigated by prosecutors, FBI agents and disbelieving historians, but they brought her an opportunity she hadn't expected.

"I never thought about college," explains Zagorodny, daughter of Ukrainian immigrants. Now, "I know I'm going to college. It's the opportunity of your life. People don't usually get a chance like this."

If you need something to look at besides bankrupt bankers, there's Ruth Zagorodny, and the program that gives her the opportunity.

Dan Blaufus, now a lawyer at Nike, spent 12 years teaching high school, the last four of them while also in law school. When he finished, and went to a Portland corporate law firm, he was "suddenly rubbing shoulders with people who knew the system. I envisioned a kid without financial advantages [having] someone who went to an Ivy League school and could mentor a kid in how to do it."

His idea was to give kids both an idea of how the system works and some financial help. "I had a kid, and I was saving for her college," he remembers, "and I said, 'What if I pretended I had another kid?'"

Shortly afterward, he went running with Jeff Cronn, another lawyer, who confided that he and his wife were looking for something to do to help kids. And on Sept. 11, 2002, Blaufus went down to Salem to charter Marathon Education Partners.

Partners would be connected with a fourth-grader, nominated by the student's school, and would put $100 a month into a college fund. They would also be in touch with the student once a month, providing encouragement and ways to maneuver through the system, and Marathon would help with some summer programs. It started with four couples.

Last weekend, partners, families and 50 of the program's 58 current students came to Marathon's annual picnic in Willamette Park, to eat hot dogs and hear some of the students tell about summer programs at the University of Oregon, and why they get up every Saturday of the school year to go sit in another classroom. The first students in the program, like Zagorodny, are now high school sophomores, but high school sophomores on a rather different trajectory than they might have expected.

"It's more than just the whole money thing," says Adrian Mayoral, a sophomore at Cleveland who's into heavy metal and computers, right after explaining to a crowd of 150 what he did last summer.

"I'm getting familiar with the college lifestyle. I've been thinking about college since the sixth grade."

For example, on the idea that colleges like students who volunteer in high school, he's been serving dinner at the St. Francis Dining Hall, and working on a mural in his Southeast Portland neighborhood. As a college admissions strategy, it's not exactly a secret; it's just something that some people know and some people don't.

Now, a few more kids do.

Nationally, it was a bleak weekend, followed by a bleaker week. The kids sitting in Willamette Park are having a few more hundred billions in national debt dumped on them, part of a bill that has doubled just since the sixth-graders started school. As we bequeath them the hideous mess we've created, it does seem we could at least give them enough education to help them pay the bills we're sending them.

Oregon, as a state, is making an effort in this direction. It's expanded its college assistance program, and on Friday, the Legislative Emergency Board came up with $4 million more to match the larger-than-expected participation in the Oregon Opportunity Program. (Students may not all have the college strategic tips, but they're not dumb.) But as the meeting of the Irish American Higher Education Research Organization earlier this month in Portland pointed out, the state is still falling behind other states, not to mention other nations in the Organization for Economic Cooperation and Development.

Discouragement all around.

Except in Willamette Park, where a lot of people looked encouraged.

"When you get together at one of our events, there's an energy and a glow to it that's highly motivating," says Jeff Cronn, Blaufus' partner in running and Marathon (www.higheredforkids.org).

Marathon's immediate goal is to get to 100 scholars involved by 2010. The broader goal is putting a lot more kids into a situation where college becomes a matter of when, not if.

"We are motivated by looking at the education gap in Oregon," says Cronn. "There's a whole group of kids being left out, and that's not good for them and not good for Oregon.

"We're leaving good, qualified kids along the side of the road, and going about our business."

To start with, that seems like a waste.

After everything else that's been happening to America's younger generation over the past week, it also looks like a dirty trick.

THE OREGONIAN, SEPTEMBER 28, 2008

Higher Education:
A Quick Way to Connect Jobs to Relief and a Route to the Future

Ted Kulongoski has something to tell Barack Obama—and may even get a chance to do it.

And it's actually a terrific idea.

Tuesday, Obama's people are meeting with governors to talk about how he can work with them to take on the economic collapse. That by itself is a pretty good idea, compared with the Bush administration's frequent attitude that the states' problems weren't the feds' problems. Now, with most states in severe budget straits as next January's legislative sessions approach, billions in cuts in education, health care and other services hang over the economy like a giant other shoe waiting to drop.

Actually, like 50 giant other shoes waiting to drop.

Almost as soon as Obama becomes president—congressional Democrats are talking about having something waiting on his desk when he returns from the inauguration—he wants to launch a huge stimulus package in the range of hundreds of billions of dollars. The challenge is to get the money into the economy as quickly as possible, while also creating jobs and producing something more permanent than credit card receipts.

So last week, the Oregon governor wrote the three co-chairmen of the Obama transition team suggesting that "the fastest, most effective economic stimulus the federal government can provide to all 50 states is an investment in deferred maintenance projects on university campuses across the nation."

It puts people to work, it's an investment in higher education (considerably useful when we get to the other side of this collapse) and it can happen quickly.

"I don't want to look away from transportation projects, but the problem is, that's two or three years of planning down the road," Kulongoski said last week. With higher education's deferred maintenance projects, "I don't have to buy land, I don't have to get land-use environmental impact permits."

And we don't have to wait until the ceiling falls in on a chemistry class.

Kulongoski says Oregon higher education, including Oregon Health & Science University, now has $660 million in deferred maintenance projects. These are not overdue paint jobs.

"Generally, the institutions are being told by someone that the places are unsafe," Kulongoski said. "They have to defer using the areas as class space," at a time when enrollment is booming.

And although Oregon may be one of the nation's more extreme examples, it's hardly alone. With state higher-ed systems squeezed across the country, there's a powerful urge to try to go a little longer with the 1920s-era insulation in the administration building—even if students report a funny smell and a tickling feeling in their throats.

There will be a lot of states on Kulongoski's side on this idea.

Last week, shortly after sending the letter, Kulongoski received a call from Valerie Jarrett, one of the transition co-chairs and a long-time close adviser to Obama, inviting him to the meeting on Tuesday in Philadelphia. When he brought up the idea, Kulongoski reported, "She said, 'You may get a chance to talk to somebody about that.'"

We might hope for a particular responsiveness from Obama on this issue. Not only did he personally use higher education to dramatically change his life prospects, but Obama spent years teaching law at the University of Chicago, making him the first professor-president since Woodrow Wilson.

(True, Bill Clinton spent a couple of years teaching law while deciding what to run for, but he probably didn't spend much time around the faculty lounge.)

Monday, before heading to Philadelphia, Kulongoski presents his proposed 2007-09 budget, reflecting the sharp drop in projected state revenues. He's trying to limit the damage.

"I have said consistently that the education issue is the highest issue," he said. "Every employer I talk to talks about work force. If I can't provide that work force, which is the fuel for the economy, I'll never be able to generate the revenues to do everything else the public wants me to do."

States all across the country are feeling a crunch on their higher-ed systems, just when demand is up and the need gets ever sharper. Kulongoski's idea could ease some of that pressure, while swiftly creating construction jobs and giving the states a chance to demonstrate new green technologies.

It could also help address a festering vulnerability in Oregon higher-education buildings—half of the state's property—and similar problems across the country.

When we talk about the roof falling in on Oregon higher education, it's not always a figure of speech.

THE OREGONIAN, NOVEMBER 30, 2008

Higher-Ed Funding:
Federal Investment at College Level Needed

As messages go, a double-page ad in the *New York Times* gets you a little more prominence than a 42-cent "Forever" stamp.

"The fact that you saw it," George Pernsteiner, chancellor of the Oregon University System and a signer of the message, reasonably points out, "shows that it got more attention than a letter to the transition team."

Whose members, one hopes, also saw it and are thinking hard about it.

Just as—one also hopes—President-elect Obama thought hard after Gov. Ted Kulongoski raised a similar point with him in Philadelphia a few weeks ago.

"As Congress and the Executive Branch consider an economic stimulus initiative," declared the letter, underwritten by the Carnegie Corporation and signed by about 50 national higher-education leaders, "it is critical that any legislation include a substantial investment in states and their educational systems, particularly public higher education."

You could see why university leaders would want to raise this subject; in the American economy right now, the expected federal stimulus package is just about the only train going anywhere, and everybody wants to be on it. But the letter also makes a point about the vital role that higher education needs to play to get the nation—and Oregon—out of this daily deepening hole.

And that the strategy has worked before.

For Oregon, recognizing that would be a clear improvement on the standard state rule that in hard budgetary times higher education is the first thing to get whacked. The real symbol of Oregon universities has been neither a duck nor a beaver but a roller coaster.

Oregon's not the only place riding it downward.

As the Carnegie Corporation points out, "The United States has now fallen from first place to 10th among nations in the percentage of our population with higher-education degrees . . . For the first time in our history, the cohort of Americans ages 25 to 34 is less well-educated than the older cohorts that preceded it."

At least Oregon's a pacesetter in that trend.

The message is about the need for the country to reinvest in higher education, to keep up with the rest of the world and to regain the research lead that once had the United States on the cutting edge of world technology. And, in the immediate future, to try to use some of the coming Obama stimulus package for the purpose that Kulongoski urges: higher education's capital needs, notably long-deferred university maintenance projects that can move quickly into the job-creating pipeline.

Asking for 5 percent of the expected package—possibly as much as $40 billion—the Carnegie message proposes, "To insure a rapid response, only projects that are shovel-ready or on which construction can begin within 120-180 days can be funded."

You don't often find folks in higher education using the phrase "shovel-ready." But these are unusual times.

"One of the things people came up with was, our buildings are falling apart," Pernsteiner says about the smaller leadership meeting that devised the letter. "It's hard to educate students when you have to patch the roof."

That's especially true in Oregon, which has a $600 million backlog in deferred maintenance on its university buildings. Monday, Pernsteiner gave Kulongoski a list of $180 million in projects that could be begun almost immediately, from fixing Portland State's crumbling heating system to a state-of-the-art geothermal well at Oregon Institute of Technology and biofuel research facilities at Oregon State.

It's not hard to imagine how this moves the Oregon economy ahead on several levels.

As Carnegie points out, investing in higher education has worked for the country in tough times before. In the middle of the Civil War, Abraham Lincoln and Congress passed the Land Grant College Act, giving the states vast amounts of federal land to set up the universities that gave the United States more college access than anyplace else in the world. During World War II—when the country's debt was higher proportionately even than it is now—Congress enacted the G.I. Bill, providing higher education to millions of veterans who'd never imagined it before the war.

By any reasonable calculation, both investments paid off like an overenthusiastic slot machine.

This is an essential strategy for the United States, whose universities, drawing students from all over the globe, may be the strongest element of its claim to world leadership. It's even more vital for Oregon, with growth staggering throughout its economy and facing major research universities to the north and south—and increasingly to the Far East.

Tuesday, Obama announced his secretary of education and talked about the importance of education in restarting the economy—without saying much about higher education. It's important that he and his team get the investment message from both Carnegie and Kulongoski, and that Oregon not let its university system become, once again, a casualty of a downturn.

The present looks bleak. But there will be a future.

We don't want to get there last.

THE OREGONIAN, DECEMBER 21, 2008

Financial Aid:

College Students' Next Lesson: Bad Economics

In 1969, Wim Wiewel was part of a mass of students demonstrating in the streets of Amsterdam against the Dutch government's raising of university costs.

The fees had shot up from $14 to $28 a year.

Last week, Wiewel—now on the other side of an ocean and a continent as president of Portland State University—had to notify 550 current and future PSU students that although they qualified for financial aid, there wasn't any money left. As Suzanne Pardington reported in the *Oregonian* Friday, the state has run out of money for the program in the middle of the school year, reducing support to existing students and preventing grants to some new ones.

Maybe Oregon college students should hit the streets of Portland.

Or at least Salem.

Everybody knows that both this year's economy and this year's legislative session are going to be excruciating to watch, that there's likely to be blood all over the floors of the capitol, and that no part of the budget—or the state—is going to go unsplattered.

But after long stretches of Oregon getting F's in college access—and gentleman's C's on much of the rest of its higher-education effort—the state has made some progress in the last few years. It would be heartbreaking, not to say self-destructive, for the state to lose that progress in the economic collapse.

And the message of this meltdown, including a national loss of 4 million manufacturing jobs since 2000, isn't that education and research will be less important in the future economy.

At least, as new state Sen. Diane Rosenbaum, D-Portland, suggested Friday, "If people are in school, we've got to find a way to keep them there."

When Wiewel speaks to politicians, businessmen and attorneys, he recounts, "Everyone seems to agree with me. But what does it mean to have leadership if you can't get followers?"

Oregon's historical indifference to its higher-education system seemed to be thawing slightly recently. The downturn hurts from all sides, from the state having less money available to current and prospective students suddenly needing more—while showing up in larger numbers. For the last two decades, Oregon universities have made up for both sudden and steady drops in state support by raising tuition; this is not an inviting time for that strategy.

At an Oregon Public Broadcasting taping Wednesday evening, President Ed Ray of Oregon State worried, "My fundamental concern is that we are at risk of creating a permanent underclass in this society that has no stake in it . . . people who don't have access to the Oregon University System because they're priced out of it."

The crunch is particularly tight at Portland State, where enrollment has doubled in the past decade, and the margins are narrower. They're especially narrow after the market has dropped PSU's endowment from $36 million—already dramatically small for an urban university—to $27 million, and when its constituency is having lots of its own problems.

"The level of need is greater than anticipated," reports Wiewel. "Some number of them will enroll anyway. Some number will decide, 'I can't afford it.'"

And some will respond to increasing pressures on campus, as PSU, like other universities, finds it harder to fill academic vacancies and maintain its quality.

"To have access to a bad education isn't worth anything," says Wiewel. "I will not cut things endlessly. A lot of our classes now are standing-room only, and you're exceeding what's a quality education."

As the Legislature convenes Monday—at least that's a public facility that isn't standing-room only—there is no quick, reassuring answer. Gov. Ted Kulongoski's proposed budget tries to defend higher education, but it's expected that this spring's revenue forecasts will be much worse—although the year should also bring a federal stimulus package that should include some good news for the states.

The challenge is that historically, when Oregon has had money troubles, higher education was the first place the Legislature looked to find some. That should—and has to—work differently in the 21st century, especially when thousands of Oregon students are besieging the state universities looking for some way in.

People might even realize that the future doesn't come cheap—or that without some effort, it doesn't come at all.

With determined optimism, Wim Wiewel insists, "I'm not in the education business believing that nothing will ever change."

In Amsterdam or in Portland.

THE OREGONIAN, JANUARY 11, 2009

Higher Education:
When Two Trends Collide on Campus Heading Toward a Collision Course

When faced with unsettling realities, higher-education officials may go so far as to say they are "concerned." When there's an actuarial chance that a building might collapse from deferred maintenance if a student drops his laptop in the wrong place, they allow that the situation is "troubling."

Deeply shaken, they might say a circumstance "requires priority attention."

But what's facing Portland State University next year, says its president Wim Wiewel, is "quite scary, actually."

Of course, he may just not have the language down yet.

Two trends are heading for the Oregon University System next year, and you wouldn't want to be the campus where they run into each other.

The first, of course, is the general state funding crisis, which last week produced a memo to state agencies asking them to produce new budgets reflecting a possible 30 percent cut. At those levels, you don't just need accountants, you need lifeboats.

But the university system got some other numbers last week, showing an 11.7 percent increase in new students admitted for next year compared with the same date in 2008. For some campuses, the numbers run higher; Portland State's new admits are up 17.3 percent, Oregon State's 21.1 percent, Western Oregon University's by 31.1 percent.

The old bumper sticker asked, "What if you gave a war and nobody came?" This situation is the reverse: What if everybody showed up, but you didn't quite have a university?

The March admission numbers don't exactly forecast September attendance; applications may be processing faster, students may be applying to more schools and this year in particular financial aid decisions may shape an entering freshman class more than SAT scores. But the overall direction seems clear: Oregon universities expect to have both a lot more students and a lot fewer resources to offer them.

"When we look at what's happening with funding made available compared to what students expect," says Kate Peterson, Oregon State's assistant provost for enrollment management, "it's not looking very promising."

In the economic meltdown, state universities are looking more attractive to students who might have gone out of state or to private colleges, and Portland State—already up 9.4 percent in spring quarter—is gaining metro-area students who might otherwise have gone down the valley.

Universities have nothing against enrollment—Portland State manages to work into every press release that it's the largest university in Oregon, at least by body count—but the resources need to be there.

"It's a huge dilemma, with a huge uncertainty attached," Wiewel says.

One uncertainty is how much of the oncoming enrollment wave breaks against the main tool the universities have to deal with it: raising tuition to replace disappearing state funding.

"It will inevitably have a chilling effect," Wiewel says. "If we get a cut like (30 percent), we will pursue a tuition increase of 15 percent in each of the next two years . . .

"Raising the tuition, even if it's the hard thing to do, is the honest thing to do. It's what it takes to give you a good education. Providing access to an affordable education that's no good doesn't help anybody."

Oregon, he points out, knows the effects of a tuition boost. Tuition went up sharply in the 1990s, after the passage of Measure 5, and Wiewel doesn't think it's a coincidence that Oregonians from 25 to 34 have lower levels of college degrees than the generation just before them.

Higher education, like everything else the state does, is going to take a beating in the next two years; things, to coin a phrase, are tough all over. But its situation is complicated by the swelling stream of students headed toward the state universities—which is, of course, exactly where we want them to go.

The universities all have formulas for admitting students and are following those formulas—although one Portland high school counselor notes that they seem more careful this year in reading the recommendation letters of students whose GPAs fall below the automatic admit level. But offering a student admission also is a kind of contract.

"It certainly establishes an expectation on the part of the student that they will have the resources to reach their degree," Oregon State's Peterson says.

Looking at next year, she thinks, it looks like an open question "whether we meet that expectation."

And a state university system that had trouble meeting that expectation would be, well, scary.

THE OREGONIAN, MARCH 22, 2009

The Universities' Budget:
In Beaver State, Higher Ed Plucked Like a Turkey

CORVALLIS—"I'm an economist," says Oregon State University President Ed Ray, a point he often makes to explain his calmness as the Oregon University System sets off on one of the fiscal roller-coaster rides that tend to leave the universities still dropping after the ride stops.

"I know what to do with money if I've got it. I know what to do if I don't have it."

Around here, of course, he's had a lot more experience with the second.

These days in Salem, there's more than enough pain to go around, and everybody's complaining that his agony is the deepest. But even in a brand-new economic situation, it's notable that some traditions are being maintained.

Such as higher ed getting particularly hosed.

As far as Oregon hosing patterns go, this one is right up there with not pumping our own gas.

"That's why we're one of four states that spend more on prisons than higher education," says Rep. Larry Galizio, D-Tigard. "From my perspective, I don't think there's any understanding of the significance of research and development and what the university system does for the state. I don't get it."

Neither, of course, do the universities.

By Galizio's count, the Ways and Means co-chairs' budget proposes cutting higher education by about 16 percent, while K-12, for example, goes down around 8.5 percent. But he calculates that actually, the universities don't do nearly that well.

Aside from the universities themselves, he reports, the chancellor's office is getting cut closer to 25 percent. Moreover, Galizio notes, one of the Legislature's strategies to get to the end of the current biennium was to draw on $48 million in university reserves: "They start 15 yards back in a 100-yard dash."

Over in Corvallis, Ray has his own reasons for thinking that losing 16 percent is too cheerful. That's for the university itself, he points out; cuts to the extension system and Oregon State's other statewide responsibilities are projected to run deeper.

Ray also has been in the business too long to rely on even doing that well. He doesn't count on the Legislature getting all the revenue it's figuring on, and even now the budget needs to find $100 million in miscellaneous savings: "I can't assume that none of that will be allocated to higher ed."

The reason the Legislature light-heartedly draws more and more out of higher education, of course, is that it tells itself that the universities can always raise tuition—the reason that since 1990, tuition has been shooting up as fast as student debt and next year seems likely to top $7,000.

One signpost for the Oregon system might be the one across the Columbia, where universities are generally better supported, but which budgeted for 14 percent tuition increases in each of the next two years and a drop of 9,000 in student population.

Ray sees one clear difference between the Oregon and Washington situations: "They have a budget. I don't," he explains, sounding like an economist whose fiscal year begins in five weeks.

Then there's the Legislature's fondness for limiting tuition increases and for budget notes telling the universities how to operate, a legislative taste that seems to be growing larger as its proportion of higher-education revenue gets smaller.

"I got to testify in February," recalls Ray, "and I urged the legislators that whatever they were going to give us, not to micromanage us. I later heard from the chancellor's office that the legislators thought it was charming that I'd said those things, but that's not the way things work."

Galizio also finds that pattern remarkable, especially since at this level of funding, the state can hardly claim to be the sponsor of its higher-education system: "At this point, without the state investing more in the university system, we're just a major donor. And then we're going to dictate to them about tuition . . . and not give them the flexibility to respond?

"I'm so fed up with the rhetoric about how we support higher education."

Still, Galizio should remember that this is an Oregon tradition. We keep higher ed on a low diet in good times, and then when bad times come—and the bad times are worse here than in other places—we cut it more than other things in the budget.

You might wonder, of course, if this attitude toward higher education is one of the reasons bad times tend to be worse here than in other places.

But after all, that's also a tradition.

THE OREGONIAN, MAY 31, 2009

Experience Corps:
With Kids, It Turns Out Experience Does Count

When Lester Strong was in third grade, growing up in the gritty western Pennsylvania steel town of Braddock, the school district told his parents he was mentally retarded. That was a while before he went to Davidson College and Columbia University business school and had a 25-year career as a TV news anchor and executive.

Things turned out different from what the school district expected, explains Strong, because of three adults who thought differently about him: the parent of a friend, a minister and a barber. What a kid needs most, Strong concluded, is an adult who thinks the kid is important.

Now, as the new head of Experience Corps, Strong is in the business of providing them.

Experience Corps recruits and trains adults older than 55 and sends them into high-poverty elementary schools to work with kids who need some more help. Portland was one of its original five programs and now has about 60 Experience Corps volunteers, including some of the longest-serving in the country.

"It's worked marvelously since I've been here," says Lemil Speed, principal of Woodlawn School in Northeast Portland. "They're affectionately called the grandmas. They help the students you know can make it if you have another 15 minutes, another half hour in the day."

To Strong, visiting Portland recently on a tour of Experience Corps programs, there is enormous potential in the baby boom generation. In fact, the potential is almost as big as the problem.

"Fifty percent of some of our populations are dropping out of school," says Strong. "The children of this generation will have a higher dropout rate than their parents. They'll be the first generation ever" to hit that landmark.

The best way to do something about that, as a lot of people have noted, is to get to kids early, before the gaps in their reading levels separate them permanently from the kids who are going to make it.

"You do an intervention with a second-grader, you're changing direction on a speedboat," Experience Corps quotes Harvard School of Education professor Catherine Snow, "but when you do an intervention with a fifth-grader, you're changing direction on an oil tanker."

Which is why having somebody come in, several times a week, to read with a second-grader veering off course is a pretty good investment.

To Speed, it helps kids hit benchmark levels. Strong sees some other advantages.

"It's the impact of hope on children," says Strong. "The kids are eager. They know the time they spend with their tutor is all about them. It's showing the child that they matter."

And for achieving that, Strong said—in words that these days baby boomers are yearning to hear—"age is an enormous asset." In guiding the way through consonants and vowels, he notes, older people bring patience and life experience.

A recent study of Experience Corps by Washington University in St. Louis found that students in the program do 60 percent better in reading comprehension and sounding out words than comparable students. The study also concluded that being in the program produced benefits comparable to having a 40 percent smaller class size.

It's part of why the Portland program, overseen by Metropolitan Family Services, is funded by the Northwest Health Fund and the Children's Investment Fund, a voter-created initiative to support proven children's programs. The money covers training and a $250 monthly stipend, covering volunteer costs such as transportation and lunch.

The record shows considerable potential for the program. So does the supply of possible volunteers.

"There are 78 million baby boomers moving toward retirement," Strong points out. "They're the best-educated generation in history. They're not ready to retire. They want to do something."

And in the Serve America Act, the feds have just provided another incentive, letting older volunteers earn college benefits for children or grandchildren.

Then there's the other benefit, the one that Strong has seen in his own life:

Treating a kid as if he's important can make it turn out that way.

THE OREGONIAN, JUNE 10, 2009

Farewell to Frohnmayer:
UO's Departing Chief Fought Funding Crises

At the end of this month, Dave Frohnmayer retires from the presidency of the University of Oregon with a victory lap that could qualify as an Oregon track event. During his 15 years, encompassing three financial crises for the Oregon University System, Frohnmayer raised a massive amount of money, expanded the size and range of the university, and the UO's enrollment and admissions standards moved higher. (Listings of Oregon bowl games will be found elsewhere in the newspaper.)

But it's worth remembering—not only to mark Frohnmayer's achievement, but as Oregon makes future decisions about higher education—that his time in University of Oregon administration didn't begin with the brightest prospects.

In 1991, when Frohnmayer resigned as attorney general to become dean of the UO law school, there was a lively debate about whether Oregon should just dispense with the school. After all, law schools are expensive—and, partly because of Oregon's traditional levels of investment, the law school's American Bar Association accreditation was in danger—and voters had just passed Measure 5. Besides, Oregon already had two functioning private law schools, so maybe it wouldn't be bad to be just about the only state without a public one.

"The law school is underfunded, like most of Oregon's higher-education enclaves, and has never been financially endowed like more prestigious law schools," the *Oregonian*'s editorial page mourned at the time.

". . . A refrain the new dean will likely hear is that Oregon doesn't need many more lawyers and state-funded undergraduate programs should not be sacrificed to triplicate the private schools' legal offerings. Unless the new dean can articulate—and sell—the rationale for a state-supported law school, the deanship may be a sinking ship."

The law school, Frohnmayer recalled last week, "needed to justify itself."

Under his leadership, the school became stronger and sounder, and Oregon still has a public law school, just like a grown-up state.

Looking back to 1991, there is a message here, and not just for someone looking for a lawyer—or looking to become one.

"There comes a point," Frohnmayer noted last week, "when you can't make unlimited cuts without cutting away the essence of what it means to be a public university."

And, no, that's not just about law schools.

It's about maintaining access to higher education—always a problem in Oregon, but one where we've made some recent progress—and trying to keep your programs competitive with the other universities, and the other states, that have already figured out what's going to drive the future. It's about a university system that can seriously contend to keep your smartest kids in-state, and provide an opportunity to Oregon kids wherever they live, and has the support and resources to give students a decent chance to graduate in a reasonable amount of time.

The challenge is to manage this even in economically difficult times, whether after the voter passage of a tax cut or in a worldwide economic meltdown.

Chancellor George Pernsteiner of the Oregon University System thinks higher education did reasonably well in this session, although it did take a $29 million add-back to its budget last week. Part of why legislators had some idea of the system's importance was that other people had already figured it out: "The fact that people are enrolling in record numbers," Pernsteiner said, "had a great deal to do with the Legislature's attitude."

As Frohnmayer points out, the debate now is different; it's not entirely about funding, but also about giving the three major universities more flexibility to operate successfully outside the state's regulations. Right now, he noted, the state bills the universities for various services almost as much as it gives them in general fund money, and those lines will soon cross.

There will always be an urge to deal with tough circumstances by lopping off programs and cutting back opportunities, by looking at certain services and deciding that the state, or the state universities, really don't have to provide those at all.

The problem is, "There comes a point when you can't make unlimited cuts without cutting away the essence of what it means to be a public university."

And without going down as the equivalent of a Legislature that closed down the state's law school.

THE OREGONIAN, JUNE 21, 2009

Higher Ed's Week:
For Students: More Help, Higher Hurdles

It seems difficult to get anything useful out of D.C. these days, but last week the House Education and Labor Committee gave it the old college try. It passed out a bill that overhauls the college lending system and expands federal scholarship grants in a way that could significantly improve Americans' opportunity for higher education.

The only problem is that as the feds try to widen access at one end, state budget crises are narrowing access at the other. Potential students could find themselves all funded up with no place to go.

"It is discouraging to students and distressing to me," says Rep. David Wu, D-Ore., a member of the committee and its higher-education subcommittee, "that as we're laying down a pile of bricks to get students closer to their goal, the states are digging a hole under that pile of bricks."

Last week, at the same time the House committee was reporting out its measure—which even got two Republican votes, passing the committee 30-17—California was cutting next year's California State University enrollment by 40,000 while raising fees by a total of 32 percent in one year.

(One Californian suggested defensively that Cal State was still cheaper than the Oregon State University system, which prefers to compare itself to the University of California.) Washington will be increasing its tuition by double digits in each of the next two years, while cutting enrollment, and Florida is increasing its public university tuition by 15 percent this year. Oregon is trying to stay in single digits for this year, but there's another legislative session coming around in February, and nobody expects it to be a happy one.

So while it's a heartening thing that the federal government may make it easier and simpler for college students to borrow money, they'll likely have to be borrowing more of it—assuming there's a place for them.

"College education will be harder to get, and for those who get it, it will be harder to pay for," observes Jon Shure, deputy director of the state fiscal project at the Center for Budget and Policy Priorities in Washington, D.C.

"We used to have a compact in this country: Since higher education benefits the students and benefits the taxpayers, we'll pay x, and the student will pay y."

Now, Shure notes, especially in an economic meltdown, we've broken that compact and shipped more and more of the bill to the students— although getting the economy back on track is going to take a lot of skilled and educated people.

They'll be the ones with the debt.

On that basis, the Student Aid and Fiscal Responsibility Act of 2009 makes considerable sense, expanding the government's role in Direct Loans instead of subsidizing bank loans to students, cutting down on interest costs and freeing up some more money to expand Pell Grants to low-income students.

The trouble is we're giving students a better ladder on one hand, and raising the walls on the other.

Wu thinks the feds have still more approaches to consider.

"The federal government can borrow money at a very low interest rate," he points out. "I think if we loaned it back out at a 1 percent bump, we ought to make as much money available as students want to borrow."

It's his idea of a shrewd strategy effort in a recession.

"My view of higher education is that it's the long-term wealth genera-tor. We ought to invest in higher ed."

That may be especially true for places not exactly starting out at the front of the parade.

"In Oregon, we're in the bottom five in higher-ed investment," the congressman points out. "It's not my impression that we're moving up the scale."

The Student Aid and Fiscal Responsibility Act of 2009 is a shrewd improvement in the way we invest in college students. But it looks like some of its benefits will get undermined by the way we're disinvesting in colleges, by state calculations that universities can make up the differ-ence by charging more tuition to students—which the students can then borrow from the federal government, until we're back where we started.

Except our college graduates will owe more, and have gotten less.

What we need is a Student Support and State Responsibility Act.

For more than just 2009.

THE OREGONIAN, JULY 26, 2009

Public Corporations:

In Colleges, Rearranging Can't Avoid Refinancing

The idea of dealing with Oregon's higher-education problems by allowing its public universities to become public corporations is a classic Oregon solution.

It's creative, elegant—and doesn't come near to solving the problem. Oregon all the way.

Former University of Oregon President Dave Frohnmayer, in his proposal for the restructuring, notes, "There are those who argue that structural reform is no substitute for restoring funding to something remotely approaching national and international norms. I agree . . ." In fact, he points out earlier in his proposal, "While structural reform, as next discussed in this report, is essential, it must be accompanied by public reinvestment to make the difference in fulfilling the state's crucial need for public access to higher education for all Oregonians."

But Frohnmayer goes on to note that he's tired of waiting for that to happen and besides, the current higher-education alignment isn't working.

You can agree with both of those statements without necessarily thinking that public corporations are likely to make up much of the difference. Asked how much of Oregon's higher-education program a restructuring would fix, Frohnmayer himself didn't get carried away, gamely telling the *Oregonian*'s editorial board only, "It's a start."

Nobody's going to disagree with Frohnmayer's basic point, that Oregon's higher-education system needs something more dramatic than a touchdown pass. At a time of exploding student demand, the system is bleeding money, with some campuses coming up short by double-digit millions and facing the same in 2011.

There is, of course, a lot of that going around.

In California, cuts in higher-education funding led to demonstrations on four UC campuses, including taking over a building in Berkeley and blockading the university regents at UCLA. In fiscal 2007, California was appropriating $7,083 per higher-education student, while Oregon was spending $4,653—a number which, Frohnmayer points out, dropped to $3,460 in the current year.

According to California's Legislative Analyst Office, California's higher-ed cuts this year amounted to 8 percent—meaning the spending-per-student that sent UC students into the streets was still way higher than anything we're spending here.

Fortunately, Oregon students are more polite—or maybe just more distracted.

We're never going to get anywhere near even the slashed California numbers—but how much of the difference are independent public corporations likely to cover?

Everyone's favorite example here is Oregon Health & Science University, spun off by the higher-education system years ago and still standing—not only still standing, but a much stronger research institution than when it was the University of Oregon medical school. Since spinning off into its own corporation, OHSU has become a magnet for research funds, partly spurred by the federal pipeline set up by former Sen. Mark Hatfield.

But there are some other aspects to the OHSU example. Releasing it from state spending rules, the Legislature has been happy to shrug it off almost entirely. While state spending is now down to 9.5 percent of the U of O budget, it's a fraction of that at OHSU.

And while OHSU has gained in research, access has been another story. OHSU now has the highest state medical school tuition in the country—even if there's an asterisk to its identity as a "state medical school"—and graduates emerge heavily festooned in debt. (Admittedly, OHSU is not unique in that.) But it doesn't seem a clear strategy to providing primary care physicians to rural Oregon.

According to Frohnmayer's figures, from 1997-98 to 2007-2008 the University of Oregon, Oregon State and Portland State together increased undergraduate and graduate degrees from 10,422 a year to 13,897, an increase of 33.1 percent. During the same period, OSHU's undergraduate and graduate degrees rose only from 547 to 627, an increase of just 14.6 percent.

It would be highly helpful, as Frohnmayer argues, for the universities to have more freedom from the state's rules and regulations—not to mention to keep the interest on their own students' tuition payments. But the major problem is money, and how little of it the system gets from the state. An imaginative restructuring that could lead to the Legislature tiptoeing further away could end up losing more ground than it picks up.

". . . I have never been a fan of reorganizing when in trouble or simply moving boxes around," Tony Van Vliet, member of the state board of higher education and longtime state legislator, wrote, responding to Frohnmayer's proposal. "Regardless of how you slice it—the pie is just so big. You can add to it by trying a high-tuition model, or more grants and research, but the problem remains the pie!"

The pie, admittedly, won't swell anytime soon. But no rearrangement, however artfully devised, makes much difference if the pie never does.

As much as Oregon always likes to think there is.

THE OREGONIAN, NOVEMBER 29, 2009

Building a Bridge to College: Offering Portland Kids a Life after High School

Just about two years ago, when he was still the shiny and boundlessly promising mayor-in-waiting, Sam Adams talked about one of Portland's seriously low output points.

"The number of Portland residents that go on to college is below the national level," Adams pointed out. If we're considered a reasonably well-educated city, he continued, it's because "We import a lot of people."

Which is, of course, a city achievement in itself.

But it's also a good idea to grow your own.

And as for the proportion of Portland's own graduates who go on to some kind of college—about a third—Adams said again on Tuesday, "It's an embarrassingly low number."

Adams got back to the issue last week—he's had a lot on his mind—in his State of the City speech. Following a pattern set by a number of cities in the country, he proposed the beginnings of a Portland program to help some of its kids into college.

After all, we need to give the transplants some competition.

Adams' proposal calls for matching contributions from the city—divided among the general fund, the water bureau and the sewer bureau—with money raised by Mt. Hood and Portland community colleges to help support students from the Summer Youth Connect program in community college.

"I'm excited by it," says PCC President Preston Pulliams, accustomed to raising scholarship money for the PCC Foundation. "I think this is an excellent strategy to help hold out a carrot to some students that maybe aren't thinking about higher education."

Pulling in the water and sewer bureaus is not just a matter of going with the flow. Both bureaus, notes the mayor, are facing a large number of retirements in the immediate future, and the students will be studying subjects like engineering technology, environmental sciences and forest resource management, and will have internships within the bureaus.

Like the economists say, grow your own.

Experience in other cities suggests that a program like this can affect a couple of other bad numbers that Portland is currently throwing up on the board. Right now, a total of 63 percent of Portland kids finishing eighth grade graduate from high school four years later, a casualty rate at bus-crash level. A program to attract kids into the summer program, connect them to job possibilities and give them a lift into college can move that number.

Some more support and assistance for Portland graduates could also boost another number: the percentage who manage to survive in their next academic program. "Retention rates in college," notes Adams, "are horrible."

Cities like Kalamazoo, Mich.; Pittsburgh; and Akron, Ohio, have found that some shrewd investment in their students can raise all those numbers.

And their programs are even more ambitious.

"My goal," says Adams, "is to get it to the four-year colleges as well." That would involve recruiting some more participants.

"We see it as a broader partnership with the business community," declares Multnomah County Chairman Ted Wheeler, who's worked on the program with Adams. "There's some door-knocking that has to be done. All of us have committed to work on our relationships here."

Increasing the flow of Portland kids into college is more than writing a tuition check. It's holding out a possibility to a high school freshman that can cause sweating through biology to make more sense, it's helping families move through the jungle-like FAFSA (Free Application for Federal Student Aid), it's providing exposure to college and to the jobs it can provide to teenagers not typically accustomed to making the most thoughtful decisions.

"To get them to college is one thing, but that's not the prize," says Jim Bosco, who oversees the Kalamazoo program at Western Michigan University. "The prize is if they're successful in college."

For a city that hopes to get to a new economy, and to bring its kids along, the prize is more than worth the investment.

"Resources have been provided," says Adams. "To some people, it's a little bit of a head-scratcher because we're cutting budgets, but when we say this is a priority, it has to show up in our budgets."

And if Portland's kids are a priority, so is this.

THE OREGONIAN, FEBRUARY 10, 2010

Globe Is Gaining:
Higher Ed Cuts True Madness of This March

This week marks the kickoff of the NCAA college basketball playoffs, perhaps the last remaining occasion when Americans use "college" and "revenue increase" in the same sentence. But this month, higher education started March Madness a little early.

March 4, college students demonstrated in Oregon and throughout the country to point out they're being charged considerably more and getting less and less, and that the basic quality of the country's higher-education system is starting to wobble.

"It's addressing a growing trend and an economic crisis facing students across the nation," explained Stephanie Rio Collier, a Portland State junior and part of a demonstration by several hundred PSU students. They were especially concerned, said Collier, about possible Oregon University System reorganizations that might produce sharply higher tuition and even more student debt.

There are two clear points to make about this:

1. The PSU students, and the ones across the country, are absolutely right.
2. They haven't seen anything yet.

The next legislative sessions around the country, when state budgets will be far from recovering and when federal stimulus money will be gone—at this point, states will be mostly on their own facing combined deficits that could top $200 billion—could be the worst moment for higher education since the end of mandatory Latin.

Warned state Rep. Chip Limehouse, chairman of the higher-education subcommittee in the South Carolina House of Representatives, "Next year is going to be an iceberg looming for higher education."

And we're already in over our heads.

Next year, we could get to March Mania.

Our situation is not only hurting our current and potential college students but becoming a looming economic threat. In a recent paper for the Center for Studies in Higher Education at the University of California, John Aubrey Douglass found that despite the worldwide recession, China, Taiwan, South Korea, Germany, France and Brazil have continued to bolster their university systems, while the United States and Great Britain have been cutting back.

At a time when our nuclear weapons are increasingly irrelevant, when our exploding debt is cutting away at our intentional economic influence, it's remained a vital American advantage that we've been the higher-education superpower—with universities that can attract the smartest people from around the world and produce breakthroughs that can drive an economy. Losing that undermines both state economies and national prospects.

This year, according to the Center on Budget and Policy Priorities, 39 states have either cut back their systems or sharply increased tuition. The national poster child, the University of California—built on several international powerhouse campuses—has increased tuition by 32 percent and cut freshman enrollment by 2,000 students. State funding for the University of Washington is down 26 percent, and Washington State tuition up 30 percent. Idaho's state spending for higher education is now down 15 percent from two years ago.

The next budget period could be as bad. George Pernsteiner, chancellor of the Oregon University System, foresees an Oregon budget gap of as much as $2.5 billion for the 2011-13 biennium, likely to land hard on higher education—at a time when every university and community college is bursting at the seams with exploding enrollment.

It's another reason why Congress needs to reconsider cutting the states loose without support, which would see sharp cutbacks in virtually every state undermining a fragile economic recovery. At the same time, degradation of the higher-ed system would weaken the economy's long term prospects.

As Douglass told the *San Francisco Chronicle*, 20 years ago the United States had the highest college completion rate of the 30 countries in the Organization for Economic Cooperation and Development. Now we're 19th, and the direction isn't encouraging.

"Over the last decade we have seen higher education elevated to a top policy concern in many nations," said Douglass, "where it is seen as vital for economic development and competitiveness."

And then there's the U.S. higher-education investment, or rather disinvestment.

Our annual tradition of Americans being glued to their TV sets for three weekends in March, of millions of people filling in brackets with names of colleges they've never heard of, of college students celebrating wildly across their campuses and maybe, after a particular victory, setting a few fires? That's just a little excitement.

Cutting back state higher-education systems when we—and every other country in the world—know that we're now in a knowledge economy?

Now that's madness.

THE OREGONIAN, MARCH 14, 2010

Oregon Governor's Race:
Higher Ed (Gasp!) Gets Campaign TV Time

Over time, TV ads for people running for governor of Oregon have included beaming spouses, rolling mountains, editorial endorsements, adorable kindergarten kids and—in a bold breakthrough offered this year by Bill Bradbury—a Segway.

But generally, one Oregon theme has never been considered ready for prime time—or even for the cable news off-hours specializing in political ads:

Higher education.

After all, what candidate would want to be seen with a scruffy college student—or worse, a professor—instead of an adorable kindergartner?

And candidates would always rather seem tough on criminals than soft on sophomores.

But this year's campaign for governor has been a different moment. Oregon universities are actually getting some TV time that's not on ESPN.

An ad for Democratic front-runner John Kitzhaber promises "two years of college for all Oregon students who have earned it," even if the film shows adorable pre-schoolers. A spot for Republican Chris Dudley talks about "transforming universities for innovation and job creation" and even shows a picture of one.

For Oregon's universities, this is unprecedented electoral attention. And even though their timing is not great—it's as if Cinderella is finally invited to the ball, just when the ball is being canceled for lack of money—it's always better to be talked about.

And the campaigns are saying encouraging things, even if not in great detail.

"It's through higher education that we can really drive the economy," said Kitzhaber policy director Scott Nelson on Friday. "Absolutely, the state needs to invest all it can in universities," although, of course, that may not be much. Kitzhaber's campaign website promises "Supporting additional resources for research infrastructure for facilities and matching grant," which may be no more than encouraging universities to find more money on their own.

Still, it's nice to be mentioned.

Kitzhaber's higher-education thinking also includes considerable attention to community colleges and more coordination among the various elements of the education system. His website talks about the principle of "40-40-20"—40 percent of Oregon's population with four-year degrees and 40 percent with other postsecondary training—a considerable upgrade from where we are now.

According to Dudley's website, "As Governor, Chris Dudley will unshackle Oregon's colleges and universities from outdated regulations that cost too much money and limit innovation and accountability of individual institutions; will reverse the decades-long retreat from higher-education investment."

Those last words could sound almost musical to Oregon universities.

"I'm a big believer in higher education," Dudley said Friday. "I would like for the state to be able to do more, especially in helping kids from Oregon to afford tuition. I think it's so important for our state going forward."

On the theme of giving universities more autonomy, something stressed by every university president in the state, Dudley points out, "We're supplying 8 percent of the budget, and they've got 6300 line-items," specific instructions from the Legislature to the campuses.

Blushing prettily, higher-education leaders say they appreciate the attention.

"It's good to see it," says Oregon State President Ed Ray, citing comments by Kitzhaber and Dudley. "There's a lot of white papers floating out there, and maybe that's drawn some attention."

University of Oregon President Richard Lariviere says he thinks the campaign mention is encouraging, and he hasn't even been here long enough to know how unusual it is.

Just to have a candidate for office talk about you, of course, is no guarantee of anything; you can get that confirmed by a lot of adorable kindergartners. Maybe the interest is just a byproduct of the sharp increase in younger voter participation in 2008 or the prospect of a November face-off between two Ivy Leaguers: Kitzhaber (Dartmouth) against Dudley (Yale).

But maybe it's also a sign of a long-delayed realization that you can't talk about the things that Oregon candidates tend to want to talk about—economic development and quality of life—without talking about higher education. It's been an afterthought in Oregon for too long, and now people are beginning to figure out that it's part of why it's better to be Seattle in this recession than to be Portland.

At least, Oregon higher education can know it's nice to see yourself on television.

It's even nicer—and maybe even encouraging—when someone else puts you there.

THE OREGONIAN, MAY 16, 2010

Resetting Expectations: Recognize the Realities of Reset—and Its Cost

There are many things—state budget projections, health insurance arrangements, iPod playlists—that can be reset.

There are other things—planetary orbits, the cost of cutting-edge scientific research, Oregonians' confidence that shrewd redesign can make up for an absence of money—that tend to resist readjustment.

On Friday, Gov. Ted Kulongoski gave the City Club of Portland his outlook on the state's economic future, and the report of his Reset Cabinet on how to deal with Oregon's being short $10 billion over the next decade to continue its current level of services. It's an outlook to make a departing governor glad that he's departing.

The situation, as he rightly declared, requires bold thinking, and many of his ideas and proposals properly reflect that. But his speech also reflected the most traditional of Oregon ideas—the belief that somewhere is the deft design, undiscovered by other states, that can achieve your goals while spending a lot less money.

"The hard truth," declared the governor, "is this: No matter who is elected in November, or who is in control of Salem in 2011—recovering from this Great Recession will be a long, slow and difficult journey for Oregon . . .

"Since a traditional economic rebound is not in the cards, Oregon will have to create the next decade's opportunities through hard work and tough choices. That means changing the way we think—our mindset—as well as changing the way government does business, because the current structure of state government is simply not sustainable anymore."

Kulongoski presented the report of his Reset Cabinet, nine prominent state figures who have spent months studying the state's condition and options, and produced proposals for surviving the storm.

Among the new realities is the certainty that the Legislature arriving in Salem in January, no matter who sits in it, will not be interested in new taxes.

And that Congress seems to be cutting the states loose like a pack of unwanted nephews.

Many of the proposals from the governor and his Reset Cabinet are plausible, if not inescapable. There have to be changes in how we pay for public employees' health care, and in state and local governments picking up the 6 percent employee contribution to retirement. We send too many people to prison for too long—although changing that will be a hard battle and, with the governor's understandable interest in expanding drug and alcohol treatment, probably not save as much as we'd like to think.

And though statewide contract negotiations for teachers have a certain logic in what's now nearly a statewide system, from all experience—such as Washington's—it's more likely to cost you than save you money. Lower-paid districts are more likely to be brought up to the average than higher-paid districts to be brought down.

"Our focus on higher education must also recognize the critical role universities play in research and innovation, which in today's economy are engines of growth and prosperity," Kulongoski said. "No matter how

294

tight our state budget, we must make room in our investment decisions for university-based research and development."

To bolster higher-education research and access, Kulongoski proposes giving universities the flexibility and freedom from state regulation that university presidents have badly wanted. This is intended to balance a 15 percent reduction in state general fund support for universities, where on a per-capita basis Oregon is already 44th in the country.

States, like everybody else, are bounded by how much money they have. If you can't afford a Mercedes, you can buy a Kia. But it's a persistent Oregon delusion to believe that through shrewd calculation, your Kia can operate just like a Mercedes.

At the end of his speech, Kulongoski talked about facing "a new reality of how government functions, an accumulation of events and the initiative process that are coming home to roost." He was talking about the mandatory minimum-sentence Measure 11, but he could also have been talking about the tax initiatives of the same decade that have steadily reduced Oregon's national ranking in what it spends on education and government.

If you've gone from 15th to 30th in spending per student, it's going to be reflected in your school system no matter how you design it.

For the immediate future, changes in Oregon's revenue system probably are unimaginable. But at some point, there will be an inescapable recognition that states, like everyone else, get what they pay for.

And we'll rediscover that it's an idea not subject to reset.

THE OREGONIAN, JUNE 27, 2010

Escaping the Legislature: Flexibility for Higher Ed, and Maybe Some Help

"This is a life's work," says Jay Kenton, the Oregon University System's vice chancellor for finance and administration. "I've been working to change this for 30 years."

"This" is not Oregonians' understanding of the importance of a national-class higher-education system, why some states regard their universities as economic engines, why it's a problem to be among the lowest higher-ed-funding states in the country. Changing that could be more than a life's work; it could take at least until Oregon State wins a Rose Bowl.

Kenton's goal, expressed in a proposal from the State Board of Higher Education earlier this month, is to loosen the Legislature's control over the state universities' budgets, control that has not lightened an ounce while the state's fiscal contribution has become almost weightless.

At this point, after 20 years of steady reductions, Oregon's per-capita general-fund spending on its university students is 44th in the country. The number comes from *Trends in College Spending 1998-2008*, a report released this month by the Delta Project on Postsecondary Education Costs, Productivity and Accountability.

The Delta Project also found that in 2008, Oregon's per-student spending—combined general fund and tuition—at its public research universities totaled $11,800, or eighth from the bottom. (As people throughout the higher-education world say, "Thank God for Mississippi.") Washington was second in the country, at $23,039, and California fourth at $22,489.

The news gets worse. In Washington, 42 percent of the cost comes from tuition; in California, 37 percent. In Oregon, tuition provided 67 percent of the cost, a percentage topped by only six other states.

Some states charge higher tuition. But no other state charged so much in tuition and contributed so little itself.

Currently, Oregon universities are holding off the cumulative effects of two decades of disinvestment with hugely increased tuition revenue —both at higher rates and with increased enrollments. It's keeping the doors open, but with visible effects.

In 1997, Curtis Bartlett dropped out of Southern Oregon University to go to work. He's been working ever since, but has recently returned to finish up, and he finds the difference striking.

In the mid-'90s, he recalls, annual tuition ran around $1,300. Now it's more like $6,000, and he expects to graduate more than $20,000 in debt.

Moreover, because of financial problems and faculty furloughs, SOU lost instructional days in each quarter of the past year, and expects to lose more in fall and winter quarters next year, although administrative adjustments worked to minimize the impact.

"We're losing education hours and can't do anything about it," Bartlett says. "We're paying more and getting less."

No reorganization of the system, of course, will fix the situation. But the changes urged by the State Board of Higher Education could at least ensure that the extra tuition paid by students like Bartlett, and by thousands of additional students seeking shelter from the Great Recession in universities, actually goes to serve the students—without a trip through the state capitol.

Funny things happen to money in the state capitol.

The change would also let the universities be more flexible in spending their money, the kind of flexibility that's useful when your numbers—in students and state support—keep changing around you.

The board's proposal also includes a request for a state funding increase, which everyone admits is hard to expect in these circumstances. But state budget requests are based on a current services level, what it would cost an agency to do the same things in the next two years—and state funding right now is already below the current services level.

This is like calculating air supply when you're already underwater.

Changing the system's status as a state agency will help it tread water, and better keep the universities and their sizable enrollments afloat. But it can't entirely replace a serious consideration of what Oregon needs from its universities—and what its universities need from Oregon.

That needs consideration of why, in what everyone calls a knowledge economy, the education level of native Oregonians is actually dropping—and why Washington, with a stronger historical higher-education commitment, seems to be weathering the recession somewhat better.

"The focus needs to be on what Oregon gets out of this," Jay Kenton says. "How does this better position the state to be competitive?"

Figuring this out needs to take less than a lifetime.

Because we don't have another one.

THE OREGONIAN, JULY 18, 2010